Florissant Valley Library
St. Louis Community College
3400 Pershall Road
Ferguson, MO 63135-1499
314-595-4514

WITHDRAWN

FOOD IN EARLY MODERN EUROPE

KEN ALBALA

Food through History

Greenwood Press
Westport, Connecticut • London

Library of Congress Cataloging-in-Publication Data

Albala, Ken, 1964–
   Food in early modern Europe / Ken Albala.
      p. cm.— (Food through history, ISSN 1542–8087)
   Includes bibliographical references and index.
   ISBN 0–313–31962–6 (alk. paper)
      1. Food habits—Europe—History.   2. Nutrition—Europe—History.   3.
Agriculture—Europe—History.   4. Dinners and dining—Europe—History.
5. Europe—Social life and customs.   I. Title.   II. Series.

GT2853.E85 A43 2003
394.1′2′0973—dc21   2002028431

British Library Cataloguing in Publication Data is available.

Copyright © 2003 by Ken Albala

All rights reserved. No portion of this book may be
reproduced, by any process or technique, without the
express written consent of the publisher.

Library of Congress Catalog Card Number: 2002028431
ISBN: 0–313–31962–6
ISSN: 1542–8087

First published in 2003

Greenwood Press, 88 Post Road West, Westport, CT 06881
An imprint of Greenwood Publishing Group, Inc.
www.greenwood.com

Printed in the United States of America

(∞)™

The paper used in this book complies with the
Permanent Paper Standard issued by the National
Information Standards Organization (Z39.48–1984).

10 9 8 7 6 5 4 3 2 1

Every reasonable effort has been made to trace the owners of copyright materials
in this book, but in some instances this has proven impossible. The author and publisher will be glad to receive information leading to more complete acknowledgments
in subsequent printings of the book, and in the meantime extend their apologies
for any omissions.

CONTENTS

ACKNOWLEDGMENTS

This book was an absolute ball to write. It would certainly have been less so without the help of numerous friends who patiently answered my seemingly endless and tiresome questions. First I must thank the University of the Pacific for a pleasant sabbatical in which to write this book, as well as the Faculty Research Committee for sending me to Italy. The staff of the Biblioteca La Vigne in Vicenza and the Biblioteca Ambrosiana in Milan were remarkably helpful, as were people in the State Library in Sacramento, the Sutro Library in San Francisco and the Bancroft Library and Biosciences Library at UC Berkeley. At Pacific's library Monica and Trish of Inter Library Loan were invaluable assets.

Thanks to Wendi Schnaufer at Greenwood who has proven a great person to work with, a great friend, and a partner on the new Food Culture Around the World series.

Thanks too to friends from the Oxford Symposium, who will recognize ideas that I have pilfered from them. To all my colleagues in Classics and Modern Languages—especially Mel Thomas, Susan and Arturo Giraldez and Katie Golsan—thanks for answering my frantic language queries. Thanks to Courtney Lehmann for ideas about Ben Jonson. And to my best old friend of over 25 years, Andrew Martin, who braved sixteenth-century Dutch. May the heavens smile upon you. Morning chats with Dylan Zorea have blossomed countless times into ideas that are scattered throughout this book. Anyone writing should be so lucky to have such a friend. To my former student Suzanne Rindell, my thanks for the great poetry and the odd anecdotes which made their way onto these pages. Thanks to Carolin Young for advice on illustrations and sharing thoughts. I only wish we had connected long ago. Thanks also to Thomas Gloning, an e-mail friend, whose website and bibliographies should be known by everyone writing about food in this period.

Thanks to all my colleagues in the history department, Caroline, Suzanne, Edie, Gesine, Bill, Greg and Wild Bill, our newest addition, particularly for encouragement and leaving me alone to write. Thanks to our department butterflies Terri Redwood and Marilyn Norton for all their help. I must also thank Bob Benedetti, an irrepressible gourmand, for the past years of support. We will all miss you as dean. Thanks also to students in my new Global History of Food course. It is so gratifying to see my research and teaching intersect. Thanks too to my compatriots in arms, those who have shared my board and indulged me in all manner of unspeakable culinary excess. Special thanks to Charles, Farley, Lori and Wally for eating such frightening things on innumerable occasions. A big sloppy wet thank you goes to two people who rescued me at the last minute from serious gaffes on eighteenth century cuisine: Gilly Lehmann and Beatrice Fink.

And to my family—Joanna, Ethan and Benjamin, all of whom have tolerated my bizarre food obsessions, shopped, cooked and eaten with me—my love.

TIME LINE

1492   Christopher Columbus accidentally lands on a Caribbean island while trying to reach Asia and subsequently becomes the first European to taste many New World foods.

1498   Portuguese explorer Vasco da Gama establishes direct contact with India and opens the way for further Portuguese settlements throughout Southeast Asia, which will dominate the spice trade in coming centuries.

1500   Portuguese explorer Pedro Cabral lands in Brazil, which will later be a major sugar-producing colony using African slave labor.

1515   English writer Thomas More describes the communal meals and food customs of fictional Utopians in his novel *Utopia*.

1517   Martin Luther's 95 Theses precipitate events that lead to the Protestant Reformation and subsequent alteration of the meaning of the Eucharist and abolition of many Christian food festivals.

1521   Spanish conquistador Hernán Cortés conquers the Aztec Empire, and Mexican foods such as chocolate are thereafter introduced to Europe.

1530   Publication of Erasmus' *On Civil Behavior of Boys*, which is indicative of growing concern over courtesy and civility at the table. Forks slowly gain acceptance, with their use originating in Italy.

1533   Florentine Catherine de Medici marries the future Henry II of France and is said to have introduced Italian cuisine and vegetables such as the artichoke.

1534   Francois Rabelais'novel *Gargantua and Pantagruel* describes the obscene amount of coarse food eaten by giants in this satirical adventure.

1541   Jean Calvin implements a theocratic government in Geneva, Switzerland, that sets the tone for later Puritan movements and their stern attitude toward pleasures in food and drink.

1541   Paracelsus dies after conducting mystical investigations of the role of chemicals in pharmacy and foodstuffs. His followers later in the century begin to revise and abandon ancient Greek dietary theories.

1545–
1562   Italian artist Guiseppe Arcimboldo goes to work for Habsburg Emperors for whom he paints his famous fruit and vegetable heads, one of which depicts corn and other New World products.

1563   The Council of Trent reaffirms the Catholic Church's position on Lenten food restrictions and other fasts.

1570   Bartolomeo Scappi's *Opera,* the first lavishly illustrated cookbook, introduces systematic and detailed recipes.

1576   The sack of Antwerp by unpaid Spanish soldiers. The city thereafter loses its preeminence as financial and trade capital of Europe.

1598   King Phillip III of Spain ushers in the Golden Age of Spainish arts and cuisine.

1602   A union of spice merchants called The Dutch East India Company (Verenigde Oostindische Compagnie) is formed and begins to muscle in on the spice trade in what is now Indonesia.

1605   Miguel de Cervantes' novel *Don Quixote* includes many scenes revolving around food.

1611   *Dieta statica* by Italian Santorio Santorio measures metabolic activity by measuring insensible perspiration.

1644   Death of Belgian Jan Baptista van Helmont, the first to investigate the chemical nature of digestion.

1650   The first coffee house opens in England.

1650 François La Varenne's *Cuisinier François* heralds the revolution of French haute cuisine by de-emphasizing spices and intensifying the flavor of the main ingredient through fat-based sauces.

1654 Béchamel sauce reputedly invented by a steward at the French court of Louis XIV. In the late seventeenth century, the court of Louis XIV at Versailles becomes the artistic and gastronomic model for European rulers.

1681 Frenchman working in England Denys Papin invents the pressure cooker.

1690s Thomas Tryon is an outspoken defender of vegetarianism.

1698 French Benedictine monk Dom Perignon said to have developed modern method of champagne manufacture.

1701 Jethro Tull invents the seed drill, among the first machines used in farming.

1703 Methuen Treaty favors English trade with Portugal and Spain over that of France. British fondness for port and sherry confirmed.

1708 True porcelain developed in Meissen, Saxony by Johann Friederich Böttger.

1725 Last major outbreak of plague in Marseilles, France.

1730 British statesman Charles Townsend introduces turnips as winter fodder for cattle. Crop rotation systems will also revolutionize agriculture in the course of the eighteenth century.

1750 French Enlightenment philosopher Jean Jacques Rousseau first criticizes the advancement of arts and sciences and in his treatise on education, *Emile,* will espouse a natural diet.

1765 Following the case of Boulanger and his legally being allowed to serve more than restorative soup in Paris the first true restaurants begin to open there, among which is the restaurant opened by Mathurin Roze de Chantoiseau in 1766.

INTRODUCTION

We are a people used to change, especially when it comes to what we eat. Although many of our favorite foods have been around for a long time, the way they are grown or raised, their preparation and in particular the way they are marketed and sold to us changes every day. There are also new technologies such as genetically modified foods, new convenience foods and preservative techniques, new scientific studies of health and nutrition and new and exotic foods from around the world. We take for granted that something new and improved will appear on our plates every day. It is safe to say that the way we eat has been completely transformed in the past century or so. Consider refrigeration and freezing, canning, industrial-scale agriculture, fast food, brand names, and giant multinational food corporations. All of these were unheard of a hundred years ago. We are living in the middle of a major transformation of food culture and technology.

Change is, of course, a constant in human history, but changes of this magnitude are something very rare. The first major transformation occurred when our ancestors gradually left their hunting and gathering lifestyle for settled agriculture and cattle-raising. Known as the Agricultural Revolution, this occurred independently at various times around the globe, but first began after about 8500 B.C. in the fertile crescent of what is today Iraq, Syria, Turkey, Lebanon, Jordan and Israel. It gradually spread, reaching Europe between 7000 and 3000 B.C. This movement was more than merely changing from a nomadic life of constantly following the herds and foraging for wild plants, to a life of farming and keeping domesticated animals like sheep, goats and cows. It also involved staying in one place, which enabled the eventual growth of cities, organized governments, specialized professions, writing and everything else we associate with civilization. This settled life also created a great deal of social stability, a rise in population, and inevitably wars of conquest. The end of transience was without doubt the single most important transformation of human food habits and possibly the most important set of events in human history.

There have been other great transformations of food culture before this but none with such a widespread impact. The Asian spice and rare drug trade during the classical era is one example of a pivotal change. The Roman technique of grafting trees to cultivate apples, pears and other fruits on a large and consistent scale is another example. In the period known as the High Middle Ages other dynamic changes such as the invention of the horse collar and a new stronger type of plow, the windmill and water wheel, can also be considered crucial developments in the transformation of food. But through all these centuries it is still true that most people ate a very monotonous, seasonally-restricted diet, often with the threat of starvation looming over their heads. Most people still grew food as a profession and most of that food was still consumed locally. Nature and animals still provided energy, and the basic diet for most people still consisted largely of grains, dairy products and a small amount of meat.

How then did we go from that simple agricultural and pastoral society to this modern fast-paced corporate one? How did we go from being intimately connected to the land and to domestic animals to a people totally separate and often willfully ignorant of where our hamburgers come from? How and why does our food now come from every corner of the globe when it used to come from our own backyards? Why do we now have various ways of eating, different types of cuisine, special diets, and complex ways of thinking about food, when in the past everyone ate basically the same thing?

This book will try to answer these questions by focusing on another crucial turning point in the history of food that occurred between about 1500 and 1800 when Europe and later nearly the whole world began to eat and deal with food in very new ways. Although the focus here will be on Europe, the impact of the events described is certainly global. These years, roughly the three centuries between the first European contact with the New World and the Industrial Revolution, have often been described as another Agricultural Revolution. There were many other changes too, far beyond merely how food was grown. For example, it is in these years that direct European trade with Asia was first established as well as the first overseas colonial empires around the globe.

Food, as we will see, was a prime motivating factor in exploration, and food products remained central to global trade. It was in these years that foods from the Americas first reached Europe: the tomato, potato, chili pepper, turkey and many more. Although many of these foods took a long time to be fully adopted, their effect on the European diet was obviously enormous. It is also in these years that new capital-intensive methods of farming made agriculture less a way to feed a family and more of a business designed to turn a profit. In these years new scientific ideas radically transformed our understanding of how food is processed and used by the body. Even such apparently commonplace things as forks and table manners were first introduced in this period. Early modern professional chefs and cookbook authors also invented new cooking techniques and a whole new culinary ideal. All of these changes should give the reader an idea not only of what it was like to eat and live in this period, but how we got where we are today, for better and worse.

Perhaps more than any other historical topic, our vision of eating in the past is liable to be obscured by an intensely thick steam rising from the soup pot of nostalgia. Close your eyes and you can picture the happy family huddled before the glowing hearth, savoring their bowls of hearty soup. Their meal is eaten slowly, unharried by the frantic pace of modern life. And the food tastes better too. The chicken was free-range; fed without hormones and antibiotics. The vegetables were grown right outside the door in the kitchen garden without the use of pesticides or chemical fertilizers. The bread is, of course, a crusty whole grain peasant bread, the kind we find today in boutique bakeries. There may be a measure of truth in this rosy picture, or at least we have a deep need to think so, but it is easy to forget that there were days of real privation, serious malnutrition and days of unmitigated toil in the fields and before the fire. There were also many other hardships such as crop failures, rotten food, food-borne illnesses and accidental poisonings. In other words, we need to season our romantic image of the past with some bitter realities, and just sometimes it pays to count our blessings, despite what we may think about industrial feeding of the modern era. In this book I will try to give a balanced picture, in spite of my own fondness for simpler and more wholesome times.

The range of this book is intentionally broad. There have appeared, especially in recent decades, superb studies of culinary history for the early modern period. There are also excellent works about agriculture, trade, the columbian exchange (the great transfer of plants and animals from the Americas to Europe and vice versa), manners, nutrition, food and religion and so on. But rarely are all these topics treated as an integral whole. It seems necessary, if we are to really understand a food culture and set it in a larger historical context, that we should know who grows the food and how, who buys it, how is it prepared and by whom, what kinds of people ate which foods? Why did people go to such great lengths for some foods—like spices, while they ignored perfectly edible plants growing at home? How did foods fit into the ritual life of the ordinary villager, and why were people expected to avoid meat for long periods? Why were noblemen and women expected to eat different food than their peasant counterparts? How did cooking methods differ from our own? Although many of the ingredients would be completely familiar to us, we will see that how they dealt with them, what they thought about them, and how food fit into the mental universe of the average European in this period was really very different from our own experience. This book will thus try to answer everything about food from field to fork.

This book is also intentionally written for a nonspecialist audience of students and the general public who have a keen interest in food, as most people ought to but may not have the time to sift through the massive encyclopedias or highly technical studies of agriculture, trade, cuisine and gastronomy. Having said that, much of this work relies on the excellent studies of historians, anthropologists, sociologists and others working in the burgeoning field of food studies. But I have also tried as much as possible to rely on primary source documents, that is, texts that were written by people in the past. Whenever possible, I have let these people speak in their own words. For example, it seems far more interesting and valuable to read an actual 500-year-old recipe than try to sift through a historian's interpretation of it, or, even worse, an adaptation of it for a modern kitchen. I would prefer the reader see the original and see what it meant in context. I should also point out that some of the recipes were included for sensational value. Unlike many cookbooks of old recipes, I do not expect readers to cook these, though they certainly may. Considering the audience, I thought it would be more interesting to see the fabulous and bizarre things people ate in the past rather than things which might please our palates—which after all tells us more about ourselves than the past. Historians will miss the lack of meticulous notes here but those interested can refer to the lists of suggested further readings at the end of the book. I have limited these lists to works in English, though obviously I have used many secondary sources in other languages. In the footnotes, I have cited only directly quoted sources from original texts and occasionally from the work of other scholars. Where no citation is provided the reader can assume that any translations are my own.

I have also consciously avoided jargon and technical terms. Fellow food historians will, no doubt, miss the precision that comes with such language, but it seems preferable here to use the clearest language possible, and when necessary to define the terms I do use. I should also explain that this work focuses exclusively on western, southern and central Europe and those countries or regions that were most heavily involved in exploration and overseas trade, agricultural innovation, and witnessed the development of distinct cuisines. This is not to say that the Scandinavian countries and all of eastern Europe were unimportant, but particularly for the latter, many of the generalizations to be made simply do not apply. For example, the nature of land ownership and the organization of agriculture was vastly different, and in fact nearly every topic covered in this book would demand separate treatment for eastern Europe. It seemed best, therefore, to focus on the places where change was most rapid and decisive.

Finally while this book can be profitably read from cover to cover, it can also serve as a reference work. For those interested in a particular region, a certain ingredient, or a specific topic relating to food, the organization should make access relatively easy. Despite this, I have used a narrative style. Each chapter can stand on its own, but the progression of chapters begins with the raw materials and makes its way to cooking country by country and finally concludes with ideas about food, providing what I hope is a full and satisfying set of courses.

CHAPTER 1
FOOD AND PEOPLE

Before discussing what foods people ate and how they cooked them in the past, it is essential to understand how food was grown and how it ultimately reached the consumer. To a great extent the business of food necessarily determined what people had available to cook, whether they grew it themselves or had to purchase it from merchants and middlemen. In many cases the rarity of a certain food drove its cost so high that only the wealthiest of people could afford it, and for others the high price of basic foodstuffs caused dire poverty. In this 300-year period, there are countless paradoxes like this: great commercial success for some and slavery for others, magnificent banquets for princes and terrible famines for the peasantry. It is not merely that the heartless upper classes munched happily while their subjects starved (although that probably happened often enough) but rather larger social and economic forces that created this unique European food culture in all its most glorious and hideous aspects. The nature of land ownership and usage and the business of food were changing dramatically. Trade connections between European countries and the rest of the world were becoming more extensive. Strange new crops and new ways of growing them were introduced both at home and abroad. All these factors made this a dynamic, vibrant and also potentially precarious time to live and eat.

POPULATION

If one single factor could play the decisive role as catalyst for all these changes it would have to be the sheer number of people in

Europe. Demography, or the scientific study of populations and the impact they have on the economy, society and environment, is not very precise for the early modern period. There were a few systematic censuses, like those in Venice and Florence, but nothing on a wider and more rigorous scale until the very end of the eighteenth century. It is difficult to draw generalizations from those that do exist, but we are able to judge the effect that population growth or decline would have on a society. At the very least humans, like any animal, live in balance with their resources. When there is an ample supply of food, the human population tends to grow and when there is little, it shrinks. Of course there are dozens of other factors involved as well, but this basic law of nature as understood by the late-eighteenth-century economist and philosopher Thomas Malthus is still very useful for analyzing this period. Malthus contended that resources can only be expanded arithmetically (plant two fields instead of one) but human populations grow exponentially (two parents have three children who each produce three and so on and so on). Therefore, there is a tendency for human populations to outstrip their resources. Nature has a series of effective checks to cut back the population: famines, diseases, even wars maintain a balance of population and resources and help to alleviate mankind's resource depletion. Most historians and demographers agree that the so-called Malthusian Scissors that cut off the population are ineffective or at least seriously blunted nowadays when we can grow much more food, have effective medicines and hopefully avoid wars. They agree though that for the early modern period this is still an important conceptual tool.

Looking at the larger picture, it is certain that the European population fluctuated dramatically in the centuries preceding, during and following the early modern period. Understanding these fluctuations is the key to understanding everything else about food and resources in this period. Let us begin in the High Middle Ages from about the year 1000 to 1300. This was a time of rapid expansion and population growth across Europe. The economy was booming and trade was flourishing because there was a greater demand for food. With prices being high, farmers and investors were willing to put more money into growing food because they knew they could make a good profit. Because business opportunities were plentiful, people tended to marry and set up households earlier, and naturally the greater number of years in marriage meant larger families. There was still an obscenely high infant mortality rate, which meant that perhaps as few as one in every two babies born would reach age ten. This explains the "average life expectancy" of about 35. It is not that most people expected to die at age 35, but half the people died before age ten, the other half maybe lived to 60 or so. That gives us an *average* life expectancy somewhere in the 30s. Despite this, the European population continued to grow.

Then things began to change when a series of crop failures caused widespread famine in the early 1300s. The population began to decrease exactly as Malthus explained it should. Then came the death-blow: A bubonic plague arrived in 1348. A species of rat that harbors fleas that carry the virus *Yersina pestis* made its way from the steppes of Mongolia, via the caravans of the great Empire of Gengis Khan, all the way to Baghdad and the Middle East. From there the rats and the disease traveled on ships to southern Italy and within a year or two the plague had hit almost every corner of Europe. The devastation was catastrophic. In some places entire villages disappeared. Some cities lost half of their populations. Most historians' conservative estimate suggests that about one third of Europe was dead at the end of this plague.

Paradoxically, the bubonic plague had a very positive effect on those people lucky enough to survive. The balance of resources had completely tipped. There was now ample housing to go around, and inheritance lawyers had a field day helping to divide the remaining property. There was now also plenty of food to go around, plenty of land to farm, and much lower prices for food given the dramatically decreased demand. A fundamental law of economics states that when demand is great and supply is low prices will be high, and when demand is low and supply is great prices will be low. So after 1348, despite a complete dislocation of the economy, the life of the average survivor was relatively good. In fact, it appears that because grains were so cheap, the average peasant diet included a much higher proportion of meat. That is, a smaller percentage of the average household income had to be spent on food, so most people ate a richer and more varied diet.

The late Middle Ages may have been rosy for the average and usually poorer European, but this depressed economy had a generally negative impact on investors and landowners. For one, the system whereby land was held and farmed in much of Europe began to break down. Although there was probably never one single model of feudalism, or as most historians now call it "seigneurialism" to refer only to the relationship of landlord to peasant farmer, some basic outlines of the system can be described. In the High Middle Ages when the population was growing and land was relatively scarce, those who owned the land, from kings, dukes and earls right down to ordinary gentlemen and even monasteries and bishops, were in a good position to dictate terms to their tenants. A typical arrangement would grant a parcel of land to an individual and his family who usually lived in a village and farmed the land communally with his neighbors. His holdings might consist of scattered strips of land surrounding the village and would include the right to feed animals on a "common" plot with the animals of other tenants. This is known as "open-field farming" and in fact the idea of enclosed private property was quite foreign to this culture. In return for the privilege of using the property, the peasant would pay a rent either in money or kind (which usually meant food), sometimes at a fixed rate for a number of years, but often rents could be raised whenever the landlord liked. More importantly, the peasant was forced to work for a specified number of days on the landlord's own plot or "demesne" which would supply the lord's household with food or it could be sold on the market. Further aggravating the situation, the tenant was also forced to pay certain fees, such as when a son inherited the land, when the tenant wanted to marry or when he needed legal services. Typically peasants would also pay fees to use the local bread oven, mill or anything else that the lord considered his personal possession. Above all, at least in the model system, peasants—or in this case more properly serfs—could not leave the property at will. They were literally "bound" to the land, and were called "bondsmen" in England to distinguish them from "freehold" tenants. Serfs were not exactly slaves, but they were hardly free economically.

There were many forms of this system throughout Europe, and in some places land ownership was quite different. In much of Italy and in the Netherlands for example, there might be share-cropping systems or peasants might even own the land outright. So generalizations are difficult to make for all of Europe. The important point, however, is that after the outbreak of plague and greatly decreased population, the peasants were now the ones in a position to dictate terms. There simply were not enough people to farm the demesne in many places. Markets for grain and foodstuffs collapsed, and it was really no longer very profitable for most landlords to directly cultivate the soil any more, let alone bring it to distant markets. Landlords did everything they legally could to keep their control of society, but labor being scarce, peasants demanded better leases and wage earners demanded better pay. Failure to meet these demands resulted in many violent outbursts, peasant's revolts and worker's uprisings across Europe. In the long term, though, peasants benefited and landlords and merchants suffered through the late Middle Ages. In effect, the wealth was spread around a bit more equally.

Then, around the sixteenth century the population started to grow again. In some places quite dramatically, and soon numbers began to return to their pre-1300 level. The population would continue to grow straight through the entire period covered by this book. With the exception of one hiatus in the mid to late seventeenth century when the population declined in Spain, Italy, and much of what is now Germany, the entire early modern period witnessed a demographic surge both in the countryside and especially in cities. Exactly why this happened is difficult to answer with any precision. Clearly either more babies were being born or less people were dying. In either case, the birthrate would have to be greater than the mortality rate to sustain population growth. We do know that people continued to die in alarming numbers. Plagues continued to hit Europe right up to the last major outbreak in Marseilles in southern France in the 1720s. Even without bubonic plague, one would think the litany of diseases attacking Europe (cholera, typhus, smallpox, sweating sickness, syphilis [thought to be a newcomer after 1492] and many more) would be enough to keep the population in check. With the lack of effective remedies, or even suitable hygiene to prevent the spread of such diseases, we cannot say that fewer people were dying. Perhaps people were living longer; maybe improved nutrition added a few years to the average life expectancy. Even if this were the case, women (who are the important factor here) are unable to bear children in later years. So one's longevity could not have any effect on the overall population growth. Another possibility is that fewer infants were dying. Perhaps better nourishment from a well-fed mother who breastfeeds her children, or even a wealthier mother who hires a wet-nurse, would mean more infants growing to maturity. Unfortunately there is no evidence that the alarming infant mortality rate lessened in the least during this time.

If however, there were a greater number of pregnancies per married couple, even given the high mortality rate, then in the end a greater number of people would be produced. If a woman became pregnant six times in her life and three children lived into adulthood, given the same infant mortality rate, ten pregnancies would leave five more people. What could account for more pregnancies though? An earlier age of marriage, promoted by good economic opportunities and favorable inheritance customs could be one factor. Perhaps there were fewer serious subsistence crises or emergencies in which the food supply runs out, usually because of crop failure, leaving a weakened populace and, in extreme cases, malnourished mothers who are either unable to conceive or breastfeed infants. These were probably important factors by the eighteenth century, but it is difficult to say exactly what triggered the population growth in the first place. There continued to be many subsistence crises, many diseases and the diet of the average European was worse in the sixteenth century than in the late Middle Ages. For whatever reason, the European population bounced back after each successive disaster.

Most importantly, this growth had a profound impact on the structure of society, on the nature of land ownership, on trade and on markets for food. Put simply, the demand for food increased. Despite efforts to farm marginal areas such as hillsides, drain swamps, clear forests and reclaim land from the sea in the Netherlands, the population began to outstrip the resources again. Given the scarcity, prices rose dramatically. Inflation was usually worst for those products in greatest demand like wheat and other grains, the staple of the European diet. This meant that a greater proportion of most people's income had to be spent on bread or gruel made with coarsely ground grain and water rather than meat, fish and other foods. As in earlier periods of higher population density, the diet deteriorated for most people, unless you happened to be a landowner or merchant who thrived on inflated prices. For the landowner there was now great incentive to cultivate the soil directly himself or even kick off his tenants and hire them as wage laborers. In England, the high price of wool led many landowners to evict tenants and "enclose" their property for sheep pasture which required very little labor and brought big profits. This is what made Sir Thomas More comment in his satirical travel narrative of 1516, *Utopia*, that in England now the sheep are eating the men. Sheep grew fat on the land that once fed many families. But even in those places where farming continued, there was great incentive to improve agriculture and increase yields. Back in the days of the renting landlord, he could not have cared less whether the peasants farmed the land efficiently, and usually they did not given the very traditional, custom-bound nature of open-field farming and the need to cooperate. Because decisions about sowing, harvesting and such were decided communally, peasants rarely took great risks or tried new crops. Now, the landlord could make a lot of money if he farmed the land directly and sold the produce himself. The tendency, therefore, from the sixteenth century on is direct cultivation and the introduction of new agricultural techniques. Increasingly farming went from a peasant way of life to a profitable business venture.

The profits made in farming and trade also opened opportunities for what we might call the middling ranks of society to rise in wealth and status. In the countryside this could be the wealthy yeoman who amassed a nice-sized holding, perhaps hired some workers and reaped good profits for his produce. Similarly, dairymen and specialized producers of wine or luxury items could all prosper in an economy with great demand for food. Merchants too increasingly took their goods further afield to fetch the best prices they could find, and many became extremely wealthy. The rise of these middle ranks of society and indeed upward mobility in general will be a central factor in European food culture, as will the general tendency for the rich to become richer and the poor to become poorer. It is not merely that there was a greater divergence of wealth, a greater concentration among a smaller percentage of the population at the top of the social hierarchy, but a greater social stratification. That means more layers, just like strata in the earth's crust, larger quantities and more diverse types of people will ultimately mean a proliferation of different ways of eating and distinct food ideologies.

AGRICULTURE AND LAND TENURES

How people grew food differed greatly across Europe. Regional variations in soil quality, average rainfall, temperature, altitude, all determined what could be grown or raised successfully. Low-lying and well-irrigated plains tended to be devoted to cereal production, and mountainous regions were often given over to pasture. Southern climates could support olive and citrus groves, vineyards and Mediterranean vegetables that could never thrive in the north. Coastal regions depended more on fishing, and densely populated areas tended to have more specialized agriculture supplying cities. Equally important were land tenure systems, taxation structures and inheritance customs because these would ultimately affect how much food a farmer got to keep for his own consumption or sell on the market.

Despite the incentives for improving agriculture caused by high prices, much of Europe retained its traditional modes of agriculture and land ownership. The typical image we might have of a farm as an isolated and self-sufficient operation was quite unusual in Europe.

Most people lived in villages and were forced to sell a good portion of their produce so they could pay rents, taxes, or merely to buy what they could not produce. In many places the local lord might also be entitled to a good portion of whatever they grew. Often, therefore, a region blessed with fertile soil and good yields might still be quite poor. Increasingly, many of the poorest Europeans worked as wage laborers on other people's plots, which meant they had to buy everything they ate, or forage for wild plants and animals when the money ran out.

For all but the wealthiest, survival was precarious. Crop failures might occur as often as every dozen years. A drought or excessive rainfall could ruin an entire season's work. Wars could completely dislocate the rural economy, both native armies and enemies being equally destructive. Before the era of well-supplied military campaigns, soldiers basically took whatever they needed as they passed through. The French wars of religion in the sixteenth century and the Thirty Years' War in Germany from 1614–1648 wrought havoc on food production. It has also been suggested that Europe became marginally colder in the latter sixteenth and seventeenth centuries. This "little ice age" meant not only lower yields, but some crops refused to grow altogether. For example, in the Middle Ages wine grapes were grown in England, which became nearly impossible in the early modern period. All these factors, compounded with unsound government policies and local customs, meant that some areas of Europe prospered while others languished.

There were literally hundreds of different systems of agriculture across Europe in this period, and only the most general outlines of a few different patterns can be described. The greatest distinction that can be made is that while serfdom gradually declined or disappeared altogether in western Europe, it grew stronger east of the Elbe River. In Russia, Prussia in eastern Germany and elsewhere, serfdom would survive right down to modern times, keeping these countries extremely backward and impoverished. As a rule, those regions where credit was available and affordable and where property laws allowed land to be bought and sold easily, agriculture was gradually improved. Where customs, government policies and powerful nobles prevented innovation, rural society suffered. Beyond these basic differences, the way land was held also varied considerably.

In Italy, or to be more precise the many small city-states, dukedoms and other administrative units that make up what is today Italy, the countryside was usually dominated by the city. Land was often owned by wealthy merchants and bankers living in cities and was then rented to peasants through the "mezzadria" system whereby a percentage of the crops, usually half, would be given to the owner. Uniquely, many peasants even lived in cities, traveling each day to their fields outside of town or to nearby vineyards and olive groves just outside the city walls. The rural peasant was often in debt to lenders within the city also, borrowing to buy basic tools, animals or other necessities. In good years, this could be a prosperous situation for the farmer. In poor years, and especially with population decline in the seventeenth century, the farmer unable to pay his creditors often lost his land.

Interspersed among such holdings there may also have been pockets of quasifeudal estates, either owned by old noble families or newly granted to military leaders. As profits from trade slackened for Italians in the course of the sixteenth and seventeenth century, wealthy individuals increasingly invested in land on which they might build a suburban villa and perhaps manage it directly or rent it out to small tenants. In southern Italy and Sicily huge estates were more important, because there were fewer powerful cities and many more wealthy absentee nobles with extensive holdings. This pattern is significant, because the south tended to concentrate on large-scale enterprises, especially growing wheat, while in the north holdings tended to be smaller and more diversified, perhaps growing vegetables, keeping cattle and producing wine.

The situation in Spain and Portugal was similar to that of southern Italy. Large holdings or "latifundia" were common, but they were rarely farmed efficiently. Land was seen more as a status symbol than a business, and absentee nobles preferred to spend their income on luxury items rather than invest in improvement. Unique to this area were the broad rights granted to noblemen to transport and feed huge flocks of sheep up and down the country known as the "mesta." This was usually at the expense of food production. An excessively high tax burden, both to church and state, mostly to pay for expensive wars, also made the life of Spanish peasants particularly difficult. From the end of the sixteenth century well into the eighteenth century Spain suffered serious agrarian decline, even depopulation as a result of custom and government policy.

In France, although most people were legally free peasants, perhaps half owned their small plots outright. Nonetheless, they were at a distinct disadvantage being small producers, and most continued to live from hand to mouth. The other half were still burdened by what we might call the remnants of feudalism, the "corvée" or time required to work the landlord's plot, as well as many "banalités" (the myriad fees and restrictions which were not abolished until the French Revolution). Significantly, peasants also paid all the taxes because the nobility and clergy were tax-exempt. This situation not only gave the nobility a feeling of inherent superiority, but also the feeling that they did not need to work, that titles and rents and hunting rights should support them in their life of leisure. Unlike England and the Netherlands, therefore, the business-minded land owner who exploits the land directly was a rarity in France. Consequently, many regions of France, particularly the south, never succeeded in escaping subsistence crises throughout the early modern period. The tradition for land to be divided up equally among all sons when inherited also tended to create smaller and smaller plots, on which survival became increasingly difficult. The overall pattern is one of polarization, large noble estates mixed with tiny holdings that could barely support a family.

If the picture seems bleak for most of southern Europe, the Netherlands and England stand in sharp contrast. The United Provinces of the Netherlands, which broke free from Spain in the course of the latter sixteenth and early seventeenth century, is in many ways unlike the rest of Europe. Apart from being a tiny country, facing the sea from which it drew much of its sustenance in the form of fish, the country is also intensely urban, with perhaps half the population living in cities. The Netherlands also never had extensive feudal traditions, so there were few restrictions on buying and selling land. Farmers here had full property rights and were able to plant whatever they pleased. Because of the scarcity of land, even with the "polders"—land drained from the sea and surrounded by dikes—Dutch agriculture became heavily specialized from an early date. Market gardening became the rule as well as intensive dairy farming. Consequently, they were forced to import much of their grain from the Baltic, and in particular Poland, which was still dominated by serfdom. In doing so, they perfected large-scale shipping in huge tub-like boats called "fluyts," which in turn would give them extraordinary wealth as the dominant mercantile power of the seventeenth century.

Important for the present discussion though, was the intensive agriculture the Dutch adopted, and which England would soon imitate. England was the first large nation to succeed in escaping the recurrent subsistence crises that struck the rest of Europe. This may be in part due to the unique nature of land ownership in England, especially in the midlands, which tended to be organized into huge estates which were rented out in large parcels to tenant farmers who used wage la-

Figure 1.1 French farmers from the countryside. *From Nicolas de Bonnefons. Les delices de la campagne, suite du Jardinier françois. Ou est enseigna a preparer pour l'usage de la vie, tout ce qui croist sur la terre et dans les eaux/[Nicolas de Bonnefons] Paris: N. le Gras, 1684. Frontispiece. EPB 14529/A. Courtesy of Wellcome Library, London.*

borers. This gave the English a great degree of economic freedom and the ability to innovate. The changes that took place were so dramatic that they have been called an Agricultural Revolution even though they took place gradually, beginning in the sixteenth century and reaching a climax in the eighteenth. Ironically, the fundamental change involved fewer people actually farming; improved methods and extensive enclosures meant more food could be grown with less labor. There was also rapid population growth in eighteenth-century England, especially in cities. To feed these greater numbers, specialization and the scientific study of agriculture and stockbreeding provided farmers with the techniques to meet the growing demand. Increasingly, farming became more of a market-oriented business, a pattern that would continue right down to the present when a tiny fraction of the population provides food for the rest, and large producers who can invest in capital improvements tend to push out the small farmer.

In what ways then did these enterprising landowners and wealthy tenant farmers improve their yields and maximize their profits? Some of the simplest solutions involve more careful management, hiring a steward to oversee and direct all the various tasks on the farm. This of course assumes that the laborers are now working for the owner rather than themselves, and are perhaps being paid wages. Improved equipment, better irrigation, stronger plows and more draught animals like oxen, or increasingly horses, would certainly be a sound investment. Keeping animals could also bring greater yields, manure being the best available fertilizer (though there was also a trade in "night soil" or human refuse), as well as other kinds of soil amendments like peat and marl. Naturally it would be only the well-off farmers who could afford such capital-intensive investments.

Another way to improve the soil was by using "green manure" or a cover crop that could be grown in off seasons and then cut and worked into the soil. Another innovation was to flood a field creating a "water meadow" which protected germinating seeds while they grew. Crop rotation systems were also one of the most important ways to improve output. As anyone who has tried gardening knows, most plants deprive the soil of certain specific nutrients, and growing the same crop in the same plot year after year leads to gradual soil depletion and much lower yields. To remedy this, the typical practice was to leave a field fallow every few years, that is to grow nothing on it (except perhaps weeds) while the nutrients are replenished. This meant that at any given time up to a third of the entire arable land (land that can be cultivated) might be left unused. As an alternative, farmers began to use crop rotation systems, some of which, ironically they learned about from scholars reading ancient Roman texts on agriculture. Crop rotation systems usually replaced the fallow field with a fodder crop like alfalfa or clover which not only replenished the nitrogen in the soil but provided food for cattle who provided manure for the fields. Although it is impossible to estimate exactly how much more food could be produced using these systems on the same amount of land, agricultural historians usually refer to the seed-yield ratio, or the number of individual grains you get on an ear of wheat for every one you plant. Unimproved agriculture probably gave three or four grains on every stalk, while the improved methods may have given six or seven, or in the best of situations double the amount of produce. (To gauge how far we have come since then, picture a wheat stalk in your mind—it will probably have ten or twelve grains on it.)

While these methods were very slow to spread across Europe, and many places remained completely unable to adopt them, the effect in the long-term was to reduce the number of crop failures and serious famines. Keeping a significant surplus also meant that the consequences of unavoidable natural disasters were mitigated. More food could be saved for times of emergency. The Agricultural Revolution also involved the systematic improvement of crops and cattle through selective breeding, as well as more efficient rotation systems that included root vegetables such as turnips, promoted by Charles "Turnip" Townsend. Toward the very end of the period, even machines were being introduced to farming, the most famous of which was Jethro Tull's seed drill which could move over a field planting an exact number of seeds in neat orderly rows.

Perhaps just as important as these new techniques, was a new attitude toward farming and a flourishing literary genre that catered to this growing interest in agriculture as a worthy pursuit for the leisured nobleman. In Italy there was Agostino Gallo's *Twenty Days of Agriculture,* in France Charles Etienne's *Rustic House* and Olivier de Serres *Theater of Agriculture.* Konrad Heresbach's *Four Books of Husbandry* first appeared in Germany. In England Thomas Tusser's *Hundred Points,* later expanded to *Five Hundred Points of Good Husbandry,* achieved great popularity.[1] The importance of these texts lies not only in the fact that they disseminated new techniques and crops, but they made the life of the gentleman farmer a worthy and admirable pursuit. This ideal of the gentleman farmer appealed most to the English, and it is probably not coincidental that there agricultural innovations and the business-like spirit took off most effectively. By the eighteenth century it is clear that the Agricultural Revolution in England made possible the sweeping economic, social and cultural changes that were just beginning in the Industrial Revolution.

TRADE AND MARKETS

Just as renewed population growth in the sixteenth century provided a catalyst for agricultural innovation, the increased demand for food and other goods stimulated trade both within Europe and to the rest of the world. Because of high prices, merchants were willing to venture further afield, to try out new trade routes and increasingly to supply a greater volume of luxury goods to wealthy Europeans who craved them. But by far the greatest volume of trade involved basic foodstuffs: grains, wine, fish, oil, as well as other raw materials like wool, timber and iron. As with agriculture, banking systems and available credit were indispensable to expansion in trade also. The ability to draw money from a bank account at a foreign branch, or to exchange or borrow money at favorable rates made international trade more secure and profitable. Also as nations granted rights to foreigners to live and trade within their borders, and as they built "bourses" or exchange houses open to all, the flow of money and goods increased dramatically.

Another important factor was the development of "entrepôts" or great storage centers where goods could be kept until they commanded a good price. Medieval merchants often had to carry their wares with them to local fairs and hope to sell them there for the best price possible. In contrast, the early modern merchant could arrange a sale in one city and have his agent in another arrange to ship the goods somewhere else. Investors were also more likely to enter into business deals after they were legally protected through contracts and eventually joint-stock companies whose shares could be openly traded. There were even insurance companies, making trade much less of a wild gamble and more of a steady ongoing business.

Most merchants in the early modern period did not yet specialize in one single product or type of venture. Typically they would diversify their investments into banking, land, perhaps an industry such as mining, as well as transport and trade. Because any one of these activities might fail, it was considered safer to spread their money around. The most risky investments were naturally those involving long-distance trade. Roads were poorly maintained and thieves were a constant threat. Maritime trade proved even more dangerous given the frequency of shipwrecks and piracy. Great fortunes could be made by those willing to take the most perilous journeys, but fortunes could just as easily be lost.

Within Europe the most important food product shipped long distance was grain, which was almost always transported by boat due to the high cost of overland travel. Being the staple of the European diet, demand for grain was high everywhere, but especially in densely populated regions where labor was relatively specialized and expensive, such as northern Italy, western Germany and the Netherlands, northern France and southern England. Not surprisingly these places imported grain from places where labor was cheap and land plentiful, and usually where landlords had the tightest control over peasants. Thus Sicily and southern Italy became wheat exporters as did eastern Germany and Poland though they produced more rye.

In the late Middle Ages the northern trade routes through the Baltic and North Sea were dominated by a commercial alliance of cities known as the Hanseatic League. It connected cities in the West such as Bruges and London with German cities like Hamburg and Lübeck and with eastern regions as far as Novgorod in Russia. Hanseatic merchants carried much of the grain from east to west as well as other foods like pickled herring, which was indispensable in the European diet during Lent when meat is forbidden. Cloth, timber and metal were also among the goods they carried. By the sixteenth century though, the Hanseatic merchants had lost much of their monopoly, especially as Dutch and English merchants began to expand their operations. Entrenched ways of doing business and a lack of flexibility hastened the decline of the Hanseatic League, especially compared with the freer business atmosphere of Antwerp and Amsterdam.

Antwerp in the sixteenth century was the great commercial hub of northern Europe offering the best interest rates and the first organized stock exchange. Consequently merchants from north and south met there to exchange goods. On any given day one could buy wines from Bordeaux, oil from Tuscany, spices from Asia, and increasingly even products from the Americas like sugar. Antwerp lost its dominance in the course of the Revolt of the Netherlands which was an attempt to break away from Spanish rule. Following the sack of Antwerp in 1576 by unpaid Spanish soldiers, commercial activity shifted to the north. In the end, Amsterdam in the United Provinces, which had successfully won its independence, became the new financial center through the seventeenth century. The Dutch also succeeded in carrying the goods themselves rather than waiting for foreign merchants to show up, making them spectacularly wealthy.

The foods carried by the northern merchants were certainly of great importance, but they still accounted for a small proportion of all food brought to market. Most produce and meats were too perishable to make such long journeys, wait in warehouses or be haggled over by middlemen, and it so was rarely transported more than 50 miles or so to the nearest city. Regions with navigable rivers like the Rhineland, the Loire and Rhone Valleys in France, or the Po Valley in northern Italy, would naturally be able to transport foods further. In the case of the Po, this enabled a lucrative trade in products like rice, cheeses and hams. Fresh fruits, vegetables and meats, the more perishable, the closer to home they would have to be sold. Most cities would also have little "islands" of intensive agriculture and stockbreeding from which farmers could carry and sell goods at markets within the cities themselves.

Another major nexus of trade was the Mediterranean Sea across which galleys, large flat ships with oars and sails, navigated by hugging the coastlines or crossing from island to island. Here the emphasis was to a certain extent on grain, especially wheat, barley and millet. Salt, oil and wine were also carried to and from ports such as Barcelona, Marseilles and Genoa, and often further into the Atlantic. The most profitable trade across the Mediterranean was far less bulky and fetched much higher prices per pound. This was the spice trade. Several cities competed in the spice trade in the late Middle Ages, but Venice proved to be the most successful. The arsenal in Venice could produce ships more quickly and they were better armed. Venetian merchants were also physically closer to the eastern Mediterranean ports such as Beirut and Alexandria where spices and other luxury goods were traded. The Venetians also built up what we might call the first maritime empire, capturing ports all the way down the coast of Illyria (what was until recently Yugoslavia) to Greece and the islands of Corfu and Crete. These were crucial stopping-off points where ships could load up with victuals and water, and from which shipping could be protected.

The spices themselves traveled from as far away as the Moluccas or India, carried overland via the great silk road or by Arab merchants along the coast of the Indian Ocean to the ports of the Middle East. There they were picked up by the Venetians and transported to the rest of Europe where they commanded astronomical prices. Naturally, only the wealthiest consumers could afford spices, and this made them powerful markers of status. To offer guests a heavily spiced dish was literally to consume one's wealth. The demand for spices would also prove one of the decisive catalysts in a series of events that would not only change the way Europeans ate, but would change the entire world.

Another factor that makes early modern trade radically different than our own stems from certain economic assumptions of the period. The reigning economic theory, called mercantilism, posited that a fixed volume of trade exists in the world, basically because it insisted that demand was not elastic. That is, once the average consumer buys his bread, you cannot convince him to buy more which would only go to waste. Of course we now know you can convince consumers to buy more than their immediate needs, and you can always create new needs by introducing new products. But early modern economists believed that if you wanted to increase the volume of trade in your country, you had to steal lucrative shipping routes from other countries. This led to several purely mercantile wars, increasingly global in range, whose goal was to muscle in on the trade of competing nations. The transfer of New Amsterdam from the Dutch to the English, who promptly renamed it New York, was a settlement made at the conclusion of one of these mercantile wars.

Importantly, nations as a whole were considered economic rivals, not individuals. It was for this reason that kings granted to merchants exclusive privileges and charters to trade in certain products or with entire regions. The Muscovy Company, the Levant Company and the East India Company are just some English examples. They believed that such monopolies would give the necessary advantages to succeed, which would ultimately bring money into the nation. They also believed, rather oddly according to our way of thinking, that the goods should be sold abroad and local consumption should be kept at a minimum. This way, money from trade would be flowing into the country, out of the pockets of foreigners. Equally, native produce should be sold abroad rather than consumed locally. A favorable balance of trade, more exports than imports was considered the only way to become wealthy. This theory is called bullionist. Bullion, meaning pure gold and silver, if kept inside the nation, equaled wealth, particularly for the crown. Following this logic, nations heavily taxed imports and offered great deals to major exporters. They made laws forbidding consumers to buy goods transported by rival countries. National governments also meddled with the economy in ways that we now believe hamper healthy competition and progress. Exclusive trading rights and charters to settle in the New World are just one good example. And it is no wonder that most kings invested first in ventures to claim the largest prize of all, the spice trade.

WORLD TRADE AND COLONIAL EMPIRES

With such enormous profits to be made bringing spices to Europe, competitors were naturally looking for a way to avoid the many middlemen, and especially the Venetians who held a virtual monopoly over the trade with the eastern Mediterranean. A direct trade route to eastern Asia would cut out all the intermediaries, but only one thing stood in their way: the vast continent of Africa.

The Portuguese had a lively interest in the West African coast since their king, aptly named Henry the Navigator (even though he had never been to sea), began to directly sponsor ocean voyages in the early fifteenth century. The Portuguese had a long tradition of seamanship, with sturdy vessels like the naõ and later the caravel with both square and triangular or lateen sails which made them suitable for ocean-going voyages. They also had a tradition of making portolan charts and sophisticated navigational instruments like the quadrant that aligned with the North Star to tell latitude. Unfortunately their maps were of no use far out to sea and the quadrant only works in the Northern Hemisphere where the North Star is visible. Use of the astrolabe, new ships and also a willingness to risk going out into the sea were required if one wished to travel to Africa. Another problem is that ocean currents run clockwise in the northern Atlantic, but counterclockwise in the south. Any attempt to sail south of the equator pushes a ship back. Strangely, a ship must travel west first in order to be brought back south, which of course meant going hundreds of miles out to sea. Eventually the Portuguese began to do just that and Africa proved to be extremely lucrative for trade in gold, ivory and increasingly, slaves. Slaves were usually only used as household servants by the wealthy in Europe, but soon the Portuguese and Spanish would find other uses for them—as workers on plantations.

The lure of even greater wealth from the spice trade led the Portuguese further and further down the coast of Africa, until Bartolomeu Dias finally rounded the Cape of Good Hope in 1488. Only a decade later Vasco da Gama sailed all the way to India, successfully making the direct connection to riches of the east, cutting out the Muslim middlemen and giving stiff competition to the Venetian spice trade. Eventually they would settle in the Spice Islands themselves, located in what is today Indonesia. The Portuguese established a pattern of erecting small fortified trading outposts or "feitoria" throughout these new lands, the most important being Goa in India, Malacca on the Malay Peninsula and Macao in China. Throughout the sixteenth century it was the Portuguese who controlled trade with Asia. Only in the seventeenth century did the Dutch and English successfully muscle in on their territory.

It should not seem strange then that when the Genoese merchant Christopher Columbus had the idea of sailing westward to reach Asia, he first approached the Portuguese. His scheme posed too great a risk, and he was turned down by several nations, including the Spanish. It was only when the news of Dias' reaching the tip of Africa arrived in the Spanish court of Queen Isabella and King Ferdinand, that they began to consider his proposal seriously. One of the greatest misconceptions people have about Columbus' plan is that his contemporaries thought it would be impossible because the earth is flat. Anyone with even the most basic scientific knowledge knew that the earth is round. Astronomy of the fifteenth century derived mostly from Ptolemy of Alexandria, writing more than a thousand years before, and although he mistakenly placed the earth at the center of the universe, he certainly knew it was round. People's real fears were that the distance was far too great to travel, a reasonable fear given their relatively good estimate of the earth's size. Columbus however believed the earth to be much smaller, and of course he knew nothing of the two continents blocking the way to Asia.

It is also important to remember that Columbus' motives were not exploration per se but rather an attempt to find a quick route to China so he could cut in on the wildly lucrative spice trade. In fact, even after bumping into Caribbean Islands and the mainland, he believed he was somewhere slightly east of Asia. From his journals, it is clear that Columbus was desperate to find pepper, cinnamon, nutmeg and anything that he might bring back to Europe, including gold. What he found instead were other foods that would have an equally important but entirely different impact on the world. Columbus and his crew were the first Europeans to taste corn, chili peppers, the sweet potato, and the first to smoke tobacco. Soon Spaniards would find tomatoes, chocolate, green beans, squash, potatoes and turkeys. Most of these foods remained botanical curiosities in Europe for some time, but in the long run they would dramatically change the way Europeans ate.

Equally important was the fact that the Spanish conquered the great Aztec Empire in Mexico and the Inca Empire in Peru. From these two focal points they eventually dominated and settled nearly all of Central and South America. Their first aim was crude exploitation, finding as much gold and silver as possible, but it soon became apparent that they could also reap profits from growing luxury items. The Caribbean islands and the Portuguese colony of Brazil were the most important places where plantations were first set up, mostly for the production of sugar cane. Sugar was among those expensive luxuries originally imported from India and later Cyprus and Crete, but it also began to be grown on Madeira and the Canary Islands even before contact with the Americas. When colonists realized that they could grow sugar in their new possessions, this became perhaps the only product Columbus originally envisioned bringing home that actually did become important in world trade. The plantations themselves tended to be huge estates because land was practically free for the taking. Unfortunately the inhabitants of the islands whom the Spanish forced to work the plantations and the heavy cane processing machinery had the habit of dying off in large numbers. Unwittingly, Europeans had introduced smallpox and measles to the Native American populations. Compounded with war and malnutrition, within a generation or so the native populations were decimated. Some tribes, such as the Arawaks whom Columbus first encountered, disappeared off the face of the earth forever. The solution to this labor shortage was to use African slave labor. In the early modern period at least 10 million Africans were brought in chains to the New World essentially to satisfy the European sweet tooth.

Despite the human suffering and misery the plantation economy caused, colonial owners grew fabulously wealthy, and it was not long before other European nations tried to snatch some of the Spanish and Portuguese possessions. There was a good deal of "privateering" in the sixteenth century, which is basically a legalized form of piracy. By the seventeenth century the French, Dutch and English were off establishing their own colonies. Each of these nations managed to wrest a few Caribbean islands for their own plantations. They also carved up the eastern seaboard of North America between them, the French taking Quebec and Louisiana, the English establishing Virginia and New England, and the Dutch sandwiched between the two in what is now New York state. Far more important for the Dutch was their seizure of practically all Portuguese colonies in Indonesia, although this was officially sponsored by the Dutch East India Company and not the United Provinces of the Netherlands. What all this meant is that eventually the trade in luxury foods like spices and plantation foods which would eventually include chocolate, coffee and rum passed into northern European hands.

NOTE

1. Agostino Gallo, *Le vinti giornate dell' agricoltura* (Venice: Camillo Borgominerio, 1584); Charles Etienne and Jean Liebault, *Maison Rustique, or the Country Farme*, translated by Richard Surflet, amended by Gervase Markham (London: Johan Bill, 1616); Olivier de Serres, *Le Theatre d'agriculture et mesnage des champs* (Paris: I. Metayer, 1600); Konrad Heresbach, *Foure Books of Husbandry,* translated by Barnabe Googe (London: Richard Watkins, 1577); Thomas Tusser, *Five Hundred points of good husbandry* (London: Richard Tottell, 1577).

CHAPTER 2
INGREDIENTS

Compared to today when supermarkets stock foods from all around the globe, we might expect that the range of ingredients available to early modern Europeans was very narrow and the diet bland and monotonous. For the poorest of Europeans this was certainly the case, and as a rule people were highly dependent on whatever could be grown in a given season or preserved for later use. But for those with money to buy imported items, and for those with access to forests and wild places that teemed with edible plants and animals, a great variety of foods were regularly eaten. If anything, the number of species consumed has diminished with the advance of agriculture and husbandry as a capital-intensive business. Many wild birds and fish, for example, have almost completely disappeared from European tables in modern times. Others have been hunted or fished to near extinction. The list of ingredients that follows is organized by major food group and importance of each food in the diet rather than by scientific taxonomy. Each entry also describes, when possible, the origin of each food, how it was prepared, its social meaning and any other ideas that may have been associated with it.

GRAINS

Wheat

Wheat was the most important ingredient in the European diet at all levels of society. The majority was ground and baked into bread which was considered an indispensable accompaniment to every meal. In fact, even the words *accompany* and *companion* derive from the Latin words meaning to share bread. Bread is also the most important food in the Christian religion. It played a central role in the Mass, a ritual in which bread offered to the congregation was said to be transformed into the body of Christ.

For regular use, the quality and nutritional content of bread varied greatly. Wealthy consumers preferred the finest and whitest flours for their bread, which was known in England as manchet. Those who could afford to often chipped off the "upper crust" as well. Thin slices of bread were used as a plate or trencher onto which other foods could be placed. It was not until the sixteenth century that individual plates came into ordinary use. Wheat was also made into cakes, pastries and pies, of which the rich were apparently inordinately fond. Physicians of the day never tired of complaining about their patients who indulged in such confections. Starch was also extracted from wheat and used in both baked goods and to stiffen the ruffs or collars of fashionable elites.

Lower down the social scale, a greater proportion of the daily diet and caloric intake consisted of bread. Less expensive bread contained more bran, or the hull of the grain, making it darker and rougher. Frequently, wheat flour was mixed with barley or rye, and the very poor might even use beans or chestnuts to make their bread go further. Ironically, whole wheat bread was probably more nutritious than white bread, or at least the roughage promoted good digestion, but stone-ground flours also contained minute particles of stone which seriously wore down people's teeth.

Baking bread was an organized profession with strict legal controls and standards, and in cities it was typically purchased. High prices, or scarcity of bread, was one of the most frequent causes for civil unrest, and ensuring a steady supply was a constant concern for early modern governments. So too was maintaining standard weight and size for each loaf, which is supposedly why bakers offered their customers a "baker's dozen"—to avoid being fined for underweight bread.

In the countryside bread was often baked within the household, but not every house could afford its own oven or the fees for using the lord's. In such cases porridge was a much more economical option. A small amount of wheat could be roughly crushed, cooked with minimal fuel and provide a nourishing meal. Among rich and poor alike, mush made of grain was considered especially restorative for invalids and the elderly.

Figure 2.1 Baker at oven. *From Nicolas de Bonnefons. Les delices de la campagne, suite du Jardinier françois. Ou est enseigna a preparer pour l'usage de la vie, tout ce qui croist sur la terre et dans les eaux / [Nicolas de Bonnefons] Paris: N. le Gras, 1684. p.1. EPB 14529. Courtesy of Wellcome Library, London.*

Flour could also be rolled or twisted into pasta of various shapes. Vermicelli, macaroni and lasagna noodles were all well known in Italy by the early modern period. Pasta was also normally made fresh at home. It was not until the industrial era that machine-made and dried noodles made from hard durum wheat or semolina flour became common. Surprisingly, the marriage of spaghetti with tomato sauce was a relative late-comer. There was also a dry flat bread made from a similar dough called *azima* (or *matzoh*), which most historical scholars associated with Jewish communities, but it was sometimes eaten by non-Jews, as we eat crackers.

A few ancient relatives of wheat were also grown widely in Europe: *spelt, farro, einkorn* and *emmer*. These plants bear only a single or double grain, and were thus considered a less viable crop than wheat, but interestingly they can contain a greater percentage of protein per grain, which is why we have seen a resurgence of them in health food stores nowadays. All of these grains, especially farro, were typically boiled in soups.

Barley

One of the oldest cultivated plants, barley was usually boiled into porridge or *ptisan* or decocted into a medicinal "barley water." Although it does not make very good bread, the grains when germinated and lightly roasted in a process called "malting" yield a thick and rich liquid that is the prime ingredient in beer and ale.

Rye

Grown almost exclusively in northern and eastern Europe, rye was most typically baked into dark, relatively dense bread. It is a much hardier grain than wheat and flourishes in the harsh weather and thicker soils of the north. It can be grown interspersed with wheat or barley, in which case the mixture was known as *maslin*. Rye can also be distilled into hard spirits such as vodka and whiskey. Rye is sometimes attacked by a fungus called ergot which is difficult to detect on the mature grain. Because the affected kernels contain the psychotropic drug LSD, it can cause intense hallucinations, violent illness and death. Major outbreaks of ergotism, a toxic condition caused by eating the fungus, have been recorded in Europe through the early modern period and into the twentieth century. It has been suggested that outbreaks of mass hysteria, such as witch hunts, may have been induced by ergotism.

Oats

Most Europeans considered oats fit only for horses or the desperately poor. Only in northerly climates like Scotland was it eaten on a regular basis. Cooked as oatmeal or baked into flat cakes called *farls,* oats are now known to be highly nutritious, but were scorned by early modern physicians for being indigestible.

Millet, Panic and Sorghum

Well known today as bird food, the minute grains of millet were boiled into a semi-solid *polenta* (a porridge) which after cooling could be sliced and reheated. This dish was more typically made with corn after its introduction in the sixteenth century. Panic is a relative of millet and sorghum is another grass native to Africa whose tiny round grains were sometimes used in Europe in ways similar to millet. All these were considered inferior grains, especially by wealthy consumers who associated them with poverty. Through the early modern period they gradually became obsolete, though they continued to be grown on a wide scale elsewhere in the world.

Buckwheat

Buckwheat is a brownish-gray triangular grain native to Asia, more closely related to rhubarb than other cereal grasses. It first arrived in eastern Europe some time in the late Middle Ages. It was grown mostly in colder northern regions and was usually cooked whole, cracked into *groats* or ground and made into pancakes.

Poppy, Sesame, Flax and Cannabis

All these seeds were eaten in Europe. Poppy was more prevalent in the north and sesame in the south. Apart from adorning bread or being baked into pastries, poppy seeds could also be pressed into oil. The latex from the opium poppy was made into medicine and was one of the most widely prescribed narcotics. The stalks of flax were normally used to make linen, but the seeds were sometimes eaten or baked into bread. Cannabis was usually grown for rope making but the seeds and young shoots were sometimes eaten too. The medical author Paulus Kyr claimed that "cannabis seeds are bad for the head if eaten in great quantity, create foul humors and dry up the genital seed; they are difficult to digest, but not harmful if crushed with vinegar and

25

honey."[1] His contemporary Charles Etienne remarked that the oil pressed from hemp seeds is "used as a condiment by paupers due to poverty."[2] Another medical author, Melchior Sebizius, insisted that "it assails the head if eaten immoderately ... and causes delirium."[3] The variety of *cannabis sativa* these authors refer to should not be confused with marijuana though; it was grown principally for its straight strong fibers.

Rice

Rice was a relatively rare and expensive commodity through most of the Middle Ages, and certainly not a staple as it was in Asia. Typically it would be boiled with milk and sugar into a dish resembling rice pudding. Only in the fifteenth century did it begin to be cultivated on a wider scale, especially in Lombard plains of northern Italy where it would be cooked as a risotto. The Moorish inhabitants of Spain also grew rice and after their expulsion Christians continued the practice. Rice could also be ground into a fine flour that was used as a thickening agent.

Corn

Corn or maize was one of the very few New World natives to be quickly adopted by Europeans. After its introduction by Columbus, corn was first grown in Spain and in the sixteenth century spread to much of Europe. It is easy to grow, bears dozens of grains per ear and can be easily dried and stored. Unfortunately Europeans did not learn how to process corn the way Native Americans had using crushed limestone or wood ash to soak the grains before drying and grinding. This process makes lysine available which is necessary for absorbing proteins. Also combining corn tortillas with beans offered a relatively complete protein package. In European regions where corn became a staple, as in northern and central Italy and Spain, malnourishment and the vitamin deficiency *pellagra* became a serious problem. Interestingly, most regions that were once part of the Roman Empire and were used to eating polenta, adopted corn relatively quickly. It became a major crop in the early modern period from Spain and France all the way to Romania. Perhaps more difficult to explain is the fact that corn was also grown as far as China by the early sixteenth century. This suggests that corn may have reached Asia from the Americas even before

Columbus' encounter. Sweet corn, the kind eaten fresh on the cob, was unknown in Europe or elsewhere until modern times.

LEGUMES
Old World Beans

The beans most frequently grown by Europeans before the six-teenth century were the fava bean and the black-eyed pea which con-fusingly was called *phaseolus* in Latin, the name soon given to new-world species. Beans were a very important food, particularly for the poor, during Lent when no meat could be eaten. Consequently, they were associated with poverty, and few sophisticated diners would condescend to eat beans for fear of debasement. For everyone else though, beans were critical to survival. When dried they could last through the winter and be boiled into soups, mashed or cooked into more substantial dishes with many ingredients. They were one of the most frequently eaten foods throughout the early modern period. Medical opinion was united in condemning beans as gross, difficult to digest and flatulence-promoting. Only laborers were thought to have stomachs strong enough to digest them. A diet high in fava beans can in fact affect some people with a disorder called favism that results in weakness and disorientation.

New World Beans

Several other species of bean, including green beans were intro-duced into Europe in the sixteenth century, but rarely were botanists consistent in distinguishing them from those they already knew. The first scientific description came from botanist Leonhart Fuchs in 1542. These new beans were grown so extensively and eaten so regularly that some people, like the Tuscans, were known as *mangiafagioli* or bean-eaters.

Peas

Peas were among the few legumes with no social stigma attached to them. The poor ate them out of necessity, usually dried and cooked as a "pease pottage" but they also came into fashion fresh among the rich. In sixteenth-century Lombardy "they are greatly esteemed among nobles and have risen to the most lavish banquets of princes" according to Italian physician and polymath Girolamo Cardano.[4] A century later, in seventeenth-century Rome, Salvatore Massonio tells us "the rich are used to eating them cooked with prosciutto, a most pleasant dish, carried to the most sumptuous suppers."[5] The court of Louis XIV of France was mad about fresh green peas. The snap pea variety with an edible shell was developed by the Dutch in the early seventeenth century.

Chickpeas

An important staple throughout the Mediterranean, chickpeas were among the first cultivated plants. In the past there were also red and black varieties, with more varied tastes and textures than modern cultivars. Chickpeas frequently appeared in soups and stews, but could also be dried into flour, added to breads or baked on its own into a *soca*, a flat pizza-like dish from southern France.

Lentils

Lentils are also among the oldest cultivated plants on earth, and along with beans they constituted an essential source of protein for the average working European. Physicians, however, believed that they were among the most crass of foods, difficult to digest and if eaten in great quantity could lead to cancer, leprosy and elephantiasis.

Vetches, Darnel and Lupins

Vetch, darnel and lupins are lentil-like plants, either cultivated in crop rotations or gathered as weeds among other crops. They can be quite bitter, and were usually only eaten in times of desperation. Flemish physician Hugo Fridaevallis contended that they may save lives in times of famine but are really only appropriate as cattle fodder otherwise.[6] Some species may even have mildly toxic properties, and both dietary and culinary writers strongly argued against eating them. In French the word for darnel is *ivraie* which suggests that it makes people who eat it drunk (*ivre*). On the other hand, there are vetch species that are nutritious and tasty and were eaten through the early modern period. Roman food writer Alessandro Petronio insisted though that *cicerchia* (chickling vetches) "pass only on the table of poor people, though sometimes they are used by the rich, to satisfy some extravagant appetite."[7] The process of removing vetches from other grains was called "garbling" which oddly has come to mean mixing something up in modern English.

VEGETABLES

Cabbages, Kale, Cauliflower, Broccoli, Brussels Sprouts and Kohlrabi

Remarkably, all these vegetables are varieties of one species: *Brassica oleracea*. Cabbages were among the most common vegetables throughout Europe. Compact and hard-headed varieties were prevalent in northern Europe and were popular either boiled or shredded and pickled as sauerkraut or dressed as a coleslaw. The English referred to cabbage as "coleworts." Looser, more leafy types were grown in the south. Traditionally, cabbage was said to prevent drunkenness, and many people would eat cabbage before a banquet so they could indulge later on. Cauliflower and broccoli were most popular in Italy. Brussels sprouts are the creation of sixteenth-century Belgian farmers who specially bred cabbage to form a tall stalk covered with tiny flowerets. Although the name suggests their origin near Brussels, who first developed them is unknown. They were first recorded in 1554 by the Dutch botanist Rembert Dodoens in his *Cruydeboek*. Kohlrabi is a variety specially bred in the sixteenth century to form a round turnip-like bulb above ground. Its name means "cabbage turnip" in German.

Cucumbers

Considered among the most harmful vegetables because of their cold and moist qualities, physicians usually recommended that they only be eaten in the summer by people who were naturally hot. For those with colder complexions cucumbers could cause shuddering fits or fevers as the noxious juice collects in the veins and putrefies. Of course most people ignored these warnings, and the fact that cucumbers were so widely cultivated is ample proof that most people ate them.

Squashes and Gourds

Many types of gourd were native to the Old World, but many of the varieties we are now familiar with, hard squashes like butternut, spaghetti and delicata as well as "summer" squashes like zucchini are all native to the New World. The name squash is derived from a Narraganset Indian word *askutasquash*. There is still a great deal of debate over the origin of the pumpkin; it may have arrived from Asia in classical times, or it may have come from the Americas. Squashes and gourds were usually cooked in a broth or fried in a pan, and as Spanish-born physician Ludovicus Nonnius relates, in Italy they were dried for winter use and "a truly new invention is to preserve them in sugar."[8]

Artichokes and Cardoons

These two plants are close relatives, one grown for the fibrous stalk, the other for its thistle-like bud. Both were cooked in similar ways, trimmed and then boiled or fried. They could also be eaten raw, thinly sliced and dipped into a sauce. Artichokes were among the more fashionable vegetables in European courts, and legend has it that Catherine de Medici introduced them to France when she married King Henry II. Artichokes also had a reputation for being an aphrodisiac. The English schoolmaster Thomas Cogan in typically modest sixteenth-century fashion said "they procure a more ernest desire both of man or woman to the venerial acte," and even specified that the hearts are better than the leaves for this purpose.[9]

Celery

Celery was well known but often described as an alternative to parsley which suggests that the leaves were most commonly used as an herb rather than the stalk. It was probably in sixteenth-century Italy that the first celery stalks were cultivated by mounding earth up the plant as it grows to keep it white and sweet, but the first author to discuss this procedure was the French agronomist Olivier de Serres in 1623. Around the same time celeriac, the swollen root of the celery plant, was also cultivated in Europe.

Asparagus

Among the few vegetables universally praised, Europeans considered asparagus very nutritious, and because of the acrid smell of one's urine after eating them, a good blood cleanser as well. They were often collected in the wild, but cultivated extensively by the time of the Renaissance. Royal gardener Jean de la Quintinie developed a way to grow them in hotbeds so Louis XIV could eat asparagus year-round. By the early eighteenth century German farmers were cultivating white asparagus, created by heaping dirt around the stalk as it grows to prevent sunlight from turning it green. Eighteenth-century English cookbook author Hannah Glasse's directions for cooking asparagus might be followed to this day, though we might choose not to eat them with our fingers.

To Dress Asparagus

Scrape all the stalks very carefully till they look white, then cut all the stalks even alike, throw them into water, and have ready a stew-pan boiling. Put in some salt, and tie the asparagus in little bundles. Let the water keep boiling, and when they are tender take them up. If you boil them too much they lose both colour and taste. Cut the round of a small loaf, about half an inch thick, toast it on both sides, dip it in the asparagus liquor, and lay it in your dish: pour a little butter over the toast, then lay your asparagus on the toast all round the dish, with the white tops outward. Do not pour butter over the asparagus, for that makes them greasy to the fingers, but have your butter in a bason, and send it to the table.[10]

Marshmallows

The sweet white confection we are all familiar with is actually a pale imitation of a plant (*Althea officinalis*) once eaten in Europe. The spongy root of the vegetable was used in candy-making and medicine. Some people even used it as a toothbrush.

Eggplant

Eggplants arrived in most of Europe some time in the Middle Ages, probably by way of Moorish Spain where they were regularly grown. Elsewhere they seem to have been associated with Jews, whose culinary heritage was closely linked to that of the Muslims. In the early modern period they were universally denounced as a dangerous vegetable that promotes an infinite number of diseases. In Italian the name *melanzana* derives from the Latin *Mali insani*—meaning "insane apples." Recipes are almost nonexistent with the exception of the Spanish, who maintained many of the foods of their predecessors on the Iberian peninsula.

Tomatoes

Despite the current enthusiasm for tomatoes in Italy, Spain and the rest of southern Europe, they were not well received upon arrival from the New World in the sixteenth century. Looking and smelling much like their poisonous relatives in the *Solanaceae* family it is not surprising that few people tried to eat them. They were usually grown as ornamental flowers, and were only described botanically in Mattioli's *Commentaries on Dioscorides* in 1544. Although wealthy diners would not eat tomatoes, it does appear that their poorer neighbors had begun to eat them out of necessity. Good evidence of this can be found in 1650 in Melchior Sebizius' *On the Faculty of Foods* in which he writes that they are so cold and moist that they must be cooked with pepper, salt and oil, but "our cooks absolutely reject them, even though they grow easily and copiously in gardens."[11] The first published cookbook recipes including tomatoes appeared in Naples at the very end of the seventeenth century in Antonio Latini's *Lo Scalco alla Moderna*. In this recipe the *cassuola* or casserole would be placed directly in the fire and hot coals would be heaped on top of the lid.

Another Dish, A Tomato Casserole

You make the said casserole with pieces of pigeon, breast of veal, and stuffed chicken necks. Stew these well in a good broth with aromatic herbs and pleasant spices, together with cock's combs and testicles. When it is properly cooked, take the tomatoes and place them to roast on the coals. Then clean them, cut them into four pieces, and put them in with the aforementioned things. Take care that it doesn't cook too much, because these need little cooking. Then add a fresh egg with a bit of lemon juice, and let it scramble. Cover it with a lid with flames below and above.[12]

Peppers

We know that Columbus was the first European to see Native Americans consuming capsicum peppers, and our word for them reveals that he was really searching for black pepper and called these "pimiento" with as much enthusiasm as he called the natives "Indians." But the very fact that they could also be found as far away as China within a few years has led some scholars to suggest that they may have reached Asia even before they did Europe. It is certain though that the Portuguese brought peppers to their colonies in Asia. Peppers were first described in Europe in the German herbal of Leonhart Fuchs in 1542, but he thought they came from India. Like several other New World imports though, it appears that poor people were the only ones willing to eat them; they are not even mentioned in cookbooks which naturally catered to a literate and elite audience.

ROOT VEGETABLES

Beets

An extremely versatile root that also yields edible leaves, beets came in a variety of colors and sizes. The round red variety was developed in the late sixteenth century. The beet could be boiled or roasted, or served sliced in a cold salad.

Carrots

The carrot was introduced from Islamic countries in the late Middle Ages, reaching northern Europe in the fourteenth and fifteenth centuries. Through selective breeding, the size and flavor of carrots were improved and eventually the orange carrot we are familiar with today was developed in the Netherlands some time in the seventeenth century. Before that carrots were either purple or yellowish. Carrots were usually served cooked, often in the form of a pudding or soup.

Parsnips

Looking much like a fat white carrot, parsnips were under cultivation since ancient times, and were accounted among those useful roots that could be stored over winter months. They were also one of the few naturally sweet foods common before the widespread use of sugar. They can even be made into wine.

Turnips

Because turnips keep very well stored in a cool place, they became one of the most important vegetables for winter. They could also be pickled or preserved in honey. As an innovation in British husbandry Charles "Turnip" Townshend introduced the idea of feeding turnips to domestic animals over the winter, thus ensuring a more regular supply of fresh meat beyond the fall when most were slaughtered. Once merely a garden vegetable, large-scale cultivation of turnips began in the eighteenth century. As economist Adam Smith noted about turnips, carrots and cabbages, such "things were formerly never raised but by the spade, but which are now commonly raised by the plough."[13] As a consequence of increased supply, the price came down significantly.

Radishes

One of the most frequently encountered appetizers, radishes were nonetheless criticized by physicians for causing stomach bloating and belching. Some thought they should only be used at the end of a meal. Others condemned them outright.

Horseradish

Although it can be cooked and eaten, the distinctive and intense flavor of horseradish is lost, so it was usually eaten raw. Melchior Sebizius noted that although its flavor is very hot "it is used very often among Germans as a condiment with meals, pounded or grated with wine or vinegar."[14]

Skirrets and Salsify

Skirrets are a long sweet root vegetable that was eaten either raw in a salad, boiled and dressed, or fried in oil and butter. Salsify is a reddish root that was peeled and cooked in a similar way, and was often known as oyster plant because its flavor and texture are vaguely reminiscent of oysters when cooked.

Sea Holly or Eringoes

The roots of this plant were often preserved in sugar or candied and were considered especially nourishing and good for the elderly. Its leaves are also edible.

Onions

Common everywhere in Europe, the onion had a strong association with the lower classes. Physicians denounced its sharp acrid odor and taste and insisted that they be either roasted or boiled twice to remove their noxious qualities. This suggests that many people ate them raw. Cooked onions were also among the most prevalent flavorings in soups, stews and ragouts, and among poorer Europeans onions may have been the most commonly consumed vegetable.

Garlic

Garlic was one of the principal flavorings of southern Europe, though it was also eaten by lower classes elsewhere. The therapeutic virtues of garlic were also recognized from an early date, and as the "poor man's theriac" or medicine, it was recommended for those who could not afford more expensive spices. But it was also thought to be difficult to digest, which is why, they claimed, it causes bad breath. Spanish food writer Lobera de Avila suggested "so that it not be so damnable, you must roast it twice."[15] One of the most typical ways of using garlic was in a green sauce made with parsley, vinegar and bread.

Leeks, Scallions, Shallots and Chives

These members of the onion family were equally derided by physicians. As Charles Estienne wrote, "onions, garlic, leeks are useless however cooked ... for they are difficult to digest, and frequently cause belching, and often repeat in the mouth, so that afterwards crass vapors rise upward, causing serious headaches."[16]

Potatoes

First sent to Europe from Peru in the latter sixteenth century, potatoes were regarded with great suspicion in early modern Europe. They resemble relatives in the nightshade family, well known in Europe and deadly, so this attitude is not entirely surprising. They also appear to have been associated with the truffle, and in many languages they bear a similar name—*tartufoli* in Italian means "little truffle." The Dutch botanist Carolus Clusius was the first to grow them in Europe as well as describe them in his *Raziorum plantorum historia*. In England, legend has it that explorer Francis Drake, or in some versions Sir Walter Raleigh, introduced them from Virginia, and hence the mistaken belief, long-held, that they originated there. They were eaten commonly in Spain, as the following comment from the seventeenth century shows. "In Spain they cook them in the coals, peel them and cut them into slices and eat them with a bit of wine, rose water and sugar."[17] But in some places they had to be forced on an unwilling populace, as they were by Frederick the Great in Prussia. In France they were not common until the eighteenth century when Augustin Parmentier became their great promoter. Having won a contest to provide a suitable substitute for grain, even King Louis XVI gave Parmentier his support by growing them and wearing potato flowers in his hat, a fashion that quickly spread. Not until after the French Revolution were they promoted as egalitarian fare suitable for Republicans and eaten on a wide scale. Apparently even the Tuileries gardens in Paris were torn up and planted with potatoes.

Sweet Potatoes (*Ipomoea batatas*)

Often called a yam in this country, they are actually two completely different plants. Yams are native to Africa, and are much bigger than the American sweet potato, which can be any color. The potatoes which were first eaten by Spanish explorers and brought to Europe were sweet potatoes. Interestingly, sweet potatoes caught on more quickly in China, where they were introduced by the Portuguese. It has been suggested that China's rapid population growth in the succeeding centuries was due in part to sweet potatoes.

Jerusalem Artichokes

As one of the very few food plants native to the eastern seaboard of North America, it was the French who first saw and tasted them in what is now New England and Canada during the expeditions of Samuel de Champlain. The French took to the tuber readily and it soon spread to England, Germany and Italy in the early seventeenth century. It was sometimes called a *topinambour,* after a tribe in Brazil. Its English name is a corruption of the Italian "girasole" or sunflower. Although its flavor may be reminiscent of artichokes, it is actually the root of a relative of the sunflower. It was considered by many to be an unhealthy food and along with potatoes and other roots was condemned as indigestible by physicians.

LEAFY VEGETABLES

Lettuce

Used extensively in salads much as we use it, lettuce was nonetheless considered dangerous cold and even mildly narcotic. The milky latex found in some species may have sedative properties, and physicians commonly recommended lettuce to help their patients get to sleep. As a cold and moist herb it was used extensively to cool people off in the summer, and even to cool down their sex drive, something especially useful for celibate priests. John Evelyn's *Acetaria, A Discourse of Sallets* written in 1699 says "by reason of its soporiferous quality, ever was, and still continues the principal foundation of the universal tribe of sallets; which is to cool and refresh."[18] Apparently people's preference for lettuce varied so widely, as it did for their choice of whom to kiss, that a common saying meaning "to each his

ARCHIDIPNO,

OVERO
DELL'INSALATA,
E DELL'VSO DI ESSA,

Trattato nuouo, curioso, e non mai più dato in luce;

DA SALVATORE MASSONIO

Scritto, e diuiso in Sessanta otto Capi;

Dedicato a' molto Illustri Signori fratelli,

LVDOVICO, ANTONIO, E FABRITIO COL'ANTONII.

IN VENETIA, MDCXXVII.

APPRESSO MARC'ANTONIO BROGIOLLO,

Con Licenza de' Superiori, e Priuilegio.

1627

Figure 2.2 Book on salads by Italian Salvatore Massonio, 1627. *Courtesy of the New York Academy of Medicine Library.*

own taste" ran "like lips, like lettuce, and that which is most mens bane, may be fittest to delight and nourish others."[19] The dedication of Buttes' *Diet's Dry Dinner* also claims "Here are lettuces for every man's lips."[20]

Spinach

Spinach was introduced to Europe in the late Middle Ages via the Moors occupying Spain, and most recipes for spinach retained traces of their origin. For example, Thomas Dawson in *The Good Housewife's Jewel* of 1596 offers the following:

To Make Fritters of Spinach

Take a good deal of spinach and wash it clean. Then boil it in fair water. When it is boiled take it forth and let the water run from it. Then chop it with the back of a knife, and put in some eggs and grated bread. Season it with sugar, cinnamon, ginger and pepper, dates minced fine, and currants. Roll them up like a ball and dip them in batter made of ale and flour.[21]

Arugula, Orach, Endive, Chicory, Cress and Purslane

All of these leafy greens were eaten young in salads, and their hot peppery or bitter flavor was thought to offset the cold and relatively bland flavor of lettuce.

Sorrel

This is another leafy green, although unlike those above, was appreciated for its sour flavor. It was frequently pounded into a green sauce that was used to accompany meat. This is a typical recipe: "Take sorrel, parsley and bread soaked in vinegar to make a sauce, to be eaten with meat, which excites the appetite."[22]

Hops

Although used primarily to flavor and preserve beer, hop shoots were also used as a vegetable much the way bean sprouts are used today. The astringent and bitter taste of hops also suggested that they had therapeutic value, and often pillows were stuffed with hops to promote sound sleep.

Mushrooms and Truffles

Fungi are one of the only foods regularly eaten that were foraged from the wild. Mushrooms were sometimes cultivated in caves, particularly around Paris, as they are today in the caves of the Loire Valley, but not on a large commercial scale until modern times. Truffles can still not be cultivated very successfully. The principal types of mushrooms found were porcini cepes, morels, chantrelles and numerous other wild varieties. Naturally incidents of accidentally eating poisoned mushrooms made some people wary of eating them. Scientists believed that they spontaneously generated from exhalations and excrements of the earth, and were therefore considered very unhealthy. Truffles were considered by many to be an aphrodisiac. In the early modern period they were typically cooked under hot coals, but as German poet Eobanus Hessus quipped "whoever loves aromatic truffles knows nothing about medicine."[23]

HERBS

Herbs were almost interchangeably used as medicines and foods. They were believed to correct the harmful qualities of foods and thus were treated as condiments—something you "add to" another food. In the sixteenth century, as medieval taste preferences lingered, spices were usually preferred by those who could afford them, and herbs as a flavoring agent were considered cheaper and more appropriate for rustics. This changed after the mid-seventeenth century as spices became cheaper and more affordable, and consequently native herbs came back into vogue, especially in classical French cuisine, in which they remain firmly entrenched.

Parsley

Parsley was probably the most ubiquitous of culinary herbs, featuring prominently in most green pounded sauces which were used on nearly any type of meat, fowl or fish needing seasoning. But because it was often gathered wild, many people were understandably apprehensive. Physician Girolamo Cardano tells a story of "a noble from Bologna who eating an herb tart in which the servant accidentally put hemlock instead of parsley, and they are very similar, died the following night."[24]

Thyme

As a flavoring agent, thyme really becomes popular in classical French cuisine, bound with other herbs in a *bouquet garni* or herb bundle that goes into a stockpot or stew, or sprinkled lightly on foods.

Rosemary

The name of this herb in Latin *ros marinus* means dew of the sea, but it also suggested a connection with the Virgin Mary whom it had by tradition sheltered on the flight from Egypt. Rosemary was also heralded as a powerful preserver of the memory, as Cordelia in Shakespeare's *Hamlet* recounted, "Here's rosemary for remembrance." It was also used strewn about houses as an air freshener. Girolamo Cardano suggests an interesting culinary use "among us sprigs are coated with flour and sugar and lightly toasted in a frying pan, and it is quite pleasant."[25] He also mentioned how nicely rosemary goes with roast meats, and its flowers in salads.

Basil

Although used extensively throughout southern Europe, it was not included among the most valuable therapeutic herbs, and consequently dietary writers recommended it infrequently. It is probably the great perishability of basil once cut that suggested to food writers that it was not very healthy to use.

Oregano and Marjoram

These two closely related plants were used mostly in southern Europe and were classified among the hot and dry herbs suitable for correcting cold and moist vegetables and meats and especially fish. Roman food writer Alessandro Petronio claimed that "over anchovies it is very pleasing."[26]

Chervil

Chervil has a very subtle licorice-like flavor. Although not widely appreciated in this country, chervil has always been a standard culinary herb, especially in France. It was thought to exhilarate the heart, comfort the mind and help resolve stoppages within the body. Like many other delicate herbs, its use in aristocratic cooking dates primarily from the latter half of the early modern period.

Sage

"Cur moriatur homo cui salvia crescit in horto" (How could one die who grows sage in his garden?) was a popular Latin saying attesting to the great faith Europeans placed on the medicinal virtues of this humble herb. As today, it was often used in stuffings with pork and was thought to "correct" the dangerous qualities of fatty meats.

Borage

For some reason borage was one of the most celebrated herbs in early modern Europe. Its taste, in the leaves and flowers, is somewhat insipid, and vaguely cucumber-like. But food writers extolled its virtues as the best herb to combat melancholy.

Hyssop

Hyssop was a popular herb in the Middle Ages, but its use gradually diminished through the early modern period until, as today, it became relatively unknown.

Tarragon

Some scientists thought tarragon did not grow naturally. Food writer Henry Buttes claimed that "This is an Artificiall herbe: for it cometh of a Lineseed put into an Onyon, or Leeke, and so buried in the ground."[27] It became especially popular in French sauces for its subtle licorice-like aroma.

Tansy

Tansy is a very bitter, green, fern-like herb that was commonly crushed, strained and used to color puddings or eggs green. It is, in fact, very dangerous and can induce abortion.

Fennel

Practically a weed where it grows wild, the seeds of fennel were used to season meats, especially sausages, or eaten candied as comfits. A particular variety bred to have a swollen stalk, called bulb or florence fennel was eaten as a vegetable either sliced raw or cooked.

Anise

One of the most popular herbs, whose seeds were typically mixed into bread dough or baked into little biscuits. Coated in sugar candy they were also eaten after dinner as a breath freshener and digestive. A typical digestive powder included crushed anise, coriander, fennel, cinnamon, oregano, licorice, galangal, mace, cubebs, musk, amber and sugar.[28] Anise was also thought to promote the flow of milk in lactating women.

Dill

Dill was not mentioned very frequently in early modern cookbooks, and its use seems to have been predominantly among Germanic peoples who baked it into bread and used it to flavor pickles.

Caraway

Used as a food almost exclusively in northern and eastern Europe, caraway was typically baked into or sprinkled on top of rye bread. It was also used in medicine elsewhere in Europe, and used in candy-comfits like anise.

Coriander

It was most commonly the seeds of coriander that were eaten, often candied, rather than the leaves, which we would call cilantro today, though the leaves were used often in Spanish cookbooks.

Juniper

Juniper berries were typically used in marinades for red meat, especially venison. They also gave their name to *genever* or gin, invented by the Dutch, in which they are the principal flavoring ingredient.

Bay and Myrtle

The aromatic leaves from these two trees were used primarily to flavor soups and sauces. They could also be used to wrap foods that would be grilled or placed on the bottom of a pan to prevent burning.

Because they do not disintegrate with cooking, they were generally not eaten unless finely ground before using.

Wormwood and Southernwood

Wormwood was typically used, as the name suggests, as a medicine to drive intestinal worms from the body. As a bitter astringent it also found its way into juleps and cordials, originally meant to be medicinal but frequently taken for pleasure owing to the alcohol content. Absinthe, one particular drink, became especially popular, well beyond the early modern period. It was only early in the twentieth century that most countries outlawed the use of wormwood after realizing that a substance called thujone contained in the plant causes brain damage. Southernwood is a related herb in the artemisia family with a bright chamomile-like scent and bitter flavor. Its root, dried and powdered, was used in the late Middle Ages, but gradually fell out of use in the early modern period, though its leaves were still used in stuffings.[29]

Angelica

This is a large celery-like plant the stalk of which was commonly candied and added to fruitcakes or used to adorn cooked dishes.

Rue

Rue is an extremely bitter herb, used sometimes in a culinary context, but more often in a decoction to clear the eyesight, which is why it was especially favored by painters. Both Leonardo da Vinci and Michelangelo claimed to have been helped by it. Rue was also used as an antidote for poison and in preventative medicines against plague.

Savory

A pungent herb, savory was only used extensively in cooking in classical French cuisine. Before that it was primarily considered a medicinal plant.

Mint

Mint was used in green sauces as an accompaniment to dishes like lamb, which might not seem very strange to modern tastes, but it also went with a wide variety of other dishes. It was most often used in Spanish cooking. In northern Europe the use of mint was increasingly relegated to sweet dishes, in which context we are most familiar with it today.

Melissa or Lemon Balm

The mystic alchemist Paracelsus believed that lemon balm was the elixir of life, and if drunk it was thought to counter depression and increase longevity. It was used primarily as a medicinal herb rather than a culinary one.

Flowers: Marigolds, Violets, Roses and Nasturtium

Marigolds, violets, roses and nasturtium flowers and several others were used to adorn tables and often found their way into raw salads, were candied, and in some cases put into soups and stews. Marigold or calendula in particular lends a yellow brilliance to a pot of simmering vegetables or soup. Gerard commented that "The yellow leaves of the floures are dried and kept throughout Dutchland against Winter, to put into broths, in Physicall potions, and for divers other purposes, in such quantity, that in some Grocers or spice-sellers houses are to be found barrels filled with them, and retailed by the penny more or lesse, insomuch that no broths are well made without dried Marigolds."[30] Other flowers, especially roses and orange flowers, were distilled into "waters" that found their way into a variety of sweet and savory dishes. Nasturtium or Indian cress is a New World flower with a spicy flavor that was eaten in salads along with the flowers of many herbs such as rosemary and borage.

SPICES

Pepper

As the most sought after spice pepper is perhaps the only one to retain its status as a universal flavoring down to the present. Pepper is a tropical shrub native to southern India that has been exported to Europe since classical times. It was still a rare and exotic commodity at the start of the early modern period, but as the Portuguese opened trade routes directly to India, an increasing volume of pepper flowed into Europe, and more and more people began using it. In fact it eventually came to be known as "everyman's spice" because anyone could afford it.

Long Pepper

This relative of black pepper, as its name suggests, is a narrow spike-like catkin, somewhat hotter than its relative. Through the early modern period it was to be found principally at pharmacists' shops as a heating and drying medicine, but was formerly used extensively in cooking.

Cinnamon and Cassia

Cinnamon and cassia are two related species that are rarely distinguished in the United States, but their flavors are distinct, cinnamon being lighter and more fragrant, cassia darker and more pungent. Europeans first gained direct control over the cinnamon trade in the early sixteenth century when the Portuguese occupied the Island of Sri Lanka in the Indian Ocean, but were displaced by the Dutch in 1636 and in turn replaced by the English East India Company in 1796. Like all spices, the demand for cinnamon stemmed not only from its culinary use, but its prominent place in pharmacy as well, as a heating drug. There was not yet the rigid distinction between medicinal condiments and therapeutic drugs that we maintain today. As the supply of cinnamon arriving in Europe increased, naturally the price fell and people lower down the social scale were able to afford it.

Cloves

Native to Ternate and Tidore in Indonesia, control of trade in cloves was increasingly controlled by the Portuguese after 1514, though the Venetian spice trade continued to flourish for many years. Ultimately it was the Dutch who completely monopolized the trade by taking over the region by force in the seventeenth century and rigorously restricting the cultivation of cloves to the Island of Amboina. On several occasions they even burned vast stocks to prevent the market from being saturated and the price falling.

Nutmeg and Mace

Native to the Moluccas in what is now Indonesia, nutmeg was the object of intense rivalry between European powers. The Portuguese were the first to carry it directly to Europe, but by the seventeenth century the Dutch had stolen their trade and occupied the few islands where nutmeg grows. The English East India Company also tried to gain a foothold in this region and successfully captured the island of Run, which they ultimately traded away to the Dutch in return for Manhattan Island. Nutmeg remained an expensive commodity because of the Dutch monopoly, and wealthy people often took their own portable container and grater with them wherever they went. The Dutch monopoly was only broken in 1770 when Pierre Poivre, the French governor of Mauritius, managed to smuggle seedlings which were subsequently planted around the world. Unlike most other spices, nutmeg also retained a prominent place in cooking savory and sweet dishes right through the eighteenth century. Mace is a yellowish netting that surrounds the nutmeg. Its flavor is somewhat different, which is why it was removed and used as a separate spice.

Saffron

Saffron has always been among the most expensive of spices despite the fact that it has been cultivated in many places in Europe, most notably in Spain but also in Italy and even in England in places such as Saffron Walden. The cost of saffron has more to do with the meticulous process of harvesting individual stamens from crocus flowers than it does rarity. Saffron was used primarily as a colorant, lending a brilliant orangish-yellow to rice or being used to paint virtually any dish a golden hue. With a subtly medicinal taste, it was also thought to have the power to "lighten the spirits" and chase away melancholy. In elite European cuisine outside of Spain, saffron was at the height of its popularity in the late Middle Ages and early in the sixteenth century. It slowly went out of fashion, especially after being cultivated on a wider scale, which brought the cost down. This meant that the affluent could no longer flaunt their wealth with rich saffron-colored dishes.

Ginger

Ginger was one of the most important spices in the medieval kitchen, It was used principally dried and ground, though there are references to "green ginger" which was presumably candied or crystallized because fresh ginger would never have lasted on the lengthy voyage from Asia. Ginger was used in practically every conceivable context and with nearly every kind of food, as well as in more familiar preparations like gingerbread. Through the early modern period its use was increasingly restricted to sweets, especially in classical French cuisine. Europeans first received accurate botanical information about ginger from García de Orta whose work was published in Goa, India in 1563.

Galangal

Galangal is a more sharp and pungent relative of ginger once used extensively in Europe, and now slowly making its way back via southeast Asian cuisines. Its disappearance early in the early modern period remains a mystery, especially considering the continuing popularity of ginger.

Grains of Paradise

Similar to black pepper but more perfumed, this native to the Meleguetta coast of West Africa was among the most sought after spices in the late medieval larder. It eventually waned in popularity as an inferior substitute to real pepper, and being cheaper, less affluent consumers sought it out. Believing it would cut into the lucrative trade in pepper with their Asian colonies, the Portuguese crown banned imports into Europe, and today it is virtually unknown there.

Cubebs

Often called "tailed pepper," cubebs are tiny dark spheres with a sharp stem at one end. They were used in both cooking and medicines, and the latter is the only place one might find them nowadays. The sixteenth-century authority on pepper, Walter Bailey, mentioned that "we do read of another kind of pepper brought out of the Indians, which the Portingals called Pimiento de Rabo ... this kind is not now bought, the king of Portugal did forbid any to bring it, fearing lest it might decay the price and sale of other kindes."[31] As with grains of paradise, profit and politics played as great a role in bringing new foods to Europe as it did keeping others out.

Cardamom

Cardamom was one of the rarest and most expensive spices in early modern times and still is today. It was never really used in a wide variety of dishes, the way it is in India for example or the way it was in the Middle Ages, but mostly added to cookies and pastries to give them an aromatic exotic flavor.

Allspice

Allspice, which is actually a single species whose flavor and odor is reminiscent of a spice mixture, is one of the few aromatics native to the New World, specifically to Jamaica. Columbus first introduced it to Europe and like many other things he encountered, gave it the name of something he was already familiar with, in this case *pimienta* (pepper). When the English took over Jamaica in 1655 they also stepped up the trade in this spice which thereafter increased in popularity right down to the present.

Carob

The carob tree flourishes through much of the Mediterranean and its sweet pods were sometimes consumed as a snack. The word "carat" as a unit of measure for diamonds derives from the Greek word for carob (*keration*), and the standard-sized seeds were once used as weights. Today carob is used as a chocolate substitute.

Vanilla

This flavor is derived from the seed pod of several species of orchids which in their native Mexico were pollinated by uniquely adapted insects. This meant that the plant would not grow elsewhere until growers learned to pollinate each individual flower by hand, a procedure only discovered in the nineteenth century and followed to this day wherever vanilla is grown, as in Madagascar and Tahiti. Vanilla was originally used as an ingredient added to drinking chocolate, and remained one of the lesser-known flavorings throughout the early modern period, especially compared to its use in a proliferation of sweets today.

Musk and Amber

Although technically an animal product, extracted from the scent glands of several species of deer found in Siberia, musk is a powerful aromatic now used mostly in perfumes, but in the past a culinary ingredient as well. Dragées, or candies scented with musk, were popular, as were pies and other savory dishes scented with musk. Amber, or rather ambergris (not the stone), was a similar aromatic extracted from sperm whales found washed up on shore, and was one of the most expensive things that could be incorporated into food with the exception of pearls and gold.

Cochineal

Another New World product, used principally as a dye but sometimes as a food colorant, cochineal was derived from the crushed bodies of a tiny insect that lives on cactus plants. Its intensely bright red color made it a more potent dye than alkermes and sandalwood, typical medieval food dyes.

FRUITS

Peaches

The name peach derives from the Latin word *persica* meaning from Persia. Physicians warned that peaches, just as they so easily corrupt outside the body, can also corrupt within. This is why they recommended that they never be eaten at the close of a meal, because the delay in the digestive process makes them prone to putrefaction. Clearly ignoring these admonitions, peaches were commonly eaten in the last course as dessert, and one way to serve them was cut in cubes and soaked in undiluted wine. Nectarines are merely a smooth-skinned variety of peach whose origin is unknown.

Apricots

The name apricot is a corruption of the Latin word *praecox* meaning precocious or early, as these were the first fruits of the spring. Apricots were often dried or made into preserves or jam, but could also be cooked with savory ingredients.

Plums

These were used much as they are today, in tarts, dried or sometimes cooked with meats. Serious cultivation of plum varieties, along with many other fruits began in late-seventeenth-century France.

Apples

It will probably seem strange to those of us who know "an apple a day keeps the doctor away" that early modern Europeans thought apples were very unhealthy. This may even be why early translators of the Bible identified the forbidden fruit of the Garden of Eden with the apple. Physicians usually recommended that they be baked, and if eaten raw, tart apples should always come at the end of a meal and sweet ones at the start. They were afraid that a sweet fruit at the end of a meal would float at the top of the stomach and putrefy before other foods could be properly digested. Their fear may have had a lot to do with the quality of apples available. Although grafting, attaching a sprig of an edible specimen to another rootstock, had been perfected in classical times, most apples were not the beautifully uniform varieties we have come to expect. Most were probably misshapen, sour and best used to make hard cider, a typical drink in western England and Normandy. Growing improved varieties did become a preoccupation of fruit growers, and with the publication of several classics in the science of pomology, the latest techniques for selectively breeding improved apple strains were spread throughout Europe. In the sixteenth century Giambattista della Porta's *Pomarium* and Charles Estienne's *Seminarium* set the trend which would continue in the next century culminating in Charles Cotton's *The Planter's Manual,* John Evelyn's *Pomona* and finally Jean de La Quintinie's *Instruction pour les jardins fruitiers et potagers.* New varieties of apples were also sometimes named for their creators or for famous people, such as the Newton Pippin named to commemorate Sir Isaac Newton's discovery of the laws of universal gravitation.

Pears

Considered cold and moist and difficult to digest, pears were generally not recommended by physicians. English schoolmaster Thomas Cogan contends "That peares may not hurt thee, take out the coares, pare them, and salte them, and cast them out of doores."[32]

Cherries

Though we consider cherry pie particularly American, there are recipes for it in most early modern cookbooks. Cherries themselves were considered a particularly luxurious and erotic fruit and luscious lips were frequently compared to them, as this poem by Robert Herrick shows. The "cry" here is by someone selling them in the market.

Cherry-ripe, ripe, ripe, I cry,
Full and fair one, come and buy.
If so be you ask me where
They do grow? I answer There,
Where my Julia's lips do smile
There's the land or cherry isle,
Whose plantations fully show
All the year, where cherries grow[33]

Sorb Apples, Cornel Cherries and Medlars

Sorb apples, cornel cherries and medlars are all small astringent fruits practically unknown in this country. They were mostly used in pies and preserves. Medlars are small bitter fruits that can only be eaten when practically rotten. The *Good Huswifes Handmaid for the Kitchen,* a sixteenth-century cookbook, offers the following recipe:

To Make a Tarte of Medlers

Take Medlers that be rotten, and straine them then sette them on a chafingdish of coales, and beate it in two yolkes of Egges, and let it boil til it be somewhat thick: then season it with synamon, Ginger and Sugar, and lay it in paste.[34]

Quince

Although not very popular nowadays, quince were considered one of the most healthy and useful fruits in the past. Because they must be cooked before eating, they were most commonly either baked or preserved with sugar or honey as a *marmelada* which is the origin of the English word marmalade. Quinces were also cooked down into a rich brick-red paste called *membrillo* in Spain and *cotiniate, cotignac* and various related terms in France. Acquiring a reputation as a medicinal, these were increasingly eaten for pleasure as an accompaniment to cheese, a practice which survives to this day.

Pomegranates

Although very popular at the start of the early modern period, especially the seeds as a garnish, or the juice as a sour ingredient in cooked dishes, pomegranates were increasingly used only in the southern extremities of Europe. They were often featured in paintings though, their many seeds being an apt metaphor for regeneration, or conversely their red-staining juice for sin.

Lemons

Lemons were one of the most sought after fruits in early modern Europe. Being associated with sunny southern Europe they were considered healthy, much the same way we think of Mediterranean foods today. Their juice was used as a condiment, especially on fish because its acidity was thought to cut through the "gluey humors" abounding in seafood, making them more digestible. Northern Europeans generally had to import lemons, but eventually a way to grow them indoors was devised. Lemon peel, grated or candied lemon was also a typical garnish.

Oranges

Along with lemons, oranges were greatly esteemed and grown in specially built orangeries. Physicians even recommended orange juice in the morning, much as we do, to prevent kidney stones. As Joseph Duchesne claimed "they are among the most beautiful fruits, and the most useful, and the juice of them is used commonly on all the best tables." He also claimed that orange juice comforts the heart and stomach when taken in the morning, and being acidic it dissolves kidney stones.[35] The most common orange was the rather tart and bitter Seville variety, better used in cooking than eating. The sweet orange, introduced from Asia, did not appear in Europe until 1529. A common salad consisted of sliced oranges, peel and all, with sugar or salt cast over them and sometimes onions and capers as well.

Limes and Grapefruits

Both lime and grapefruit were foreign to Europe, limes originating in southeast Asia and grapefruits from the Caribbean. Limes were recommended on ocean-going voyages to prevent scurvy as early as the sixteenth century, but were regularly issued to British sailors, or "limeys," after James Lind's research showed how effective they are at preventing the disease. Grapefruits, probably a mutated form of the pomelo introduced into Barbados from southeast Asia, were practically unknown to Europeans until the end of the eighteenth century.

Citrons

The oldest of the citrus fruits, citrons were known to most Europeans as candied peel which they used in both cooking and as a garnish. When they are fresh, they resemble lemons and were used much the same way, though they contain little juice.

Pineapples

Native to the New World, the fruit was not enthusiastically embraced by Europeans, probably because they are difficult to ship and can only be grown in tropical climates. Europeans do not seem to have known what to do with pineapples either. The very name in English suggests how strange people thought they were. They vaguely resemble the cones that yield pine nuts. Charles II was depicted in 1670 with the first one grown in England, but not until the eighteenth century did it appear in a recipe book. By that time, the excitement over pineapples mounted steadily, and carved wooden ones were even featured on houses as a symbol of hospitality.

Figs

Thought to cause less harm than other fruits, figs could nonetheless harm the liver or spleen if eaten in great quantity, or could even engender lice, which were thought to spontaneously generate on the scalp.

Dates

As just about the sweetest food available to Europeans, dates were highly valued but also quite rare and expensive since there is nowhere in Europe where they will bear fruit. Physicians warned that excessive consumption of dates can rot the teeth, which is true.

Jujubes

These are tiny oval fruits somewhat like dates in texture and flavor. They were a popular garnish in Renaissance Italy.

Currants and Gooseberries

Although relatively rare in the United States currants and gooseberries have always been common in Europe. Currants, tiny tart red fruits, were used to make a "rob" a kind of medicinal syrup used in times of pestilence, but also in soups and salads in summertime. What we call "zante currants" in this country are actually raisins made from tiny grapes. Both currants and gooseberries are also excellent in jams.

Raspberries and Blackberries

Most common in northern Europe, raspberries and blackberries were used exactly as we do today, eaten fresh or in preserves. They were also made into electuaries, or confections, and syrups of a more medicinal nature.

Mulberries

Mulberries are an intensely sweet berry, either black or white, that grows in clusters on a large tree. Because they are almost impossible to ship, and go bad very quickly, they are not well known in this country except for those who own a tree. The principal reason mulberry trees were grown in Europe was not for its fruit, but rather for its leaves on which silk worms live. Any country with a nascent silk industry, as many countries were in the sixteenth and seventeenth centuries, had to plant mulberry trees.

Grapes

Table grapes used for eating were relatively difficult to come by outside grape-growing regions. This may be one reason why they were so often depicted in Dutch paintings, because only the affluent could afford them. Another explanation is that they served as symbols of Christ's sacrifice because after being consumed the seeds spring back to life, and the grapevine seems to completely die before budding in the spring. One culinary setting in which grapes are often found is in combination with small birds. The coolness of the grapes was thought to counteract the inherent heat of the birds. Raisins, especially those imported from the Middle East were also a highly valued commodity and made their way into a variety of recipes. Passum, a wine made from raisins was also very popular.

Strawberries

The small wild strawberry was native to Europe and excellent in preserves, but not as comely on the table as the large strawberries brought from the New World. It appears that after their introduction and commercial cultivation, strawberries became a more common fruit eaten at dessert with cream, especially in England. The English name derives from the practice of heaping straw between the rows as mulch.

Melons

Physicians of the early modern period considered melons one of the most dangerous fruits. The very fact that they go bad so quickly suggested to them that they do the same inside the body, causing fevers and a variety of illnesses. They argued whether wine with melons was a good idea, would it prevent putrefaction of the fruit, or would it force the semi-digested food into the veins prematurely? Should melons precede or follow other foods, or should they be eaten alone? These arguments were probably ignored by most people, but they may also have had the effect of increasing the allure of this delicious fruit, much the same way doing anything forbidden provides a satisfying transgression. Perhaps for this very reason, melons were celebrated in European courts, cultivated in royal gardens, and graced the most elegant banquets. Apart from an accompaniment of wine, eating salty foods such as prosciutto ham or aged cheese with melons to prevent putrefaction, is a custom whose origin may be medicinal. As physician Prosper Calanius recommended "after melons use Piacenza cheese [like Parmesan] or some salted meat, or even salt or sugar" to prevent putrefaction.[36]

NUTS

Almonds

Almonds were an imported and relatively expensive item for most Europeans. They were used in cooking in Europe in much the same way that they were among Arab peoples. In the sixteenth century they were still being used to make almond milk, which was a thick liquid strained from ground and soaked almonds. It could replace regular milk in Lenten dishes. This procedure gradually went out of fashion in later centuries. Almonds were also ground with sugar into almond paste or marzipan, which made its way into dozens of confections as well as savory dishes and could be molded into shapes. Green immature almonds were also a delicacy during spring in places where they grew.

Chestnuts

A very important food in mountainous regions such as the Cévennes in France and in much of Italy and Spain, chestnuts were often associated with poverty and were considered by physicians to be very difficult to digest. Nonetheless, people of all social classes did consume them roasted in a perforated pan or under the coals, boiled, candied or in the form of a chestnut purée. Chestnuts could be baked into bread as well. A thriving trade also existed, transporting chestnuts from southern Europe to northern ports.

Walnuts

According to the doctrine of signatures, the shape and color of a given food will offer clues about its therapeutic value. Because of their similarity to a brain, walnuts were therefore considered good for the mind. As a food, walnuts figured prominently in many pounded sauces, of which the Ligurian (Italy) *pesto* is a modern example made with basil, garlic, olive oil, cheese and nuts—either pine nuts or walnuts. Walnuts can also be pressed into a delicate salad oil. E. Smith gives an eighteenth-century recipe "To Pickle Walnuts." Note that the walnut, its shell and the green outer covering are all pickled whole before the nuts ripen.

To Pickle Walnuts

Take walnuts about midsummer, when a pin will pass through them, put them in a deep pot, and cover them with ordinary vinegar; change them into fresh vinegar once in fourteen days, for six weeks; then take two gallons of the best vinegar, and put into it coriander-seeds, carraway-seeds, and dill-seeds, of each an ounce grossly bruised, ginger sliced three ounces, whole mace one ounce, nutmeg and pepper bruised, of each two ounces; give all a boil or two over the fire, and have your nuts ready in a pot, and pour the liquor boiling hot over them; repeat this nine times.[37]

Hazelnuts and Filberts

Hazelnuts and filberts are very closely related species, the former American and the latter Eurasian. Filberts are named for St. Philbert whose feast day falls on August 22 when the nuts are said to ripen.

Pine Nuts

The large edible seeds contained in the cones of several species of pine tree, pine nuts have always been used as a food in southern Europe. They can be ground into sauces and even milky soups such as the white gazpacho of Spain, baked into cookies and other confections, and used as a garnish for nearly any kind of dish, sweet or savory. It was also believed that pine nuts increased sperm production and were thus recommended for couples hoping to have children.

Pistachios

Pistachios were an imported luxury item and relatively unknown except for those who could afford them. The height of their popularity as a cooking ingredient appears to have been during the seventeenth century in Italy. Bartolomeo Stefani, for example, in his *L'Arte di Ben Cucinare* (The art of good cooking) of 1662 uses them pounded in sauces, as a garnish and in an interesting cauliflower dish in which the par-boiled vegetable is fried in butter with nutmeg, egg yolks, lemon and crushed pistachios.[38]

Peanuts

Peanuts are a South American plant probably originating in Peru, and are technically not a nut but an underground legume. They were brought by the Spanish and Portuguese most notably to Africa and thereafter to Asia. They thrived in both places, but never seem to have caught on in Europe, although they were grown to a limited extent in Spain in the early modern period. They arrived in North America from Africa, where they were brought by the Portuguese.

CONDIMENTS

Salt

Salt was probably the most important food flavoring for early modern Europeans. It was equally indispensable as a preservative agent and most families would probably not have survived the long months before harvest without salted meats, fish and pickled vegetables. Without refrigeration or canning, it was the only way to store most foods, apart from drying. Salt was typically either mined from deep tunnels bored into the earth in which water was pumped to dissolve the salt laden walls (as at "Salzburg" in Austria) or evaporated from sea water in a series of shallow pools along the coast (as in Brittany and in much of the Mediterranean). Quite different from the bright white iodized salt we are used to, salt was typically grayish, damp and smelling sharply of the sea, something gourmets are once again coming to appreciate. A tax on salt, the *gabelle,* was also an important source of revenue for the French crown and would be a point of contention preceding the French Revolution.

Olives

Olives were grown around the Mediterranean since ancient times, and some huge specimens can even survive for centuries. For eating, they must be cured in salt or a brine solution to remove their bitterness, either green and unripe or black. Preserved in this way, they were exported throughout Europe and used as an appetite stimulant, and sometimes were eaten throughout a meal, or even at the end along with desserts. "On account of the astringent faculty they have, they are included with desserts in the last course" as Hispano-Flemish food writer Ludovico Nonnius tells us.[39] A good proportion of olives were also pressed into oil which was a staple of the diet throughout southern Europe and also an important export item in its own right due to the prohibition of butter during Lent. Many northern Europeans paid the church for a dispensation from eating olive oil, but others bitterly resented this imposition, and it became a major point of contention in the Protestant Reformation.

Mustard

Strangely, the word mustard comes from "must" or grape juice which was typically used to make a *mostarda* in Italy, a combination of preserved fruits and spices. Mustard as we know it was also a typical condiment, especially in northern Europe, where it was usually matched with pork. The sharp flavor of mustard was thought to cut through the crass texture of the pork. Mustard was also eaten in southern Europe and Francisco Nuñez de Oria offered the following advice. "Usually we make with it a sauce called *mostaza* with honey, vinegar and the soft insides of bread, eaten with gross meats that are difficult to digest, like beef, because it cuts and diminishes their fattiness."[40]

Capers

These are the pickled buds of a shrub native to southern Europe. They were used much like olives, to stimulate the appetite, but could also be cooked into a variety of other dishes. In the eighteenth century capers were especially popular as a flavoring in sauces all over Europe.

Samphire (*Crithmium maritimum*)

Samphire is a thin plant that grows along the south and west coasts of England and elsewhere. They were usually pickled and eaten as an appetite stimulant and as a condiment. As herbalist John Gerard said "The leaves kept in pickle, and eaten in sallads with oile and vineger, is a pleasant sauce for meat."[41]

Laver

A type of seaweed commonly eaten in coastal areas of the British Isles, it could also be baked into bread. Its use was not very widespread outside of Britain.

Sugar

Considered one of the rarest and most precious of spices through the Middle Ages, sugar was used only sparingly as a flavoring, sprinkled on a variety of foods, like meat and fish, and in many sauces. It also featured prominently in medicines, there not yet being a sharp distinction between condiments and pharmaceuticals. In fact, most people bought sugar in conical loaves from the apothecary's shop.

Most sugar was imported from Asia, hence the great cost, but there were experiments by the Spanish and Portuguese to grow it in Madeira, the Canary Islands and other sub-tropical locations in the Old World. The fate of sugar changed in the sixteenth century once it began to be cultivated on plantations in the Caribbean and Brazil. The price dropped and more people began to use it. Writing near Antwerp, a major center of sugar refining, the Flemish Hugo Fridaevallis noted, "no type of food becomes more insipid with the addition of sugar. No magnificent feast, nor everyday food will please without sugar."[42] Its culinary role only slowly shifted in the late seventeenth century from a universal flavoring to something used exclusively at the end of meals in desserts, or eventually in coffee, tea and chocolate. This happened just as the British, French and Dutch began processing sugar themselves in the Caribbean on a much larger scale using more efficient processing methods.

Honey

Before sugar became the universal sweetener, honey was probably the only intensely sweet substance most Europeans were familiar with. It featured prominently in a number of medicines designed to combat colds, many of which can be traced back to the ancient Greeks. Honey was also fermented into mead, a drink not unlike beer in consistency and alcohol strength. The most extensive discussion of mead was *The Closet of the Eminently Learned Sir Kenelm Digby Opened* published in 1669 which offered dozens of recipes. The following is one of his shorter and simpler versions. A runlet or rondelet is a round wooden cask that holds liquids.

fürung. Alle geräuchte Fisch/so am rauch
getrücknet werden/soll mann / als schäd-
lich vnd vngesundt / vermeyden/ꝛc.

Von der Natur vnnd Eygen-
schafft des Honigs.

DEn rohen Honig allein vnd ohn
Brodt genossen/treibt von seiner
schärpffe wegen den Bauch/ aber
gesotten Honig führet.

Honig/wiewol es alten Leuthen/vnnd
allen denen / so kalter Natur vnnd Complexion sehr nützlich vnnd gut ist / so ist es
dargegen jungen Leuten/ vnd fürnemlich
denen/so in blüendem Alter seindt/schäd-
lich.

Figure 2.3 Honey. *From Ryff, Walther Hermann d. 1548.
Spiegel unnd Regiment der Gesunndtheit. Frankfort : Heirs
of C. Egenolff [for A. Lonicerus, J. Cnipius & P. Steinmeyer],
1574 p. 77. EPB 5679. Courtesy of Wellcome Library, London.*

To Make Meath

Take three Gallons of water, a quart of Honey; if it be not strong enough, you may add more. Boil it apace an hour, and scum it very clean. Then take it off; and set it working at such a heat as you set Beer, with good yest. Then put it in a Runlet, and at three days end draw it out in stone bottles; into every one put a piece of Limon-peel and two cloves. It is put into the Runlet, whilest it worketh, to avoid breaking of the Bottles.[43]

Vinegar

As a "cold" corrective seasoning, vinegar was used far more extensively in cooking than we normally use it. It was thought to balance meats and fowl by counteracting their inherent "heat" creating a far more healthy dish. Vinegar was also thought to aid digestion and the distribution of nutrients throughout the body and because it constricted the body's passages was thought to be a good preventative against plague. At the start of the early modern period sweet and sour sauces using vinegar were very popular as a legacy of medieval cuisine. By the latter seventeenth century, however, cooking tried to accent and intensify the flavor of the main ingredients, and vinegar was increasingly banished to salads and as a preservative agent.

Verjuice

In grape-growing regions, and especially after summer thinning of the vines, unripe grapes would be pressed into a sour condiment used in a variety of recipes, much as vinegar was used. Even in places beyond grape cultivation, crab apples or gooseberries could be used to make verjuice.

Sapa

This is the boiled down must or juice from pressed ripe grapes. It is thick and sweet and used both in cooking and as a condiment drizzled on other foods. It is not very different from real balsamic vinegar which is made from a reduction which is essentially *sapa* turned into vinegar and then aged in a succession of wooden barrels. The first major book devoted to wine by Andrea Bacci explains that *passum* is basically evaporated grape must, *defrutum* is cooked and reduced to one half. *Sapa* is usually reduced to a third or more, and thus would be a kind of thick grape syrup.[44]

MEAT

Although the average European ate relatively little meat through the course of the year, wealthier people consumed a good deal, and were advised by their physicians that meat was the ideal food to maintain the body in health. Compared to today, a much wider variety of meats were consumed, both domesticated and wild, preserved and fresh. Unlike today, people were also not very squeamish about consuming parts of animals that would remind one of the animal in life, such as the head and eyes. In fact, scarcely any part of the animal would be wasted, and on those rare opportunities that poorer people got to eat fresh meat they would typically consume every last morsel in one form or another down to every organ and bone and even the blood.

Pork

Probably the single most common meat eaten across Europe at all levels of society, pork was also considered the most nourishing food available because of its similarity to human flesh. Foods most similar to us were thought to be those most easily converted into our own flesh, and thus for well-exercised people who could digest it, pork provided the ideal aliment. Unlike other animals, pork was raised solely for its flesh. A common saying ran "avari suibus similes dicuntur: quoniam nemini utiles sunt ante obitum" (pigs are like misers since they're of no use to anyone until dead). While quite revealing about the importance of inheritance to early modern Europeans, this saying also points to the fact that pigs were used for food and nothing else. Pork was also essential for survival because it could be preserved in so many ways: as smoked hams and bacon and in countless sausages. It could also be pickled, made into salami, liver paté, and most importantly its fat could be preserved as lard, used in cooking. Before refrigeration, these were the only means of preserving meat after the annual slaughter in autumn.

Boar

Boar was a delicacy usually only eaten by noblemen who had the right to hunt it. It could be cooked and preserved exactly as pork, but had a stronger, wilder flavor. Boar's head was a typical dish presented with fanfare on courtly tables and "brawn" was a popular preserved product made from boar's flesh.

Beef and Veal

Because of the great cost of raising a male steer to maturity, in most of Europe veal was the preferred meat. It was considered one of the healthiest foods, easy to digest and extremely nourishing, but because veal cannot be easily preserved, it was almost always consumed fresh. It was therefore quite expensive. A roast joint could last perhaps a week, and would usually be eaten in successive meals before making its way into the soup pot. A large cut of veal could also be "seethed" or gently boiled in water yielding a rich broth for one course and a tender pot roast-like dish for the next. Veal head was considered an especially elegant dish cooked in this fashion. Veal can also be made into sausages or can be baked into pies. Cows were mostly raised for the dairy, but were usually eaten when they grew too old to produce enough milk, or when desperation forced a family to sell the cow. The tale of Jack and the Beanstalk is a familiar example of this. Oxen, or castrated males, were typically used as draught animals, pulling plows, carts or even hitched to huge rotary mills for grinding grain. But they too were eaten, as were steers, which are males before they have reached maturity. As a rule though, beef was considered a food appropriate for the lower classes because of its supposedly tough indigestible texture. Keeping in mind that there were few breeds raised specifically for their flesh until the eighteenth century, this aversion is not difficult to understand. The only country that excelled in scientifically raising specific breeds for the table was England, whose obsession with roast beef is legendary, but other regions also had renowned examples such as the Charolais of France and the Val di Chiana of Tuscany. Salted beef or "corned" so called after the grains or corns of salt with which it was preserved was one way of preserving beef or its tongue, but was consistently condemned by physicians.

Buffalo

Buffalo is not the American bison we are familiar with but a large species of cattle raised in marshy regions in the lower half of Italy. Although they principally provided milk made into mozzarella, they were also eaten and considered much like cows in taste and texture.

Lamb and Mutton

Lamb was one of the most important foods in Europe, probably because sheep were one of the most valuable animals for both cheese making and for the wool industry. Suckling lamb was not considered very healthy, but after a year a young *wether* was deemed one of the best meats available. Mutton, the flesh of a full grown sheep, usually a castrated ram or *vervex,* although much more assertive in flavor, was also highly esteemed.

Kid, Goat and Mountain Goat

Kid was considered among the healthiest meats of all by physicians, especially those who depended on medieval Arabic authorities like Avicenna and Averroës. It was consumed primarily in Spain, Italy and southern France. Kid was thought to be drier than lamb, more easily digested, and thus perfectly appropriate for sedentary people and thinkers. It was usually roasted whole on a spit. As a mature animal, however, male goats were thought to be too lascivious, and their flesh rank and harmful. Female goats, on the other hand, were kept primarily to make fresh cheeses. Wild mountain goats were often hunted, and the great amount of exercise they get and the clean air and pasture was thought to render their flesh more tempered and digestible.

Venison

This is a general term once used to cover all wild meats, but has come to refer solely to various types of deer: red deer, fallow deer, stag or hart. Venison was a food explicitly associated with the nobility, who had the leisure and often the exclusive legal right to hunt it. Serving it to honored guests or even sending one to friends or business associates, thus became a visible symbol of one's power and status in society. Venison was usually roasted or marinated in wine, cut up and baked into a pie. Hartshorn was used as a jelling agent but also eaten on its own. Food writer Ludovico Bertaldi mentions that "princes eat the soft points of the horn, the ears, extremities of the lips and nose, along with onions, aromatic spices, fat and lemon juice."[45] Another practice, condemned by most physicians, was to serve deer fetuses extracted from the womb of a pregnant deer.

Rabbit and Hare

The principle difference between the two is that rabbits are smaller and can be domesticated, while hares are larger and wild. Both were typically skinned and roasted, sometimes covered with spices and

Figure 2.4 Trussed hare. *From Martha Bradley. The British housewife: or the cook, housekeeper's, and gardiner's companion. Calculated for the service both of London and the country: and directing what is necessary to be done in the providing for, conducting, and managing a family throughout the year. London: Printed for S. Crowder and H. Woodgate, [1770?]. vol. 2. Courtesy of Wellcome Library, London.*

breadcrumbs to keep in the moisture. Jugged hare was a procedure in which the whole animal was cut up, placed in a clay vessel with bacon and onions and the animal's blood, sealed and then cooked in a kettle of water. Another dish, rather unsavory-sounding to modern palates, was young rabbit fetuses roasted.

Hedgehog, Porcupine and Dormice

Hedgehog, porcupine and dormice were hunted and roasted throughout Europe, though not considered a particularly healthy food. There is also evidence of people in remote regions eating foxes, martins, marmots, squirrels, badgers and other wild animals, but most Europeans in cities and villages would have considered these very unusual foods. Dormice were a delicacy in ancient times, but it is clear that people continued to eat them well into early modern times as well. Cookbook author Domenico Romoli suggests that they are best in winter when fattened, and served roasted on toast points.[46] In size, and probably in flavor, they are somewhere between a rat and squirrel.

Bear

Hunted wild in mountainous regions like the Swiss Alps, bear was certainly not considered a typical food for most Europeans. But chef Bartolomeo Scappi did offer a recipe for roasted bear's legs nonetheless, and admits that though it is little used "I have cooked it."

Cat and Dog

Although certainly not a typical food through Europe, many writers at the time referred to people customarily eating cats and dogs in various locations. Certainly in times of famine people would not have had the abhorrence to the practice found today, and in some places they seem to have enjoyed it. For example one jingle from northern Italy goes "Padovani gran dottori, Veneziani gran signori, Veronesi tutti matti, Vincenzini mangia gatti" (Paduans are great doctors, Venetians grand nobles, Veronese are all crazy and Vincenzans eat cats). According to Edward Topsell in *The History of Four Footed-Beasts*, "In Spain and Gallia Norbon [southern France], they eat Cats, but first of all take away their head and tail, and hang the prepared flesh a night or two in the open cold air, to exhale the savour and poison of it, finding the flesh thereof almost as sweet as a cony [rabbit]."[47]

Horse

There was a religious prohibition against eating horses since the times of Pope Gregory VII in the early Middle Ages, and there is little evidence of people eating it unless out of dire necessity. They were far too valuable as draught animals, for transport and of course for war. Horsemeat was, however reintroduced as a food, particularly in France and Italy, in the nineteenth century and is still eaten there today.

Organ Meats

The internal organs of most quadrupeds, fowl and even some fish were enjoyed throughout Europe in the early modern period. It is only relatively recently that we have acquired an aversion to some of these foods, and very recently that several of them are no longer considered edible, lung and spleen being the best example. Liver was the most common of organ meats and found its way into a variety of dishes and most frequently in patés. Kidneys and various glands including mammary, testes and thymus or "sweetbreads," brains and bone marrow were all considered good and delicate foods, even elegant if well prepared. Some organ meats were associated with lower classes, particularly tripe, the lining of the stomach and intestines. Blood was also typically consumed in the form of blood sausages, or *boudins* in French, "black puddings" in English. Interestingly, these were given away to friends in France as a symbol of friendship.

FOWL

Chicken and Capon

Chicken was universally praised as the healthiest food for people of all complexions, ages and regions. Whether most people ate them regularly is doubtful though considering that King Henry IV of France only wished that every Sunday there could be a chicken in every pot. Those who did eat chicken regularly distinguished between young chickens or pullets, what we call today fryers, and older chickens as well as castrated capons which were usually roasted or boiled into restorative broth. Perhaps one of the most versatile of foods, there were literally thousands of ways to prepare chicken in early modern times. There were even efforts to preserve chicken by freezing. The philosopher Francis Bacon actually caught pneumonia and died after an experiment in which he stuffed a chicken with snow.

Peacock

Although rarely eaten today, peacocks were considered one of the more elegant party dishes and were frequently served at weddings and important banquets. One particularly grand way of serving the bird involved skinning it, roasting the flesh and then sewing it back into its own feathers. There was a superstition, held by many learned food writers, that peacock's flesh would not corrupt and there circulated stories of peacocks being cooked and then eaten years later without any apparent change in taste. Peacocks went out of fashion in the middle of the early modern period and were largely replaced by turkey.

Duck

Ducks were not considered a healthy food principally because of their diet of lake muck, bugs and other unsavory creatures. Physicians believed that the noxious properties of these animals would be ultimately passed into whomever ate duck. Nonetheless they were one of the most frequently served foods on tables all across Europe.

Goose

Among food writers geese were often associated with Jewish communities who salted and smoked goose flesh much as the Christians did pork. This treatment was not considered particularly healthy though, and many writers ascribed the melancholic character of Jews to eating this dish. The practice of "cramming" or force feeding geese to increase the size of their livers was already well established by early modern times. From such geese the prized *foie gras* was taken. One particular type of goose, the barnacle goose, grabbed the popular attention solely for the bizarre way people thought it was born. Even reputed scientists insisted that the creatures spontaneously generate and immature goslings emerge from a barnacle fastened to the sides of rocks or trees in remote places like Scotland.

Swan

Although its flesh is said to be dark and foul-smelling, swans were considered a very grand presentation dish in the courts of European rulers. One can only guess whether their principal attraction was seeing or eating the swan.

Turkey

Originating in the New World, Turkeys were one of the few foods immediately accepted and praised everywhere in Europe. This is not entirely surprising, considering that it is similar to other fowl regularly eaten and never really seemed exotic or unusual. Guinea fowl is a similar bird and was often confused with it. Guinea fowl originated in Africa and was introduced to Europe about the same time as turkeys, early in the sixteenth century or slightly earlier.

Pheasant and Partridge

These fowl were considered superior to all other wild fowl, and pheasant in particular were the most prized on fashionable tables. In fact, medical writers like Tobias Venner suggested that partridges are actually unhealthy for country laborers, "wherefore when they shall chance to meet with a covie of young Partridges, they were much better to bestow them upon such for whom they are convenient."[48] The logic of this was that delicate birds would only burn up in the powerful digestive system of the average worker, and so it was best left to the leisured classes. The usual way to catch these birds was with a trained hawk or falcon, which was a favorite pastime of nobles. These birds were also "hung" before being cooked, which means that they were left to decay for several days or longer, which not only tenderized the flesh but also imparted a unique rich flavor to it.

Woodcock, Grouse, Snipe and Ortolan

These medium-sized wild fowl were all prized across Europe. Traditionally snipe was cooked whole and ungutted, after which the contents of its intestines would be spread on toast and eaten. This practice prompted food writer Melchior Sebizius to comment: "Such is the furor and stupidity of gluttony, that bite-size pieces of toast are placed in a pan, then the snipe is roasted, and the excrement from its belly is squeezed out, and it is afterwards avidly and sweetly devoured."[49]

Crane, Heron, Stork and Plover

All wild waterfowl, most are no longer eaten in Europe but formerly were enjoyed despite their tough fibrous flesh. Cranes were usually hung from the neck with weights tied to the feet in order to tenderize it. The eggs of plovers in particular were gathered on the coasts of Britain and Holland, and were an esteemed delicacy.

Pigeons and Turtledoves

The idea of eating a pigeon of course revolts most modern Americans but they were considered one of the most healthy birds, and were often kept in coops, towers or *dovecotes* and fattened expressly for the purpose of eating. In fact, in France, it was an aristocratic privilege to keep pigeons, and this was one of the first things provincials complained about when writing to the Estates General at the start of the French Revolution. Their complaint stemmed from the fact that pigeons will eat up freshly sown seeds, thus destroying the farmer's livelihood.

Figpecker, Sparrow, Thrush, Starling and Swallow

All these are tiny wild birds that were caught in nets or trapped with a sticky lime mixture spread on tree branches. In some regions they were an important part of the diet. They were usually larded (strips of fat are sewn into the skin), a procedure that prevents them from drying out and then roasted over a flame on a rotating skewer. The tiniest of these birds were sometimes eaten bones and all. Such birds were also baked into huge pies, of which the famous "four and twenty blackbirds" is one example.

Quail

Quail are also tiny birds, but were often considered very unhealthy, purportedly because they eat a poisonous herb called hellebore. People ate them regardless, without any harm, and unlike similar fowl they gained a reputation for being especially dainty.

Puffins

Puffins are arctic seabirds that were usually heavily salted and eaten as a kind of cocktail snack. They are featured in early modern cuisine, strangely enough, because scientists categorized them somewhere between fish and flesh, and the Catholic church offered dispensations for people to eat puffins during Lent, when all other fowl was officially forbidden. Popular medical author Thomas Moffett explained that "Puffins being Birds and no Birds, that is to say Birds in shew and fish in substance, or (as one may justly call them, feathered fishes) are of ill taste and worse digestion; how dainty so ever they seem to strange appetites, and are permitted by Popes to be eaten in Lent."[50] By the same logic beaver tail was considered akin to fish, and also allowed during Lent.

FISH

An innumerable variety of fishes were consumed in early modern Europe. The following section lists only the most important species. Fresh fish was relatively hard to come by far from the sea, though those with money could afford to have them shipped inland, and many major waterways throughout Europe as well as lakes provided fresh water species. Fish ponds were also not uncommon, especially connected to monasteries. The importance of fish stems primarily from the 40-day period in the Christian calendar from Ash Wednesday to Easter, called Lent, during which meat eating was prohibited. Other fast days were also liberally sprinkled throughout the year, and a meatless Friday is one tradition that has lingered into the present. For the majority of the population, if they could afford fish, it would probably have been dried or preserved. Even in the Mediterranean, where one might expect fish to be abundant, people depended on dried cod or *bacala* from northern waters because it would last indefinitely. It is also interesting that although fish was eaten in significant quantities by both poor and wealthy families, physicians believed fish to be generally unhealthy due to the abundance of phlegmatic humors which they contain. These cold and moist humors were thought to disturb the body's inherent humoral balance, leading to illnesses like colds and coughs.

Perch, Carp, Bream and Pike

These fresh water fish were considered healthier than other species because of the great exercise they get swimming through fast rocky currents. Their white delicate flesh also suggested that they were easier to digest than other fish, and contained fewer "superfluous excrements"—something oily fish were said to abound in.

Sole, Flounder, Turbot and Halibut

These are all related flat fishes that range from about the size of a hand to the enormous halibut which could weigh over 100 pounds. Sole, because extremely light and crumbly, was often called a "sea capon" or the original chicken of the sea, and was considered among the more delicate fish. Turbot were typically sold in *popinae* (Latin for cook-shops), places where people could take out ready cooked food.[51]

Tench and Bleak

Tench is a particularly slimy fish and for this reason was considered ignoble and only fit for the table of paupers. Bleak, a fish with similar texture was even called *schnotfisch* in German, and was equally scorned by the well-off.

Eels and Lampreys

Eels and lampreys were believed to be among the most harmful of foods because of the gummy viscous texture of their flesh. It may have been this very prohibition that made them the object of intense gastronomic interest though, and records of royal banquets frequently included eels, and many kings were even said to have died from a surfeit of eels. Some food writers thought that eels generate spontaneously, without parents, from rotting organic matter. The practice of using a dead horse's head thrown in the water to catch eels may have suggested that they were generated from the decaying flesh itself. Eels and lampreys were usually grilled on a sheet of paper to prevent burning, but they were also pickled, smoked, served cold in a jellied aspic or baked into pies with sweet and savory ingredients.

Salmon and Trout

The Rhine River provided an abundance of salmon in early modern times, but both salmon and trout could be caught in dozens of waterways that connected to the sea. Over fishing since then has seriously diminished stocks and some European species are even in danger of extinction.

Tuna and Mackerel

Tuna was fished throughout the Mediterranean and the techniques of Sicilian fisherman using a maze of nets to corner the fish are legendary. Its eggs could be preserved as *botarga,* a hard dry ingredient sliced or grated much like salted meats or cheese.

Sturgeon and Caviar

Sturgeon can be enormous fish, and those caught in the Danube could weigh up to 400 pounds. At one time most European waterways contained sturgeon, which because of their size and the difficulty of transporting them fresh were among the most expensive foods. Their flesh was often salted and exported, but equally important were the fish eggs or caviar which was among the most esteemed delicacies among European elites. The following simple recipe for sturgeon comes from *The Sensible Cook,* a Dutch cookbook first published in 1667:

To Roast a Piece of Sturgeon

Remove the fin and scales, stick it with Cloves, let it roast; baste it well with Butter, when it is done take it from the spit, place it in a pot, then do stew it with Rhenish wine, Vinegar, Cinnamon, and Nutmeg. When dished up like this it is good.[52]

Cod

It was cod that in large measure inspired European voyages of exploration past Greenland to Nova Scotia and the east coast of North America. The Basques, French, English and even the Portuguese all scrambled for control of the valuable shoals where cod could be caught. As the most important of preserved fish, either salted as bacala or dried into stockfish, it provided the most durable and long-lasting form of protein for many Europeans, and was typically associated with Lent. Preparation of stockfish involved beating it with a mallet, then soaking for several days with repeated changes of water, after which it could be cooked like other fish or mashed into a puree with oil and garlic as in *brandade de morue.* Cod roe, the eggs salted like caviar, was also a delicacy, as were the tongue and cheeks. The air bladder was rendered down to make *isinglass,* a jelling agent used much like gelatin, and the liver provided a valuable oil. Related species such as haddock, whiting and hake were also eaten in similar fashion.

Herring

Second perhaps only to cod in importance, pickled herring provided major wealth to several cities facing the North Sea and the Baltic, who regularly sent out major fleets to catch herring. Beyond pickling in brine, herring could also be smoked or dried, or a combination of all these preservation techniques. The most significant breakthrough in the processing of herring came from the Dutch in the fifteenth century, who began to salt their catch on board ship so as to avoid returning to port before it spoiled. Trade in pickled herring thereafter became extremely lucrative.

Sardines and Anchovies

Both these small oily fish travel in huge schools through the Mediterranean and off the coast of Spain and Portugal, and although they could be eaten fresh, they were usually salted for preservation. Anchovies in particular were a major flavoring ingredient throughout Europe, added to sauces, ragouts and fricasées, or enjoyed with drinks as an appetite stimulant.

Sharks and Rays

Sharks were commonly eaten, but were usually considered a low and peasant-like food. Rays, because they were so cartilaginous, were thought to improve with age, which is why French dietary writer Nicholas Abraham suggested that they are better at Rheims than Abbeyville, better in Paris than Rouen and better in Lyons than Marseilles. The river journey inland to market presumably improved the texture of the flesh and let its disagreeable odor dissipate.[53]

Porpoise and Whale

Although we now know these to be mammals, they were thought to be fishes well into the early modern period. They were also eaten, though because of their size and the difficulty involved in catching and transporting such huge creatures, they were enjoyed only at the most lavish of banquets at which they were presented baked whole. In some regions however, as in the Basque provinces of France and Spain, whales were fished and eaten by the general populace. Both animals went completely out of fashion in the latter part of the early modern period.

SHELLFISH, MOLLUSCS AND OTHER CREATURES OF THE SEA

Oysters

Oysters have always been considered an aphrodisiac, though food writers of the past were hard-pressed to explain why. Some claimed it was the saltiness that created an artificial itch through the body; others insisted that because eaten raw their crude juices inflate the body, particularly the extremities. On a more prosaic level some contended that it was merely the pepper and other aromatics that caused this effect. As one food writer put it "Good Fellows cook them on the grill in their shells, adding butter and a bit of pepper, to excite the appetite for Venus."[54] It is perhaps this view of oysters as an inevitable part of a rich and luxurious life that led them to be depicted so often in still life paintings among the "vanities" of this world.

Clams, Cockles, Mussels and Scallops

These shellfish abounded on the coasts of Europe and were consumed primarily in these regions. The idea that they are best consumed in months containing the letter "R" was current even in the early modern period. It was believed that they spawn in the summer and this weakens their bodies and ruins their taste. The scallop, being the symbol of St. Iago, was consumed along the pilgrimage route across northern Spain to the Cathedral of Santiago de Compostella.

Lobster, Crayfish, Shrimp and Crab

Lobster, much as today, was considered especially elegant and appropriate food for lovers, being an aphrodisiac. There is a common perception that lobster was considered a poor man's food, and this may have been the case in colonial New England but not back in Europe. In fact English man-about-town Samuel Pepys's diary records that an elegant dinner he threw in 1663 included a fricassee of rabbit and chickens, carp, lamb, pigeons, various pies and four lobsters. All these shellfish were considered exquisite garnishes for other dishes as well. Lobster was cooked either by roasting, boiling or by removing the meat from the shell and cooking it separately.

Snails

Eaten mostly in Spain, Italy and France, snails were not considered either flesh or fish. They were also reputed to have special restorative properties, and sick emaciated people were often given snail broth to revive them.

Frogs

Frogs were eaten primarily in southern Europe, and not merely the legs, either. Whole young frogs, eaten bones and all, were considered a dainty dish, though physicians condemned them because the bones could pierce the stomach lining. Northern Europeans found the idea of eating frogs repulsive. The French on the other hand found them delectable and food author Nicolas de Bonnefons offered several ways to prepare frogs:

How to Skin a Frog

You skin them and leave only the two thighs and the backbone, throwing away the rest which is bad; Then wash them well, and cook them with bouillon to make soup, or you can place them in a fricasée; Or reserving the legs [still connected], you remove the bone of one, and leave the meat on the other, then dunk them in a batter for beignets and fry them and serve; these are called Frogs in Cherries, because at one end of the bone it looks like the dimple on a cherry, and the bone seems like a stem.[55]

Sea Turtles

The sweet flesh of sea turtles was used only rarely through the early modern period, but in the eighteenth century, and especially in England, turtle soup became all the rage. Turtles could also be roasted or baked, but the difficulty of preparing them meant that only the best equipped kitchens could deal with them. Hannah Glasse offered explicit instructions for the intrepid on how "To dress a Turtle the West India Way" which involves bleeding, dissecting, soaking and cleaning the guts, then boiling, stewing and baking various parts. The procedure yielded several different courses: a soup, a fricasee, fins and the *calapee* or flipper meat and *calapash* which is the meat from the upper shell that is greenish and gelatinous.[56]

Squid, Cuttlefish and Octopus

Squid, cuttlefish and octopus were all classified as "bloodless" fishes and hence were thought to be tough and difficult to digest. No doubt this opinion was framed by people who did not know how to properly cook them. Both pounding and long cooking were two ways, though so too was quickly frying them.

Sea Urchins

These spiny members of the echinoderm family were eaten both cooked and raw. Their use was mostly restricted to southern Europe and to the first half of the early modern period.

DAIRY

Milk

Milk was not generally considered an appropriate food for healthy adults, but it was given to children and also the elderly for whom it was said to be particularly nourishing and easily digested. "Common experience prooveth that Womans mylke sucked from the brest, is without comparison best of all in a consumption,"[57] contended Thomas Cogan in a medical recommendation. Interestingly, many southern Europeans are lactose intolerant, which may account for the aversion many had toward drinking fresh milk.

Cream

Cream was really not a typical ingredient in cooking and cream sauces are relatively rare before the eighteenth century, but *béchamel* (a white sauce of flour, butter and cream or milk) was reputedly invented in 1654 by one Louis de Béchamel, a steward in Louis XIV's household. Cream was often poured over fruit, especially strawberries, but usually it was churned into butter, which could be stored for several months. The early modern period did see the very first ice cream in Europe though, and ice houses were often built on sumptuous estates just to keep ice or snow for making ices and ice creams. The technology of using a container suspended in ice and saltpeter greatly interested scientists and was gradually perfected in the course of the late-sixteenth and seventeenth century. Ice cream spread from Italy to France in the late seventeenth century and from there to other European countries, but it remained an expensive and rare dessert through the early modern period.

Figure 2.5 Dairy. *From Scappi, Bartolomeo. Opera/di Bartolomeo Scappi M. dell'arte del cucinare. In Venetia: Presso Alessandro Vecchi, 1610. verso R2. EPB 5812/B. Courtesy of Wellcome Library, London.*

Butter

Butter was a staple food in the diet of northern Europeans, and Flemings and the Dutch were proverbially fond of it. Although physicians warned that butter was only to be eaten at the start of meals, the French typically ate it at the end. English physician Andrew Boorde believed that eaten this way the butter "doth swim above in the brinks of the stomach: as the fatness doth swim above in a boiling pot, the excess of such superfice will ascend to the orifice of the stomach, and doth make eructions [belches]."[58] Butter was not a typical ingredient in most of southern Europe where whole milk was usually made into cheese.

Cheese

Most milk produced in Europe, whether from cows, goats or sheep, was made into cheese. The ability to store cheese for months or in some cases even longer made this an eminently practical solution for dealing with large volumes of milk. Once the milk was curdled, usually using rennet, an enzyme taken from a calf's stomach, it could be separated into curds and whey. The curds would then be drained, cooked, pressed, salted and then aged, and the whey or liquid left over could be fed to pigs, or even recooked to make ricotta cheese. Every region produced its own local varieties, many of which survive to this day.

Physicians often recommended cheese at the end of a meal to seal off the contents of the stomach while it "concocted" the food and to prevent noxious fumes from rising to the head. This may be the origin of the current European custom of finishing a meal with cheese.

Eggs

Eggs were among the most prevalent foods in Europe at all social levels. They were believed to be among the most nourishing of foods, easily digested and eminently versatile. The best way to prepare them, according to most food writers was poached, but they were also typically fried, boiled, scrambled, roasted in the embers and even cooked on a spit. Omelets were considered a particularly elegant dish as well.

BEVERAGES
Water

Water was not commonly consumed as a beverage except by the poorest of families. For good reason, physicians discouraged people from drinking water, though they did not yet understand the dangers of infectious diseases that were easily spread through water supplies. At the very least, they recommended that water should first be boiled and strained, or combined with wine which would at least have provided a small antiseptic effect. An exception to this rule, however, was made for medicinal springs and mineral bath waters which were consumed for various ailments, especially gout and gallstones. Ordinary water was, of course, used in the household for cooking and other purposes and could be drawn from wells, cisterns that collected rain water or running streams and springs.

Wine

Wine was the principal beverage for most Europeans particularly in the south, but even in north where and when people could afford it. Wine was also central to the Christian Mass, making it absolutely indispensable for worship, even though the entire congregation might not be offered wine, which was a matter of controversy in the Reformation. By the early modern period manufacturing and retailing wine had become big business in many regions, though small producers continued to manufacture wine for local consumption too. Imported sweet wines such as Malmsey, Madeira and other varieties produced throughout the Mediterranean also fetched high prices throughout Europe. By the mid-sixteenth century the courtly fashion of drinking wine with ice or snow in it had spread through most of southern Europe, and was viciously denounced by physicians. Wine was considered an essential nutrient, in fact a meal without wine was called a *prandium caninum* or dog's dinner because only dogs have an aversion to wine. Wine was also drunk with breakfast, first thing in the morning.

Although there had been lightly sparkling wines in Europe for centuries, the invention of the cork stopped bottle containing champagne is credited to the Benedictine monk Dom Perignon in 1698, though this story was largely made up by nineteenth century champagne manufacturers as a marketing ploy. The bubbles in champagne are the product of a second fermentation inside the bottle, which not only creates the "pop" but is also dangerous if the bottle explodes. Champagne became wildly popular at the court of Louis XIV and from the eighteenth century down to the present has been known as the drink of luxury and refinement.

The popularity of port, especially among the English stems from a period in which war with France cut off supplies of wine from Bordeaux.

Under the terms of the Methuen Treaty in 1703, the English sponsored trade with Portugal in the fortified sweet wine by severely lowering tariffs. Thereafter, most wine drunk in England came from either Portugal or Spain. Sherry, a corruption of the name of the Spanish town Xeres de la Fronteira, was also a common drink in England throughout the early modern period. Sherry can be either dry or sweet and is usually slightly more alcoholic than ordinary wine.

By the eighteenth century the use of corked bottles meant that wine could be stored and aged properly. Up until then most wine was consumed within a year of harvest, and was drawn from a cask.

Throughout the early modern period, in places where wine was made, a weaker drink was also made from previously pressed grapes. In France it was called *piquette,* in Italy *acquarello* or *aquata.* Wine expert Andrea Bacci called it *lora* in Latin. Most writers considered it a drink for peasants, who often sold the wine they made and consumed this weaker kind of wine themselves.

Beer and Ale

Differing only by method of fermentation and the addition of hops in beer, beer and ale were not only a drink for social occasions, but a regular food in most of northern Europe. They were usually made from malted barley, but could also be made from wheat, rye and even oatmeal. Hopped beer was first introduced into England in the 1520s, and one version of a common rhyme ran "Turkeys, Reformation and Beer, Came hopping into England All in a Year." Physicians, following precepts framed in Mediterranean climes, usually condemned beer as something only appropriate for rustics and laborers. But often northern physicians did champion their native brew, as did the German Johannes Brettschneider (Placotomus in Latin) who wrote a whole treatise on the virtues of beer. Rural households typically produced their own beer, but in cities it was manufactured as a commercial enterprise and was already strictly regulated by the government and guild regulations. The famous Bavarian *Reinheitsgebot,* a purity law of 1516, is one of these. Alehouses were gathering places in cities and villages alike, often run by women, known as "alewives." In the course of the sixteenth and seventeenth centuries beer was increasingly produced outside cities in large capital-intensive factories which eventually made the small family-run alehouse that brewed its own beer obsolete. Glass bottles, used extensively in the eighteenth century, also meant that beer could be stored for longer periods and shipped further distances, which only intensified the trend toward beer brewing as a big business.

Cider and Perry

Cider made from apples, and perry made from pears, were common drinks in areas like Normandy in the north of France and through the west of England. Physicians believed that these were harmful and excessively "cold" drinks that made people's faces pale and bodies languid.

Mead

Mead is brewed from honey, and is perhaps one of the oldest alcoholic beverages on earth. It was promoted since classical times, with various additions such as herbs, as a medicinal drink, and this was its principal use through most of Europe in the early modern period.

Aqua vitae

The art of distillation had been perfected by alchemists in the late Middle Ages who probably learned it from Arabic authors, which is why we use the terms alcohol and alembic (the vessel in which it is distilled) which derive from Arabic. Ultimately what they were trying to make was a volatile "spirit" that would be analogous to the "spirits" that were thought to course through the human body. This artificial spirit would thus prolong life, hence the name water of life, which is what aqua vitae means. The term whiskey derived from the Gaelic *usquebaugh* means the same thing. Though hard alcohol was first introduced to Europe as a medicine, it soon became clear that people were consuming it for pleasure, and by the sixteenth century many of the liquors we are most familiar with were already in commercial production. Aqua vitae could be distilled from wine, yielding a clear and fiery liquid, but also from fruits as French *eau de vie* often is. Aqua vitae could also be flavored with medicinal herbs, and often it was monasteries that manufactured such "cordials" and "elixirs" meant to strengthen the heart and ward off disease. Benedictine and Chartreuse are both modern descendants of liqueurs first made by monks in the sixteenth and seventeenth century respectively. Grappa or marc is a clear and strong alcohol distilled from the residual pits and skins left over after a grape pressing.

Brandy

The term brandy derives from the Dutch *brandewijn* or burnt wine, which implies that ordinary wine must be distilled with fire. What distinguishes brandy from *eau de vie,* is that it was usually aged in wooden casks, giving it a golden hue and nutty flavor. Because it was more easily transported than wine, it became a staple on long ocean voyages, especially among the Dutch who encouraged vineyards outside of Bordeaux in the southwest of France, whose trade was then controlled by the English. Cognac, to the north of Bordeaux and Armagnac to the south, thus became the most revered of brandies. Many of today's cognac producers started business in the eighteenth century: Martell in 1715, Rémy Martin in 1725 and Hennessy in 1765.

Whisky

As the national drink of Scotland, whisky was manufactured primarily at the local level in small household stills. Several attempts to tax Scottish whisky production from the late seventeenth century met with resistance and small-scale producers in the highlands managed to completely evade taxation. Whisky was relatively unknown outside Scotland and was not produced on an industrial scale until the nineteenth century, when it began being exported in large quantities.

Gin

Invented by the Dutch and manufactured commercially by the Bols company since 1575, but arguably perfected by the English in the eighteenth century, gin is merely grain alcohol either distilled with or flavored with juniper and sometimes various other aromatic spices and herbs. It became so popular among the working classes in England that it prompted the artist William Hogarth to produce a series of satires depicting the brutal effects of gin drinking on the populace when compared to the more nutritious and wholesome beer.

Rum

Of central importance in the so-called triangular trade route between England, North America and the Caribbean, rum was one of the most important and valuable commodities in eighteenth-century Atlantic trade. Rum, distilled from molasses, was one of the principal uses for the sugar grown on plantations. It also became standard issue to sailors in the British Navy who mixed it with lemon or lime juice to make "grog."

Coffee

Native to Abyssinia, coffee was adopted in Muslim lands in the Middle Ages as a sober alternative to alcohol which is forbidden by Islamic law. Europeans might read about it in exotic travel accounts such as Leonhart Rauwolf's *Journey to the Land of the Orient* published in 1582, but they did not taste it until the middle of the seventeenth century when it became extremely popular, both as a medicinal and as a social beverage. Sylvestre Dufour in his *Traitez Nouveaux et Curieux Du Café, Du Thé et Du Chocolate* confidently exclaimed that "among all the healthy things that [trade] has procured for us, the best and most universally good is in my opinion coffee."[59] While physicians argued about its physiological properties, and moralists proclaimed its wonderful sobering effects, the fashion for coffee drinking spread down the social hierarchy until it eventually replaced beer or wine as the standard morning draught. One story recounts how it was introduced to Vienna: the fleeing Turkish army after the unsuccessful siege of 1683 left behind sacks of coffee beans, and before long Vienna opened its very first café. The first café in Paris, Le Procope, was opened by the Sicilian Francesco Procopio de Coltelli in 1686. Coffee houses, such as Lloyd's in London, also flourished as meeting places for middle-class businessmen and merchants. Lloyd's eventually became the renowned insurance firm, while other coffee houses attracted writers, artists and politicians, making them the focus of eighteenth-century urban society. So popular was coffee that Johann Sebastian Bach composed the "Coffee Cantata" which exclaimed "Ah! How sweet coffee tastes! Lovelier than a thousand kisses, sweeter far than muscatel wine!"

Tea

Consumed in Asia for hundreds of years, tea was also virtually unknown in Europe until the seventeenth century. Europeans could read about tea in such works as Antoine Balinghem's *Apresdinees* of 1624, in which the author describes the Japanese tea ceremony. He also claims that the hot beverage "augments and nourishes the interior fire, opens the conduits of the body, which is why it penetrates and refreshes better and quenches thirst quicker" than cold drinks.[60] It only began to displace coffee in England in the eighteenth century, prompted by the vigorous trade in tea of the East India Company and lowered tariffs. It was the very same company which tried to foist a cargo of tea on American colonists, only to have it dumped in the harbor in the Boston Tea Party. Ironically, it was at the same time that tea was becoming established as an article of mass consumption in England, and even the poorest workers spent their hard-earned money on tea sweetened with sugar.

Chocolate

It was on a latter voyage in 1502 to the New World that Christopher Columbus first encountered chocolate, but it was not until after Cortés' conquest of Mexico, that the drink made from cacao beans was successfully introduced to Spain in 1528. The Aztec nobility drank their chocolate mixed with ground corn, chili and vanilla (and they even used the beans as currency) but it was the Spanish who added sugar and cinnamon, and sometimes more exotic flavorings like musk, spices and aromatic flowers. The popularity of chocolate spread through Europe by the seventeenth century along with coffee and tea, but always remained the drink of choice in Spain where it was sipped through the morning by indolent noblemen and women. Although it was incorporated into desserts and even savory dishes in the early modern period, eating chocolate as we know it today was invented in the nineteenth century.

NOTES

1. Paulus Kyr, *Sanitatis studium* (Brasov, Romania, 1551), E4.

2. Charles Etienne, *De nutrimentis* (Paris: Robert Stephanus, 1550), 69.

3. Melchior Sebizius, *De alimentorum facultatibus* (Strasbourg: Joannis Philippi Mülbii et Josiae Stedelii, 1650), 241.

4. Girolamo Cardano, *Opera Omnia*, vol. 7 (Lyon: Huguetan et Ravaut, 1663), 56.

5. Salvatore Massonio, *Archidipno overo dell'insalata* (Venice: Marc'antonio Brogiollo, 1627), 365.

6. Hugo Fridaevallis, *De tuenda sanitate* (Antwerp: Christopher Plantin, 1568), 66.

7. Alessandro Petronio, *Del viver delli Romani*, tr. M. Basilio Paravicino (Rome: Domenico Basa, 1592), 141.

8. Ludovicus Nonnius, *Diaeteticon, sive re cibaria* (Antwerp: Petri Belleri, 1645), 67.

9. Thomas Cogan, *The Haven of Health* (London: Thomas Orwin, 1589), 57.

10. Hannah Glasse, *The Art of Cookery,* facsimile (Bedford, MA: Applewood Books, 1997), 35.

11. Sebizius, 349.

12. Antonio Latini, *Lo scalco alla moderna* (Naples: Antonio Parrino e Michele Luigi Mutii, 1692), 551.

13. Adam Smith, *The Wealth of Nations* (Chicago: University of Chicago Press), Book I, 87.

14. Sebizius, 401.

15. Luis Lobera de Avila, *Vergel de sanidad* (Alcala de Henares: Joan de Brocar, 1542), Lxxviii.

16. Estienne, 59.

17. Giovanni Domenico Sala, *De alimentis* (Padua: Io. Bapt. Martinum, 1628), 12.

18. John Evelyn, *Acetaria,* reprint (Totnes, Devon: Prospect Books, 1996), 27.

19. Thomas Moffett, *Health's Improvement* (London: Thomas Newcomb, 1655), 165.

20. Henry Buttes, *Dyets Dry Dinner* (London: Thomas Creede for William Wood, 1599), dedication.

21. Thomas Dawson, *The Good Housewife's Jewel,* Introduction by Maggie Black (Lewes, East Sussex: Southover Press, 1996), 42.

22. Ugo Benzi, *Regole della sanita,* annotated by Giovanni Lodovico Bertaldi (Turin: Heirs of Gio. Domenico Tarino, 1618), 130–131.

23. Elius Eobanus Hessus, *De tuenda bona valetudine* (Frankfurt: Heirs of Christian Egenollf, 1556), 60.

24. Cardano, *Opera Omnia,* 58.

25. Cardano, *De sanitate tuenda* (Rome: F. Zanettus, 1580), 143.

26. Petronio, 109.

27. Buttes, fol. H.

28. Benzi, 114.

29. Sebizius, 426.

30. John Gerard, *Herbal,* reprint (London: Studio Editions, 1994), 169.

31. Walter Bailey, *A Short Discourse on the Three Kindes of Peppers,* facsimile (New York: Da Capo Press, 1972), A8r.

32. Cogan, 91.

33. Robert Herrick, "Cherries Ripe," see *Food for Thought,* ed. Joan and John Digby (Hopewell, NJ: Ecco Press, 1987), 400.

34. *Good Huswifes Handmaid For the Kitchen,* reprint (Bristol, England: Stuart Press, 1992), 38.

35. Joseph Duchesne, *Le pourtraict de la santé* (Paris: Claude Morel, 1606), 406.

36. Prosper Calanius, *Traicté pour l'entretenement de santé,* tr. Jean Goeurot (Lyon: Jean Temporal, 1533), 60.

37. Eliza Smith, *The Compleat Housewife,* facsimile (London: Studio Editions, 1994), 104. There is no concrete evidence that this was the author's name; most culinary historians refer to her as E. Smith.

38. Bartolomeo Stefani, *L'Arte di ben cucinare* (Mantua: Apresso gli Osanna, 1662), 80.

39. Nonnius, 135.

40. Francisco Nuñez de Oria, *Regimiento y aviso de sanidad* (Medina del Campo: Francisco del Canto, 1586), 206.

41. Gerard, 122.

42. Fridaevallis, 54.

43. *The Closet of Sir Kenelm Digby Opened,* ed. Jane Stevenson and Peter Davidson (Totnes, Devon: Prospect Books, 1997), 44.

44. Andrea Bacci, *De naturali vinorum historia* (Rome: Nicolai Mulii, 1598), 23.

45. Benzi, 285.

46. Domenico Romoli, *La singolar dottrina ... dell'ufficio dello scalco* (Venice: Giovanni Battista Bonfadino, 1593), 28.

47. Edward Topsell, *The History of Four Footed Beasts* (London: E. Cotes, 1658), 81.

48. Tobias Venner, *Via recta ad vitam longam* (London: Edward Griffen for Richard Moore, 1620), 64.

49. Sebizius, 933.

50. Moffett, 108.

51. Nonnius, 349.

52. *The Sensible Cook,* tr. Peter Rose (Syracuse: Syracuse University Press, 1989), 66.

53. Nicolas Abraham, *Le gouvernement necessaire a chacun pour vivre longuement en santé* (Paris: Marc Orry, 1608), 41.

54. Abraham, 49.

55. Nicolas de Bonnefons, *Les Delices de Campagne* (Amsterdam: Jean Blaev, 1661), 316.

56. Glasse, 227–229.

57. Cogan, 154.

58. Andrew Boorde, *A compendyous Regyment,* reprint (London: Early English Text Society, 1870), 46.

59. Sylvestre Dufour, *Traitez nouveau et curieux du café, du thé et du chocolate* (Lyon: Jean Girin et B. Riviere, 1685), 4. Available online at http://www.bub.ub.es/grewe/showbook.pl?gw026.

60. Antione Balinghem, *Apresdinees et propos de table* (Saint-Omer, France: Charles Boscart, 1624), 272–287.

CHAPTER 3

COOKING AND THE FOOD PROFESSIONS

PROCEDURES, EQUIPMENT AND UTENSILS

Procedures

Although there was considerable variation from country to country and between rich and poor households, certain basic cooking procedures were common throughout early modern Europe. The method of cooking was largely dependent on a reliable source of fuel. In regions where wood became scarce due to deforestation, quick cooking methods such as frying and sautéeing were more popular and small pieces of wood, twigs, or plant debris could provide a quick but hot fire. In many places trees such as willows would be regularly pollarded, or trimmed of branches that could be used for fuel and then harvested each season after they grew back. The right to gather wood, "by hook or crook," or merely through "windfall" was thus an important consideration for most families. Roasting on an open hearth, or keeping a large cauldron simmering for hours meant either an abundant supply of hardwood or enough disposable income to purchase it. Similarly, baking required a good deal of wood to bring an oven to temperature and thus most urban families purchased their bread. In some places, particularly in Ireland, peat, a kind of rich fossil-laden soil, could be burned for warmth and cooking. Dried dung might also be similarly used. Elsewhere coal provided fuel, but it was not until regular mining and transport in the industrial nineteenth century that it was widely used in iron ranges. Gas ranges also are only found after the early modern period.

Figure 3.1 Outdoor cooking over open fires. *From Scappi, Bartolomeo. Opera/di Bartolomeo Scappi M. dell'arte del cucinare. In Venetia: Presso Alessandro Vecchi, 1610. Verso Q4. EPB 5812/B. Courtesy of Wellcome Library, London.*

Roasting is probably the oldest and certainly the simplest method of cooking; all that is required is a fire and a skewer to hold the food. Technically roasting should be defined as cooking over or in proximity to an open flame or hot coals. Through the Middle Ages and well into the sixteenth century roasting was done either outdoors or in colder climates indoors in the center of the kitchen. Smoke escaped through a hole in the roof. For most households the kitchen was also the common gathering space, so one can imagine the inconvenience, let alone the difficulty of cooking should it rain. It was not until the mid-sixteenth century that chimneys became more common, and hearths were regularly set into the wall. Because of the inherent danger of fire, kitchens were often situated far from the dining space in wealthier households, which meant that food had to be carried a considerable distance before it reached the guests. This is, no doubt why covered vessels were the preferred way to transport hot food. Around the fireplace itself could be gathered several small pans, while over the fire a spit with a hunk of meat or whole birds could be slowly turned, manually of course. Mechanical turnspits, powered by a clockwork mechanism or hot air rising up the chimney, became common in the seventeenth century, though there were various other ways they could be powered, even by dogs on a treadmill. Typically a dripping pan would be placed beneath the meat to catch any juices and fat. This could be used to baste the meat or could be made into gravy. Small morsels of food could also be cooked directly in the hot drippings. Apart from the spit, food could also be roasted directly on or underneath the hot coals. Eggs were sometimes roasted this way, as were potatoes and truffles. A perforated pan held over the fire, as was used for chestnuts, was considered another type of roasting. So too was a portable metal open-faced oven placed in front of the fire.

Another way to cook on an open hearth without bringing food in direct contact with the flames was to use a covered earthenware vessel or metal pot that was placed in the burning coals. The coals would also be heaped on top to provide more even heat. To prevent burning, the pot would usually contain some liquid and thus this method would today be defined as **braising,** though this verb did not enter the English language until 1797 in *The London Art of Cookery*. The term derives from the French *braise* meaning charcoal. A related procedure was to seal the pot lid with dough to prevent any steam from escaping and then place it in an oven. Many pies were also cooked with a lid made entirely of a flour and water dough which would be discarded. Both meats and vegetables were cooked this way, indeed

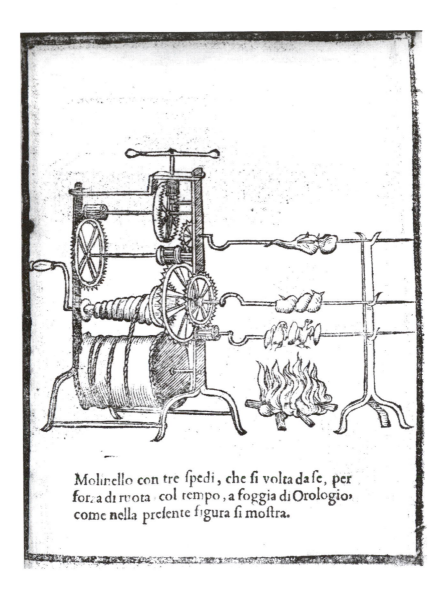

Molinello con tre ſpedi, che ſi volta da ſe, per
forza di ruota col tempo, a foggia di Orologio,
come nella preſente figura ſi moſtra.

Figure 3.2 Spit. *From Scappi, Bartolomeo. Opera/di Bartolomeo Scappi M.
dell'arte del cucinare. In Venetia: Presso Alessandro Vecchi, 1610. Recto R8,
verso R6. EPB 5812/B. Courtesy of Wellcome Library, London.*

anything that could withstand long slow cooking was braised. Today, we still refer to a large cut of beef cooked this way as a "pot roast" which is perhaps a linguistic remnant of this procedure.

Also using an open hearth, **boiling** foods in small pots or larger cauldrons suspended over the fire by hooks and chains was a method that demanded less direct attention. Sometimes a ratchet mechanism was used to lower or raise the vessels, or even a crane-like arm that could be swung in and out of the fire. If all this sounds dangerous, that is because it was. Serious burns were a frequent occurrence, and even accidental deaths if a boiling kettle overturned or if someone fell into the fire. In cold months embers would be kept burning continuously and the pots left for days to heat and cool, containing a soup or gruel such as the pease porridge in the pot "9 days old." Apart from meats, grains and vegetables, puddings were also cooked in cloth bags within the cauldron. A pudding was essentially anything cooked in this way: a plum pudding of dough, or a chopped meat or blood pudding cooked encased in an intestine or stomach. Small earthenware vessels could also be placed inside the cauldron. Perhaps surprising, because seen practically nowhere today, many foods were subjected to two different cooking procedures. For example, a cut of beef might first be boiled and then roasted, roasted then simmered with a sauce, or stewed and then grilled wrapped in paper.

Stewing is really only one step away from boiling. The only real distinction is that boiled foods are served separate from the cooking liquid which is either discarded or served as a soup, stewed foods are left in the cooking medium which is usually reduced and thickened. Thus a pot of boiling meat and vegetables can become a stew if left on the fire. In classical French cooking, however, the ingredients are usually browned first, and the addition of a roux made from fat and flour is used to thicken the mixture. In Spain the *olla podrida,* literally "rotten pot," was a stew made from a wide variety of meats, fowl, fish and root vegetables simmered together. In England and elsewhere this method, there known as an *olio,* became fashionable in the eighteenth century.

Poaching is also a variety of boiling, only the water is left at a very low simmer. Usually called "seething" in English, it would be used either to cook foods that would fall apart in a boiling vessels, such as fish or dumplings, or for foods that require only minimal cooking, such as eggs. Slowly boiled fruits like apples or pears in a spiced liquid are also referred to as being poached. This procedure was first recorded in the Middle Ages, and probably goes back much further.

Figure 3.3 Open fire. *From Scappi, Bartolomeo. Opera/di Bartolomeo Scappi M. dell'arte del cucinare. In Venetia: Presso Alessandro Vecchi, 1610. Recto R6. EPB 5812/B. Courtesy of Wellcome Library, London.*

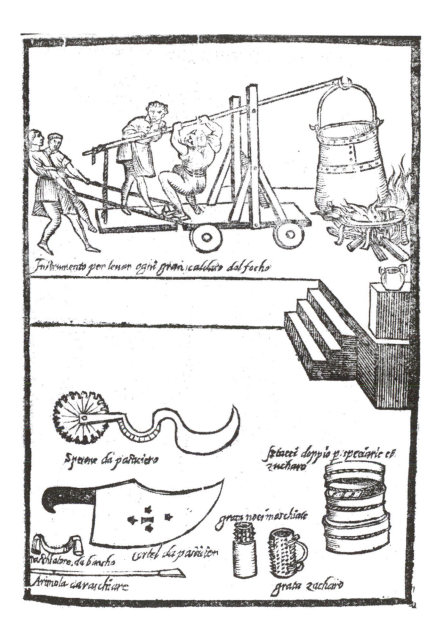

Figure 3.4 Cauldron on a crane. *From Scappi, Bartolomeo. Opera/di Bartolomeo Scappi M. dell'arte del cucinare. In Venetia: Presso Alessandro Vecchi, 1610. Recto Q3. EPB 5812/B. Courtesy of Wellcome Library, London.*

Although what is called **grilling** in Europe today we would call broiling because the food cooks underneath a heat source, grilling used to be precisely that. Food was placed on a grill or iron grate set above coals or an open flame. Generally a quick method of cooking, used for small cuts of meat or vegetables, it could be done both outdoors and indoors, in which case the grate would usually be set on an iron braisier containing hot coals. Delicate foods, or those that might stick to the grill, like fish, were sometimes wrapped in greased paper before placing on the grill.

Probably the most economical method of cooking was **frying,** food being cut into small pieces or cutlets that cook quickly in fat, either oil, butter, lard, suet or even fat from a goose or duck. Surprisingly though, frying was a relative newcomer to Europe, probably introduced some time in the Middle Ages. In places where fuel was scarce this became one of the most typical procedures, as a frying pan could be set on a trivet over a small fire. Some pans were made with legs so they could be placed over coals raked from the fire. In wealthier households a brick range containing several small fires could hold many pots and pans. With the ability to cook many dishes at different temperatures, smaller cuts of meat were not a matter of economy, but rather of refinement. Food writers often did not distinguish between sautéeing in a small amount of oil placed in a pan and what we would call deep frying in a large quantity of fat, but it is clear they used both procedures, the latter especially for fritters. Either iron pans or earthenware vessels could be used to fry. Physicians, incidentally, found frying to be the least healthy of all cooking methods. A fricasée is one type of frying which involved cooking the food in a sauce. In the end it would resemble a stew, but used meats and vegetables, or most typically chicken, that did not require long slow cooking. It was often difficult to distinguish from a ragoût, which had a sauce added at the very end. The word ragoût, in fact, comes from the French verb *ragoûter,* meaning to pick up the taste.

Baking was only generally done by those who could afford an oven and the fuel to heat it. Ovens were often set in the wall beside a hearth, but they could also be free standing beehive shaped brick structures, built outdoors or in a separate bake house. To heat them a fire would be made inside and kept burning, often all day, until the oven reached the desired temperature. Then all the ashes would be swept or mopped out, the bread dough placed inside, and the oven door sealed. After several hours other foods could be placed inside, casseroles or pies being the most typical baked foods. A larger oven

Figure 3.5 Baking equipment. *From Scappi, Bartolomeo. Opera/di Bartolomeo Scappi M. dell'arte del cucinare. In Venetia: Presso Alessandro Vecchi, 1610. Verso R6. EPB 5812/B. Courtesy of Wellcome Library, London.*

would be required to bake cuts of venison, or porpoise, and these were naturally only owned by the wealthiest of households. In smaller ovens, a baking stone or metal griddle could also be set, on which various quick breads or pancakes could be cooked.

Although really a method of preservation, **smoking** was absolutely essential to maintain a supply of meat through the year. For many households, smoked meat was probably the only kind they ate. Smoke dries food, and in combination with a previous soaking in brine, it prevents bacteria from forming and flavors the food as well. The addition of saltpeter (potassium nitrate) to the brine gives many smoked products their pinkish color. Pork products such as ham, bacon and sausage were the most common foods to be smoked, but fish and cheeses could be too. Some smoked foods were meant to be eaten raw, like Bayonne ham of France, while others were cooked. The simplest smoking method was to merely hang the food in the chimney. A separate smokehouse, in which a slow smoldering fire could be kept going for days, was a more efficient method, and was usually adopted for the commercial production of smoked foods.

Drying is a related procedure, sometimes used in tandem with other preservation techniques. But some foods, if treated properly, usually with salt, could be air dried and preserved without smoking. In Italy dried beef or *bresaola, prosciutto* and *serrano* ham from Spain are preserved this way. Stockfish is also merely air dried, but this procedure only works in the cold and dry climate of the extreme north, in places like Norway. Fruits were also typically air or sun-dried: raisins, figs, dates, plums as well as other botanical fruits like tomatoes and peppers. Herbs were often dried in bunches hung from the ceiling in the kitchen, which could be snipped whenever needed. Mushrooms were also typically dried after spring gathering, to be used throughout the year. Apples and pears in colder climates were often dried in a warm oven. Other products dried for storage include beans and peas, corn, pasta, as well as dried biscuits or "hard tack" bread carried on long ocean voyages.

Pickling was another method of preserving food. In a salted and sometimes acidic environment that inhibits bacterial growth, almost anything can be pickled, including meats, vegetables, fish, olives. Pickling was frequently done within the household, but there were also large-scale operations that supplied barrels of pickled fish, for example. One step beyond pickling are those foods which are both preserved in brine and that also ferment, such as sauerkraut.

Perhaps one of the oldest preservation techniques, immersing fruits or other foods in honey which keeps out air and bacteria, creates what is called a **preserve.** With the increased availability of sugar in the sixteenth century, the art of making preserves came into full flower, and manuals designed for country gentlewomen offered hundreds of recipes for everything imaginable. Preserves also had a lingering medicinal reputation. Marmalade, probably first concocted from quince and later from orange peel, was one preserve that made a smooth transition from a medicine to a condiment. Fruits could also be preserved in alcohol, ideally in an *eau de vie* made from the fruit itself. Meats preserved in fat, either by "potting" or in a confit or pâté, could also be considered a type of preserve.

Apart from the various syrups and juleps that were used primarily as medicines and citrus concentrates on ocean voyages against scurvy, there were also attempts to **concentrate** other foods to make them both portable and long-lasting. One such successful attempt involved cooking down a rich stock into a gelatinous concentrate known as "portable" or "pocket" soup because it could be carried wrapped in a cloth and reconstituted as needed. It was essentially the ancestor of the bouillon cube. Concentrated grape must or *sapa* was also a popular condiment and cooking ingredient, not unlike balsamic vinegar, though without the acidic bite.

Remarkably, the **pressure cooker** is a contraption invented in 1681 by Denys Papin, and was then called "The New Digester, or Engine for Softening Bones." It was designed to render old tough animals and fish and even their bones tender and edible. The device was exhibited before the Royal Society, of which Papin was a member, but it remained merely a scientific curiosity for many years.

Equipment

Probably among the most important vessels in the kitchen were the basins and pitchers for holding and transporting water. We might find it hard to imagine a kitchen without running water, but it remained a rarity through most of the early modern period. The wealthiest households might have running water drawn from a cistern or pumped in from a well or spring, but most people had to carry their water directly from the source. This naturally made washing dishes a more difficult and odious task, especially as dirty dishwater had to be dumped somewhere. In cities it must have been a pressing concern, especially in those without good drainage or sewage systems.

Naturally all kitchens contained pots and pans, and these were not terribly different from those we use today. But, unlike modern pots

Figure 3.6 Work tables. *From Scappi, Bartolomeo. Opera/di Bartolomeo Scappi M. dell'arte del cucinare. In Venetia: Presso Alessandro Vecchi, 1610. Verso Q5. EPB 5812/B. Courtesy of Wellcome Library, London.*

and pans, they would have been made of iron or copper, lined with tin and would need to be considerably thicker and heavier to withstand direct exposure to flames. Various spits, skewers, chains, hooks, grates and trivets would also have made the cooking apparatus more heavy than that used today, and much more charred with wood smoke. To stoke the flame, bellows would also have been necessary.

Obviously every kitchen would also have to be supplied with a panoply of knives, spoons, spatulas, the more lavish the kitchen, the more utensils. Bartolomeo Scappi's *Opera* provides illustrations of utensils that were considered requisite for the best kitchens in the sixteenth century, including a good dozen knives for chopping, peeling, cutting pies, dismembering joints and opening oysters. There is even a notched pastry cutter. In other words, the wealthiest households had kitchens with innumerable gadgets though nearly all were, of course, manually operated.

The mortar and pestle played a much greater role in the early modern kitchen than it does today. Made of wood, marble or ceramic, it was where spices, nuts, herbs and anything requiring pounding was processed. But by the latter seventeenth and eighteenth centuries when pounded and sieved breadcrumb-based sauces were gradually replaced with flour and fat-thickened sauces, the quintessential chefs' tool went from mortar to whisk. Graters also played a large role, and separate graters were used for cheese, nutmeg and sugar, which was grated from a conical loaf when needed. Rolling pins were also ubiquitous, both the smooth sort and notched varieties that could be used for cutting long strips of pasta, or ravioli into separate squares. Slotted spoons and colanders were also thoroughly familiar. Perhaps less familiar today, were various irons for waffles, wafers and other confections that were thrust directly into the fire. Sieves were also important in the early modern kitchen for straining stocks and sauces, and especially for pureeing ingredients. They were usually made of horsehair or wool tightly set in a hoop-shaped frame.

Early modern chefs were also extremely fond of using molds for creating towering presentations set in gelatin, or indeed of anything that could hold its shape. By the eighteenth century, cookbooks included illustrations of a whole variety of shapes and sizes, and it seems that chefs vied with each other to create the largest quivering mass that could defy gravity.

Another tool, rarely seen nowadays, was the larding needle. Drier pieces of meat intended to be roasted were often studded with thin

Figure 3.7 Knife sharpening. *From Scappi, Bartolomeo. Opera/di Bartolomeo Scappi M. dell'arte del cucinare. In Venetia: Presso Alessandro Vecchi, 1610. Verso R5. EPB 5812/B. Courtesy of Wellcome Library, London.*

strips of pork fat, which themselves could be rolled in spices. This kept the meat moist and flavorful.

Many households also owned a small copper pot still for distilling alcohol, flower essences and medicines. In its simplest form, the still or alembic merely heated the contents of the pot, and the steam traveled up a long angled tube where it condensed, and the resulting alcohol or essence then dripped into another vessel. Many cookbooks and guides on household management contain long sections on how to use the still to prepare various syrups, juleps and cordials whose use was both gastronomic and medicinal.

Utensils

At the start of the early modern period, a typical table would be set with a platter or bowl of food in the center. Each diner would remove a portion and place it on a bread "trencher" or slice of bread and proceed to eat it with his or her fingers. There were no forks and if food had to be cut it was customary for each diner to use his own personal knife, which could be rather elaborate. As might be imagined, this was a rather messy affair, and the tablecloth was usually completely soiled from greasy fingers by the end of the meal, which is why it was removed before the dessert course, sometimes itself called a "remove." More liquid foods, of course, had to be contained within bowls and, fortunately, spoons were provided. These tended to be quite different from modern spoons though, and usually consisted of a thin narrow shaft extending directly from a deep tear-shaped bowl.

Although there were two-pronged forks used for carving and picking up small delicacies much earlier, forks as a regular table utensil were introduced first in sixteenth-century Italy. Even then, they were elaborate expensive utensils, used by only the most fastidious of diners. Their use spread gradually to France in the reign of Henry III and then to England in the seventeenth century, but they were still widely viewed as something effete and unnecessary. It was not until the eighteenth century that they were widely used. It is also interesting that in Europe the fork developed quite differently than it did in America. The tines were longer and sharper and were used to skewer food. The fork was, and still is, held in the left hand with the tines pointing downward, and the hallmark is on the curved inside rather than the back. The knife was held in the right hand, and thus no switching of utensils was required. The American custom of using the fork as a scoop in the right hand with the curve facing upward is a unique development. In Europe there was also a vast variety of portable utensils. Traveling gentlemen were expected to bring their own cutlery, not only to public eating houses, but also as guests in others' houses. It was only toward the end of the early modern period that tables were set with a full range of utensils as a matter of course.

In poor households, the eating vessels would be made of wood or low-fired earthenware pottery. Even in wealthy homes, and especially in southern Europe, earthenware was the most prevalent material used for eating vessels. The hand-painted majolica of central Italy and the lusterware of Spain are two notable examples, though the beautiful examples which have survived were more likely used for display rather than holding food. With the expansion of the economy in the sixteenth century, individual dinner plates gradually replaced the bread or wooden trencher, and this meant that food could be served with a sauce on the plate rather than in a separate vessel or dipping bowl. Each individual was also now given his or her own plate rather than sharing as was the custom in previous centuries. Plates were also used as covers over other plates of hot food, and they were sometimes stacked end to end into towering columns secured with ribbon and brought to the table. One can only imagine the plight of the poor servant who happened to drop one of these.

For the very wealthy, porcelain dishes imported from Asia were preferred, and it was not until the early eighteenth century that Europeans learned to make real porcelain themselves. What is called "soft-paste" porcelain had been made in Italy and elsewhere, and the blue and white "delft" pottery made in the Netherlands imitates porcelain. But it was not until 1708 in Meissen, Saxony, that Johann Friedrich Böttger learned to make true porcelain using kaolin, a white clay that becomes hard and translucent when fired at extremely high temperatures. The kiln technology to fire at such temperatures had been known since the late Middle Ages in Germany, and salt-glazed stoneware was typically used there for drinking vessels, pitchers and other tableware. It was much harder and more durable than low-fired pottery, and thus many examples still survive, especially large beer steins.

Glass was another widely used medium, most obviously for drinking glasses, but also for vases, pitchers and platters. Drinking glasses at the start of the early modern period tended to be squat relatively unclear and greenish and were often studded with little gobs of glass, no doubt to prevent them slipping from greasy fingers. The Dutch and German *rohmer* is a good example of these, coming in various shapes and sizes with or without a stem. Gradually glass manufacturing techniques produced clearer and thinner vessels that more closely resemble modern stemware. Colored glass was also perfected, the glassworks of Murano (outside Venice) became especially lucrative in supplying delicate intricately blown glasses. Interestingly, in the earlier part of the early modern period glasses were often shared between diners. After that the custom of having servants bring a drink to the guest and then remove and clean it prevailed. That is, individual glasses for each diner left on the table were not common until the end of the period. This of course refers mainly to aristocratic and royal tables; in more humble settings people drank at will from whatever they had.

Cups and goblets were also made from more expensive materials, cut crystal, sea shells, wood burls rimmed with silver and even coconuts. These creations, often monstrosities, were seen as a way to show off the metalsmith's skills, and were often enameled and studded with pearls as well. The cup made by the Mannerist artist Benvenuto Cellini is perhaps the best known of these, though it is unlikely that it was ever actually used. Unlike today, many cups, mugs and steins were covered, usually with a metal domed cap connected by a hinge. This was probably of great use in keeping away flies, which apparently in poorer households was done with a slice of toast, hence the origin to drinking "toasts" to someone's health.

Metal serving vessels appearing on the table could be made either of pewter, a relatively soft metal made from tin and lead, or of brass, which is a combination of copper and zinc or another alloy. Cast bronze vessels were heavy and extremely expensive, and naturally silver or gold plates were only owned by the wealthiest people. Particularly toward the latter half of the early modern period a set of silver, among the most prized possessions in a middle-class family, was often given as a dowry, and of course could be melted down and sold in times of emergency. From the late seventeenth century on terrines and matching serving vessels became more important and were set on the table in carefully arranged symmetrical patterns. A common feature of cookbooks at this time was illustrations of just how such settings should be designed. Among the table paraphernalia were a number of metal vessels that have since become obsolete. Shallow square or rectangle plates, probably meant to replicate the bread slices formerly used, were gradually replaced entirely by the more familiar round one. The porringer, a small bowl with one or two flat handles extending vertically from the lip is another relic. Shortly thereafter, bowls lost the handle when diners were discouraged from picking them up off the table as doing so was considered bad manners. The egg cup is another vessel that, though not obsolete today, has diminished in importance. The *surtout,* a kind of silver tray holding condiments and often used as a centerpiece was another fixture that is now obsolete.

There were also a number of other vessels used on the table with which we are no longer familiar. Although water was rarely drunk on its own, it was mixed with wine, so pitchers of water were typical. A pitcher and basin for hand washing or a bronze *aquamanile,* often in the shape of a lion or some other animal would also be passed around at the start of a meal. The water would often be perfumed with flowers or musk. Through the early modern period ewers for water became much grander and elaborate, sometimes so ornate that one wonders how they could have been used. Table fountains were also a popular set piece often decked out with mythological figures, *putti* (little naked cherubs) and sea creatures. To keep water cool ice buckets were also very common as well as the *cantimplora,* an earthenware vessel with a round bottom and long neck in which is contained a hollow chamber for snow or ice, which had a separate opening to prevent the wine from diluting.

Also appearing on more elegant tables were small salt cellars or a larger *saliera* from which diners could take a pinch of salt. These could sometimes be elaborate affairs made of gold and precious gems, often in the shape of a boat, in which case they were called a *nef.* By the seventeenth century the *nef* became more of a ceremonial decoration than a practical piece of tableware, and it was carried into the dining chamber with great pomp before the kings of France. The placement of the salt cellar on the table was also a matter of great concern, more respected guests were placed in its proximity while others were "below the salt" meaning they were deemed of inferior status. We must not forget the central importance that candles set on the table would have had, especially for evening meals and banquets. In many noble households there was a special officer appointed just to ensure that the candles were kept burning. Like all other table wear, candelabra grew to fantastically elaborate size and shape in the course of the seventeenth and eighteenth centuries.

Another interesting feature of grand dining was the layering of several tablecloths on the table which could be removed between courses. This might occur several times, or at least once for the last course—the "dessert" when the table was totally cleared. The term itself comes from the French *desservir,* meaning to clear or "un-serve" the table. At formal dinners, especially those of royalty and nobility, guests were seated on one side of a long table and were served from the opposite side, though some people preferred to sit at square tables to foster conversation. Surprisingly, tables were usually not permanent fixtures in a separate dining room devoted solely to eating until the end of the early modern period. More typically, tables would consist of planks laid on moveable trestles that could be set up wherever the head of the household chose to dine. This could change season to season, and in hotter months it was not uncommon to dine in an open *loggia* or porch, or even out in the garden or in a grotto. Many estates even had small banquet houses built in the garden or along the roof of the mansion where diners could retire for sweets after a meal. These were especially popular in seventeenth- and eighteenth-century England. A credenza, or side table, was also important for laying out cold salads and the antipasto course before guests arrived. In fact a separate staff was usually charged with arranging the credenza that would have been different from the kitchen staff in the largest households. On wealthier tables, napkins were also extremely important in the days when people ate with their fingers, and servants might be expected to replace them after every single use. They were also folded into elaborate shapes and laid on the table among other implements. Flowers might also grace the table, though interestingly, blossoms were often scattered on the table haphazardly.

FOOD SERVICE PROFESSIONALS

It should go without saying that most of the cooking done across Europe in ordinary households was done by the woman of the house. Unfortunately we have scant record of the details of her duties, except by way of books about household management which were usually written for women who had servants and did little actual cooking themselves. The general impression these books give is that the literate housewife would instruct her staff, explaining recipes and procedures, and sometimes perhaps taking part in the actual preparation. Making preserves or medicine seems to have been among the duties of the housewife which lay beyond the responsibilities of the kitchen staff, though it was obviously connected to the kitchen. We should not assume from the presence of servants that this practice was exclusively the province of the wealthiest families. Even middle-class households in the country and city could hire servants, which was really one of the few options available for young women from poorer families. They might, when they grew older, marry and start their own modest household, or might use their experience as a stepping stone to seek employment elsewhere as a confectioner or cook for a larger patron. Only in the eighteenth century in Britain do we have ample evidence that independent women made a living as chefs, sometimes composing their own cookbooks. But this was not the case for the rest of Europe.

The only evidence of formal training available for women was the cooking school opened by Françoise d'Aubigne, the marquise de Maintenon and King Louis XIV's mistress. The Institut de Saint-Louis, as it was called, was intended to train the daughters of impoverished nobles, presumably either to make them more marriageable despite their small dowries, or to find employment as cooks. The training appears to have been in earnest though and at age 17 the senior girls were entitled to wear a blue ribbon or "cordon bleu" as a mark of their status. The cordon bleu is still the symbol of the trained chef in France.

The ideal position for an aspiring chef would naturally have been employment in one of the great kitchens of the nobility or royalty. Some of these men, and they always were men, reached celebrity status, especially if they were fortunate enough to publish a cookbook which offered proof of their skills and conferred a reputation for discernment and largess upon their patrons. Sometimes wealthy statesmen would even compete for the services of a particular chef of renown, trying to lure them in with larger salaries and better facilities. Such a position would come only after years of working in such a kitchen, perhaps moving up the ranks from serving or cleaning dishes, to assistant chef and so on.

We can get a good impression of the staff employed by such a household from the many books about how to manage a banquet that proliferated throughout this period. Addressing the *scalco* or *maitre d'hotel* this literature recounts the numerous responsibilities of the post, as well as the chain of command. In fact, the *scalco* was in charge of all the dining personnel or *officiers de la bouche* (Officers of the Mouth) as they were called in France, and was even above the head chef. According to the many carving manuals published in Europe the *trinciante* was a high ranking courtier who displayed his dexterity by holding large joints of meat and huge birds aloft on the end of a carving fork. He would then slice delicate pieces that ideally dropped onto the platter in neatly ordered rows. Aside from the carver, there was also the *credenziere* or pantler who bought preserved foods and fruits for the buffet table. Then there was the *spenditore* whose task was to shop for fresh foods, a butler who took care of the butter, dairy goods and the like, and often a separate wine steward. Beneath all these was a small army of pages, servants and water-bearers. For the typical banquet it seems like there were more people serving than eating.

Retailers and the Guild System

Today we take for granted the right of every individual to pursue his or her own best economic interest by entering a profession freely chosen. This is an assumption that would only have been possible after the theories of economist Adam Smith became implemented widely after the late-eighteenth century, and rigorous control of the economy by nation states was abandoned. In other words, today, in the era of relative free trade, anyone can go into any business and is free to sink or swim. Smith believed that open competition, while it might be bad for those who fail, ultimately benefited everyone, because manufacturers would be forced to offer the public the best products at the most competitive prices. This way of thinking was totally foreign to the mindset of the early modern era. Rather than let everyone do as they please and hope the "invisible hand" of nature provides a livelihood for everyone, the early modern labor force was strictly controlled by a complex system of guilds, each operating like a tiny government with its own statutes and ruling elite.

The guilds were essentially a closed club of individuals working within a particular profession. They carefully controlled the number of people allowed to practice the craft in a city so as to prevent competition and lowering the value of their work. They fixed wages, so that members of the guild would be assured of a decent living, and protected jobs so members could not be randomly laid off. They even provided social services and pensions for the widows and children of deceased guild members. Many of the safety nets now provided by the federal government were in the past offered by guilds. Which is fine, as long as you could get into the guild.

Prospective candidates were forced to spend several years (often as many as seven) as an apprentice to a guild member, during which time they were treated little better than slave laborers. Apprentices were usually quite young, and considering that few people were educated formally, an apprenticeship might begin when a boy was eight or ten years old. They would often live in the house/workshop of the master, where they were clothed and fed and presumably where they learned the craft. They might be given a small allowance, but otherwise were not paid. After the period of apprenticeship, the candidate was usually turned out of the workshop and was sent as a "journeyman" to another shop where he was expected to perfect his skills. Here, fortunately he was paid and might even begin thinking about setting up his own household. But this could only happen after a fixed term of years, and after completing a "masterpiece" to the satisfaction of the guild's ruling body. But if there were already enough people practicing the trade, he might have to wait many years before he was allowed to open a shop of his own.

At the start of the early modern period nearly all trades were controlled by guilds. In many professions, the power of the guild was broken by either moving manufacturing processes outside the confines of the cities, as happened with the clothing industries in many places, or by finding ways around the guild restrictions. Specializing in a trade not legally defined as falling under one particular guild's jurisdiction was one way to accomplish this. But the food service guilds, being long-entrenched and necessarily confined to cities where they could sell their goods, remained in force through most of Europe right to the end of the early modern period. Which means that if you wanted to be a baker, a butcher, a green grocer, wine-merchant or an apothecary (who sold many luxury foods), you had to submit to the restrictions of the relevant guild. Even professional cooks, unless they were hired directly by a noble household, had to belong to one of the many cooking guilds—whether it be the roasters, pastry-makers and confectioners, caterers or whatever. Imagine throwing a large party, say a wedding, and having to subcontract every single different type of food from a different supplier. Guild organization, though cumbersome and sometimes litigious, did offer job security. The only profession still governed by guild-like controls is higher education.

The supply of raw ingredients was controlled in a somewhat different fashion than the food guilds. Because not considered a craft per se, but merely the retailing of an individual's produce, whether it be vegetables, fish or livestock, these items fell outside guild restrictions. But they were subject to the rules of the market place. In most European cities, and in many right down to this day, on a specific day or two of the week the town square would be jammed with farmers, fishmongers, people selling local cheeses, directly from farm to consumer. Because they had no permanent shop or retail establishment, usually only a table, wheelbarrow or piece of cloth spread on the ground, they were not controlled in the same way guild-dominated trades were.

They might be expected to pay a small fee to set up a table, and their produce might be subject to the inspection of a market official appointed by the city to prevent fraud, rigged scales or rotten food. But otherwise, any farmer who could get his product to the market was free to sell there.

Another unique feature of the food supply system of the early modern period stems from the fact that governments typically legislated prices. The size of a loaf of bread and its cost, for example, would have been fixed, a measure intended to insure that everyone could afford bread and would not be rebelling against the government, although that frequently happened when the price was too high or the supply of bread inadequate. By fixing prices and wages, states believed that they could control the food system, ostensibly to the benefit of everyone. Only when crop failures or wars disrupted production were the inadequacies of this system made painfully apparent. Sometimes governments were not so beneficently paternal, and being chronically short of hard cash they often made arrangements with suppliers in return for loans, or more notoriously they granted monopolies to court favorites when they could find no other way of rewarding them.

A monopoly is very simple. In return for a sum of money, or in lieu of some other owed debt, an individual or corporation was granted exclusive rights to supply a certain commodity. It might be soap, playing cards or a food item, usually a luxury like sweet wine or raisins. Without competition, the holder of a monopoly could charge whatever price he liked and people were willing to pay, and there was no possibility of being undersold. Naturally such people became fantastically wealthy, and it should be clear why in this country we are so vigilant in breaking up monopolies, even though they arise without being officially granted. The effect of food monopolies was that many items, although they may have been in abundant supply, nonetheless remained expensive. The monopoly of the East India Company in the spice trade is one example. But even on a smaller scale, the right of an individual courtier to exclusive fishing rights in a given area could also be lucrative. Patents worked much the same way, though we now grant them to inventors for a fixed term to encourage innovation and progress, they used to be given out for a whole variety of services, many relating to food.

Another right, claimed by kings through the period, though occurring in many forms and known by many different names was purveyance. This was the right of the monarch to buy up a certain supply of food at a low price. It was intended originally to feed armies in times of emergency, but in practice it was used to supply the royal household. It could be disastrous for a merchant who expected a decent price for his goods in the market only to be forced to hand them over to the crown. An odd relic of this practice still survives, in fact. Note how some foods made in Britain, like tea or biscuits, bear the queen's seal and read "by appointment to her majesty .... " Presumably the queen pays the going price, but it is still purveyance, one of the few rights left to the British monarch.

DINING ESTABLISHMENTS

A good proportion of those working in the food service sector owned or were hired by a variety of places where one could buy cooked meals. The distinction between different types of eating establishments was never very rigid. Naturally, they proliferated in cities and towns where a concentration of customers provided steady business, though an inn situated prominently on a major thoroughfare might also do very well. For many urban dwellers cooked food purchased at a shop or eaten on the premises may have been an economical option if the cost of fuel was prohibitive. Some people lacked cooking facilities entirely and thus depended on such establishments. While what we know as a restaurant offering patrons a variety of dishes on a menu appeared only at the very end of the early modern period, there were many places a person might find cooked food outside the home.

Cookshops were one type of business that sold prepared food to be taken away, usually dishes that could be left out on the counter like hams, pies or sausages. In the minds of many food writers and medical authorities, the cookshops or *popinae* offered the aesthetic and dietary equivalent of what we today call "fast food." It may have been convenient and tasty, but usually oversalted, overspiced and laden with all sorts of unhealthy ingredients like garlic and onions. However, some of these shops must have approached something like a gourmet store selling prepared dishes, because some authors associated them with braised ox shanks, turbot and other simple but delectable foods which clearly had to be cooked each day. Many cookshops, like bakeries, might also offer facilities to their customers who could bring pies or bread dough to be baked. This is no doubt the origin of the nursery rhyme: "Patty Cake, Patty Cake, Baker Man, Bake me a cake as fast as you can, Roll it and knead it and mark it with a B, Put it in the oven for baby and me." Presumably marking your loaf meant that you could identify it when you came back to claim it.

Although their main business was selling alcohol, most **taverns** also offered a variety of foods. These were usually salted or preserved food, which not only could be consumed without heating but caused thirsty patrons to drink more. Food writers throughout Europe are fairly consistent in mentioning that taverns served hams, sausages, anchovies and other preserved fish. They might also have on hand a roast joint of meat, various pies and any other food that would not require last minute preparation or attentive service. Taverns and alehouses were also places for social interaction between regular customers, and in small villages the local tavern might be the most important place for gathering, competing only with the local church. Here business deals could be made, marriages arranged and most importantly gossip could spread like wildfire. Taverns, alehouses and bars that served wine elsewhere, were also strictly licensed and taxed, not only as a way to gain revenue, but often as a way to control what authorities considered potentially disruptive drunken behavior.

The fare at **inns** was usually more elaborate than at taverns though guests at the inn were usually not offered a choice of dishes and meals were served at a specified time. Here hot meals, soups and stews as well as roast fowl and fish could be served. Because catering to travelers, probably unfamiliar to the host, the prices for each dish were fixed and prominently posted. Travelers themselves were equally cautious of being robbed, but also of eating tainted food or drink while on the road. There were even books written advising travelers how to eat en route, such as Guliermo Grataroli's *De regimine iter agentium* (Regimen for going on the road) of 1561. Grataroli suggested that counter to normal custom, travelers should eat a small morning meal, because the bumping around on horseback or in a carriage can cause upset stomach and fevers. He also recommended that one avoid fish served at inns because it is usually kept cold and reheated and especially avoid fruits and vegetables which can corrupt and foul one's humors. Ever cautious, "for who can trust an innkeeper," Grataroli even offers recipes for light and nourishing snacks that travelers could bring with them, such as marzipan, cookies and various pastries.[1]

Street vendors were also a familiar sight in most European cities. Naturally they served foods that could be picked up and eaten by hand, and sometimes drinks such as lemonade or ices.

As professional chefs, **caterers** often belonged to their own guild, and who could enter the business was strictly regulated. They could be hired to arrange an elaborate party, a wedding, state dinner, or whatever. In France there were also organized guilds for *rotisseurs* (roasters), *pâtissiers* (pastry chefs), and *aubergistes* (innkeepers), none of which were allowed legally to infringe on the others' trade. In fact, in order to serve food, innkeepers would have to be supplied by roasters and pastry chefs, who would be paid by patrons separately.

True **restaurants** that accepted customers as they arrived, seated them at a private table and offered a wide choice of cooked dishes at fixed prices only appeared in the mid-eighteenth century. The very first was opened by a tavern keeper named Boulanger in 1765 at his Champ de Oiseau Tavern in Paris and served various soups meant to be "restorative" which is the origin of the term restaurant. But when he served a dish of sheep's feet in a white sauce, the *traiteurs* (caterers) of Paris sued him, believing that this establishment cut into their exclusive privileges. The publicity ultimately only attracted customers, especially after he won the case. A restaurant opened by one Mathurin Roze de Chantoiseau in 1766 is also sometimes considered the first, although there were probably others equally deserving credit. In 1782 the first true restaurant La Grande Taverne de Londres was opened by Antoine de Beauvilliers, serving a wide variety of dishes. It was only the abolition of the guild system during the French Revolution, however, that paved the way for dozens of restaurants to open in the capital, especially as chefs to aristocratic households suddenly found themselves out of work. Restaurants in other cities also only proliferated in the nineteenth century.

NOTE

1. Guliermo Grataroli, *De regimine iter agentium* (Basel: Nicolas Brylinger, 1561), 19–24.

CHAPTER 4
CUISINE BY REGION

There really was no such thing as a "national" cuisine in the early modern period. The very idea of a nation-state first emerged in this period, and to suggest that everyone throughout a country, from every social class, ate the same foods prepared in similar ways would be false. The idea of regional foods comes a bit closer to the truth, but even then rich and poor had radically different diets. In the end one must say there were cuisines based on class with regional variations which were sometimes adopted on a wider scale and at times associated with a particular nationality by outsiders.

The cuisines discussed here were almost always intended for the wealthiest segment of the population, for kings, nobles and sometimes other wealthy people who emulated them. In fact cooking can be considered a visual and gustatory expression of power, a form of propaganda intended to impress. Unfortunately, elite cuisine is all most cookbooks record. Sometimes they offer a glimpse of ordinary eating habits, but in the end, this story is primarily about courtly cooking.

The very existence of a thriving court is one of the very reasons early modern Europe had such a brilliant culinary culture. The fact that the middle classes, townsmen and professionals had access to that court and spread its ideas in turn gave the court reason to invent new fashions in order to remain distinct. Once an ordinary commoner can buy a cookbook and prepare a dish enjoyed by nobles, it is no longer interesting to the nobles. And to eat something common would be an act of debasement. This is never a problem in an isolated court whose ranks are closed in a society with no social mobility. They never have reason to innovate. But Europeans devised a dazzling repertoire of recipes precisely to reinforce their superior status, which would not have been necessary if their "natural" superiority were not in question. In all the countries to be discussed, in some places and times more intensely than others, this urge to be distinct fueled culinary experimentation and innovation.

On the other hand, national rivalries, prejudices and stereotypes sometimes push individuals to cling to the familiar, local and traditional. These are what separate and protect them from those they perceive to be dangerous and foreign. Customs and eating habits reinforce group solidarity, they define precisely who is in and who is not. So we can at least begin to speak of distinct national foodways, even if they are sometimes conscious fabrications or the stereotypical impressions of outsiders.

Interestingly, cookbooks of the Middle Ages like the *Viandier* of Taillevent (attributed to Guillaume Tirel, chef to King Charles V of France) or the *Ménagier de Paris* a bourgeois cookbook that evidently emulates courtly cooking, or Master Chiquart's *Du fait de Cuisine,* do not exhibit strong regional or national cuisine different from other places in Europe. They are much like cookbooks from England, Spain and Italy. One gets the distinct impression that one culinary style dominated Europe, much as gothic architecture can be found everywhere with local variations. The heavy use of spices, sweet and sour sauces, pounded, strained and brightly colored dishes are found in practically all existing cookbooks of the period. This uniformity may be more apparent than real, and certainly only reflects elite dining which consciously sought to reproduce the most dazzling international recipes. Nonetheless, what we know of medieval cuisine reveals few major regional variations.

Whether significant variations appeared in the early modern period as a result of heightened national awareness and prejudices, or whether cookbook authors, now seeing their works printed and reaching a much wider audience, felt confident in describing their local culinary traditions is not entirely clear. It probably has something to do with trying to consciously forge a national identity as these new nations were first emerging, as a way of defining precisely who is included or excluded. In any case, it is true that only in the sixteenth century do distinct regional cooking patterns emerge in the culinary literature, and increasingly recipes are labeled French, German, Spanish and so forth.

It is also clear that at different times through the early modern period different countries took the lead in gastronomic matters, much as they did in the arts. In the sixteenth century it was Italy that became the culinary vanguard. By the early-seventeenth century Spain dictated the precepts of taste, and by the end of seventeenth century the France of Louis XIV reigned absolute in all fashions, including cooking. These shifts are equally discernable in cookbooks of the era, when as much as they might defend their native habits, as did the English persistently, cooking methods, the formal structure of meals and the very definition of fine dining were influenced from the outside.

Thus we see two competing tendencies, the urge to eat local produce cooked in traditional ways, and the irresistible draw of new fashions set by the fabulous courts of powerful monarchs. Equally contrary were two different but related impulses: whether to present foods prepared in richly elaborate ways adorned with a complex variety of expensive luxuries or to serve food simply prepared with sauces that accentuate rather than mask their basic flavors. Just as in painting and architecture, some periods favored the wildly elaborate ornate and fantastic. Others tend to simplify and refine. Either can be a way to create distance, depending on who is being excluded: social climbers imitating their superiors, or strange and threatening foreigners.

The recipes included here to illustrate these trends may sound strange or revolting. There are odd flavor combinations and ingredients we find disgusting today. But it should be kept in mind that most cultures throughout history have had no problem combining sweet, spicy and savory flavors, like sugar and cinnamon on meat. Nor did they expect to eat only a tiny select portion of a slaughtered animal, as we do. In the history of eating on this planet, modern Americans are the real odd balls. More specifically, the notion that rich meaty flavors should be radically segregated from sweet ones, and main courses separate from desserts, is a legacy of classical French cooking which began to develop in the period covered here. But it really has little to do with any absolute universal principles of good taste. It could just as well have turned out that all salty foods should come at the end of a meal, or all sour ones. That early modern chefs usually mixed all flavors in all dishes and all courses is not a lack of refinement or discernment, just a different conception of taste, one that most people in the world would still agree with.

ITALY

The geographical and political entity we now know as Italy did not come into being until 1860. Through the Renaissance and at the start of the early modern period the peninsula was ruled by a patchwork of small city-states vying for power. The strongest of these states, both militarily and economically, gradually came to dominate: the Dukedom of Milan, the Republic of Venice, Florence, Rome and the Papal States and lastly the Kingdom of Naples. Beyond these five powers which ruled the surrounding countryside as well as smaller cities in their region, there also existed a number of other city-states, which were quite often the aesthetic trend setters in matters artistic and culinary. The Gonzagas of Mantua, the Este family of Ferrara and the Montefeltro of Urbino are three good examples of independent and culturally vibrant late Renaissance courts. Many of the surviving cookbooks we have from Renaissance Italy come from these small courts.

Milan

The geography and economy of the five major powers determined to a great extent their culinary traditions. Milan and the region of Lombardy in the north occupied a flat plain through which the River Po flows. It was thus a rich agricultural region with a tradition of highly diversified cultivation of fruits and vegetables and dairy farming. Rice cultivation was also important since the late Middle Ages, and the *risotto alla Milanese,* a thick dish of short-grained rice cooked with stock and saffron, was and remains the most famous dish of the region. Unlike most of central and southern Italy, the region used butter as a cooking medium rather than olive oil, often in prodigious quantities. Also unique was the cultivation of corn, which was typically coarsely ground and cooked into a polenta or cornmeal mush.

Venice

Venice was the other powerful city-state of northern Italy. It remained an independent republic for a good 1,000 years and was ruled by what is often termed a merchant oligarchy (government by the wealthy). Literally perched on pilings in lagoons at the upper end of the Adriatic Sea and possessing a maritime empire stretching down the Dalmatian coast and as far as Crete, Venice drew her wealth from the spice trade with the eastern Mediterranean. Its galleys, huge and well-armed oar and sail-powered vessels, plied the routes laden with Asiatic products, making the ruling elites of Venice among the wealthiest of Europe. Not until well into the sixteenth century did the direct sea-route to Asia cut into their lucrative trade, giving incentive for landed investment. By the seventeenth and eighteenth century, Venetian nobles preferred to live in luxury on their estates on the *terra firma* (dry land), which while it may have benefited the culinary arts, left the bulk of the population, and the entire economy, in a relatively weak position.

Because of their position on the sea, it is not surprising that seafood played such a prominent role in Venetian cuisine. Venice's links to the east also meant that spices like nutmeg and cinnamon, raisins and other luxuries featured prominently in their cooking. Venice also drew from its landed holdings where corn was grown as were rice and wheat for bread and pasta.

Florence

Florence was the cultural and financial capital of Renaissance Italy ruled by the Medici family. Medici power derived from their massive international banking network that had branch offices throughout Europe. Though twice ousted by popular uprisings in the early sixteenth century, the Medici eventually returned and gained the title of Grand Dukes of Tuscany. As a requisite stop for traveling gentlemen on the Grand Tour, its fashions were imitated throughout Europe. Fresh from their travels, young nobles returned home with a taste for salads, vegetables and other Italian foods.

The region of Tuscany was renowned even in early modern times for its olive oil, particularly that of Lucca. Wine, on the other hand did not reach international repute until more recent times because most wines, such as Chianti, were produced and consumed locally. Often called *mangia fagioli* (bean eaters) because of their fondness for beans, Tuscans were also known for being great consumers of vegetables. Antonio Cocchi, in his *Del vitto pitagorico* of 1743 which promoted a vegetarian diet, claimed that the Florentines were among the healthiest people in the world because they ate so little meat.[1] The Florentine Giacomo Castelvetro has even left us a detailed description of the vegetables of his homeland that he longed for while exiled in England. Tuscan cooking was in general relatively simple, and the bulk of the population continued to subsist on beans and vegetables. If anything, Tuscans became increasingly impoverished through the early modern period, and their largely vegetarian diet was the product of scarcity more than any conscious choice.

Rome and the Papal States

Rome and surrounding regions stretching up into the Emilia Romagna were ruled by the papacy, forming the "Papal States" of which the Vatican City is the last remaining remnant today. Under papal patronage, Rome became the magnet for Renaissance artists like Raphael and Michelangelo, and it was also here that the very first printed cookbook and health manual *De honesta voluptate* (On honest pleasure) was composed. The papal curia continued to be one of the great culinary centers of Europe, producing the most famous chefs and most comprehensive cookbooks through the sixteenth century.

The cuisine of Rome itself was largely based on immature meats like lamb, veal and kid. All three were consumed fresh and thus became status foods, distinct from the preserved salamis and pork products of the poor. Pecorino, a hard grating cheese made from sheep's milk was a product of sheep rearing. Fish, both from the Tiber River and from the nearby coast were also central to the Roman diet. Alessandro Petronio, a native food writer of the sixteenth century, noted that Rome is set in a very humid and swampy region and this makes the food more watery and less nutritious, which is why there are so many thin people, he believed.[2] But he also thought that the city, crowded as it was with foreigners, scholars and priests was more addicted to pleasures of the gullet than any other place. Within the Papal States was the university town of Bologna, long recognized as the culinary capital of Italy with its mortadella sausage and innumerable fresh pasta shapes like tortellini and lasagne.

Naples

For most of the early modern period, Naples, in the south, was ruled by a viceroy appointed from Spain and thus was part of a vast empire that stretched from Europe to Mexico City to Manila. This meant that at court one could eat lavish meals, influenced by both Italian and Spanish traditions, as well as by New World foods. But it also meant that outside the corridors of wealth and privilege, there was serious poverty. In both Naples and Sicily the disparity in wealth was perhaps more pronounced than any other place in Europe. While nobles and courtiers kept well-stocked larders purchased through heavy taxation and noble privileges, their subjects often starved, even though Sicily was one of the most prolific grain producers in Europe.

Thus Neapolitan cuisine was lavish at one end of the social spectrum, and extremely frugal at the other.

Many of the foods Americans so readily associate with Italian cooking come from Naples: tomato sauce, mozzarella, macaroni and spaghetti, and pizza. Yet all these foods are quite different today and in this country than they were in the past. Pizza was basically just a flat bread with herbs, oil and perhaps cheese. *Mozarella di bufala* was a soft creamy fresh cheese made from water buffalo milk quite unlike the rubbery cheese made from cow's milk in this country. Tomatoes themselves, although probably eaten by the poor out of necessity, did not appear in a cookbook until the end of the seventeenth century.

Italian Chefs and Cookbook Authors

The cuisine of Italy, and especially the impact of its cookbooks was also greatly influenced by political events that shook the peninsula in the sixteenth century. The five major powers and many smaller ones had managed to coexist through the fifteenth century. This was due to a relative balance of power among the major states, and the tendency for all of the states to gang up on any one that grew too large and powerful. Thus a tenuous peace was kept. This equilibrium fell apart however at the start of the early modern period, and would have long-lasting consequences for both Italy and the rest of Europe.

The territorial ambitions of the small Italian city-states essentially drew their larger neighbors into the peninsula. France and Spain fought a long series of wars in Italy from 1494 to 1559. Milan, after being occupied by successive armies, in the end became a Spanish possession. Naples and Sicily too were annexed to the Spanish Empire. But equally important was the influence Italy had on the rest of Europe. Italian arts and literature set the trend throughout Europe, and Italian artists were imported to decorate European courts. It was in Milan that Leonardo da Vinci met King Francis I and followed him back to France. Many artists and even some Italian chefs were hired at courts throughout Europe.

Thus in the sixteenth century, despite these wars, Italy became the aesthetic vanguard of Europe. Late Renaissance culture had enthralled the Europeans who first arrived in Italy as invaders, and then found themselves imitating Italian art, literature and to a certain extent cooking.

Platina

A good example of this is the first printed cookbook by Bartolomeo Sacchi (known as Platina): *De honesta voluptate* (On honest pleasure). Although first printed in 1474, and actually incorporating an earlier vernacular cookbook by Martino of Como, the Latin text was soon translated into Italian. It then appeared in an expanded French version, and then a German one. It was also pirated or incorporated into several other cookbooks and remained in print through the sixteenth century. The name Platina became associated with complex cuisine everywhere in Europe. The recipe sections were mostly medieval in the techniques employed, the ingredients used, and the general repertoire of dishes. But Martino was innovative in several ways. He offers the very first recorded instance of egg whites being used to clarify a broth, as well as the first instructions for making an edible short-crust pastry. Before then pastry toppings were meant just to keep the contents of a pie moist, but they were not eaten. There is also the tendency to present individual ingredients whole rather than pounded up and disguised as medieval cooks were so fond of doing. Apart from the recipes, the sections penned by Platina were more of a grab bag of natural history and dietetics than a cookbook per se. But what made this book so different is that it was printed and widely distributed through Europe in dozens of editions. And the rest of Europe, just as they sought out Italian fashions in art and architecture, also began to follow Italian culinary fashions. They began to cook more vegetables, especially artichokes, asparagus and mushrooms. They also began to serve meals and carve meats the Italian way. What is more important, perhaps, is that the late Renaissance esthetic began to pervade the overall flavor of aristocratic dining.

There has been a great deal of debate among food historians over the precise nature of this influence. Many have pointed out that the marriage of Catherine de Medici to Henri II of France, long held to be the crucial mode of transmitting Italian cuisine to France, probably had negligible effect. Others have doubted the importance of Platina's book being translated and read everywhere. Few food historians have been able to muster tangible evidence of Italian cooking in French cookbooks, of which, in any case, there were very few in the sixteenth century. Some have even pointed out that French cuisine may have influenced Italian, noting the number of recipes labeled as French appearing in Italian cookbooks. These appear among recipes from many nations though. Perhaps it would be safest to say that European countries had a mutual influence upon each other, that there was a wider exchange of ideas and customs, especially when printed books were widely circulated. That most of these books were Italian, or translated from Italian does lend evidence to the idea that Italy was the forerunner in gastronomic matters. Whether Italian cuisine had a European-wide impact or not, it is certainly the case that Italy was the real innovator in the sixteenth century, as a closer look at its cookbooks will show.

The cooking of the early sixteenth century was very much attuned to the arts of the period. This is the case because aristocratic feasts always involved music, food sculptures and various other forms of entertainment such as plays and dances. The leading artists were usually commandeered to contribute to these multimedia events. The dominant style of this period is called Mannerism by art historians, and can be described as a self-consciously elaborate and sophisticated style that abandoned the balanced and rational compositions of the Renaissance by depicting figures in twisted positions sometimes placed into illogical settings. By using odd juxtapositions, surprising and densely packed surfaces, and a staggering variety of forms, Mannerist artists hoped to display their wit and inventiveness. Titillating the viewer with marvels and obscure allegories not only displayed the knowledge of the artist, but flattered the spectator who "got it." For the Mannerist, artificiality and the depiction of impossible, contrived and deliciously perverse subjects was a positive virtue. That this style influenced the cutlery, table settings and presentation of food is undeniable. It also, arguably, affected how and what foods were prepared.

One could also compare the cooking of this period with the polyphonic music that flourished in Italian Renaissance courts, especially the madrigals of composers like Arcadelt, Verdelot and Josquin du Prez. Although strange to modern ears used to homophonic music in which a dominant melody hovers above a progression of chords, polyphony involves many different voices given equal emphasis and often intricately intertwined offering a wealth of variations on simple themes often piqued with dissonant accents. The cooking and overall presentation of late Renaissance meals is much the same and could also be called polyphonic. Sweet, sour and savory flavors vie for attention and in each course simple themes are repeated with subtle variations and surprises.

Messisbugo

Although the basic outlines of Italian cuisine at the start of the sixteenth century were inherited from the middles ages—there is still

the heavy use of spices, sugar and medieval sauces based on vinegar—
something began to change noticeably. If we look, for example, at the
Banchetti of Cristoforo di Messisbugo printed at Ferrara in 1549, the
description of banquets thrown reveals that a diversity of dishes bordering on perversity, spectacles and surprises, and ingenious novelties,
all show that Mannerist esthetics were at play. Although grand presentation pieces had been a feature of courtly dining for centuries, and
even such oddities as invented creatures and peacocks resewn into
their feathers were seen on medieval tables, there is something different about the sheer profusion of delicacies that appear in every course.
A typical banquet, some with as many as a dozen separate courses, included salads, soups, vegetables, pastries and pies, sweets—especially
little allegorical scenes made of sugar called *trionfi*—and fish and
meats in nearly every single course. Rather than presenting an orderly
procession of dishes, the diner is meant to be overwhelmed by the variety and elegance of each successive presentation. Many foods appear
in every single course, though presented in a slightly different guise,
and only the barest hints of order are discernable—cold foods to start
and fruits and sweets to conclude. Again, as in the madrigal, only at
the end do the text and notes come to some resolution after their er-
rant meandering.

Take for example the banquet thrown on January 23, 1529 by the
son of the Duke of Ferrara for his father and various dignitaries. The
total guest list numbered 104. Sugar sculptures of the labors of Her-
cules appeared first, in deference to the host himself, named "Her-
cole." The antipasto course consisted of cold dishes: a caper, truffle
and raisin salad in pastry, another salad of greens with citron juice and
anchovy salads. There were also radishes carved into shapes and animals, little cream pies, prosciutto of pork tongue, boar pies, mortadella and liver pies, smoked mullet served several different ways, and
gilt-head bream. The first hot course had capon fritters sprinkled with
sugar, quails, *tomaselle* (liver sausage), capon liver stuffed into a caul
(netting of pork fat) and roasted pheasants, an onion dish, pigeons in
puff pastry, tarts of fish milt (spleen), fried trout tails and barbel (a
fish), eel pie, and pike in broth. The second course had franklins
(bird), quails, meatballs, white cervelat sausage, veal, capon German
style in sweet wine, pigeon pastries, carp, turbot, shrimp, trout roe
pies, a yellow almond concoction, and pastries. The third course had
partridge, rabbit, turtledoves, sausages, boned capon, pigeons and
more fish. This goes on to a fourth course, again with birds, fish, a rice
pie, and other dishes. A fifth course with some suckling pig, veal and

more birds and fish as well. A sixth course with more veal prepared a different way, peacock, goat, boar and also more fish. The seventh course finally sees some vegetables, fennel, olives, grapes, pears and parmigiano cheese. The eighth course has 2,000 oysters, oranges, and other pastries; the ninth citron, lettuce, cucumbers and almonds in syrup, various fruits and confections. There was also a play by Ludovico Ariosto to start and musical interludes between each course.

What is immediately striking is that guests were given individual plates for many of the dishes, only larger foods or presentations of several ingredients together came out in multiples of 25 or 50, and would have been divided up and served. Many of the foods came out in multiples of 104 on 25 larger plates as well. Because Messisbugo specified the number of plates needed for each food in each course, they can be counted. This meal used 2,835 plates.

The recipes themselves are no less staggering for their variety and profusion. This recipe for *sosamelli*, a kind of cookie, is among the simpler ones, but gives a good idea of the flavors appreciated by the Ferrarese court. Note the use of contrasting sweet, spicy and aromatic flavors.

To Make Perfect Sosamelli, Around 36 in Number

Take 1 pound of white flour and 2 pounds of fine sugar, and pass it well through a sifter with 1 ounce of finely pounded cinnamon and two pinches of crushed pepper. Add three egg yolks and one white, an eighth of long pepper, and rose water mixed with a little salt. With diligence make your dough a little stiff and roll it out well. Then take the stamp and cut them out. If you put a bit of musk on them they'll be better. Then put them to cook in an oven over a small flame.[3]

Some of Messisbugo's recipes contain crushed coral or pearls, deemed to be restorative, but they would certainly have been impressive for the cost alone. The sugar, spices and rose water that flavor so many of the dishes would have been considered just as luxurious. The appearance of foreign dishes, German, Spanish, Turkish, French and Hungarian, show that these were adventurous eaters eager to taste the new and exotic. Obviously there are no national food prejudices here, perhaps because there is no nation state. Even a "Hebraic" dish of chopped veal, herbs, raisins and spices formed around a hardened egg yolk and cooked in a broth, made an appearance in the recipe section.[4] But not all the recipes were so outlandish. There is a *maccheroni* and cheese dish not very different than our own, though the pasta was shaped by hand rather than purchased in a box, and probably looked more like gnocchi or a dumpling than tubular pasta. There is also an intriguing sweet fried dough dish Messisbugo calls "pizza."

We cannot leave Messisbugo without sampling one of his more extravagant perversities. Note that there was nothing unusual about cooking fish with fruits, nuts and sugar. It was not for more than another century that sweet and savory flavors were kept separate, and in Italy the combination persisted through the entire early modern period.

Lenten Eel Pie

Take clean spinach and fry it in a pan, then dry it of all water and fry it in 4 ounces of good oil. Then take a pound of almonds, half a pound of raisins, half a pound of pine nuts, 7 or 8 sweet apples and pound it all together. Moisten it with some fish broth, and pass it through a sieve. Put everything in a vessel, put in the spinach and 7 ounces of sugar, an ounce of cinnamon, a fourth of pepper, four ounces of jujubes [a small date-like fruit] cut along the side with the pit removed. Incorporate everything together. Then take a sheet of pastry dough, and put it in a baking pan well greased with good oil, and put the mixture on top. Then take 3 or 4 skinned eels, pre-boiled, and cut them up, removing the spine. Add it to the mixture. Then put the other pastry sheet on top and cook it like other pies, with sugar on top.[5]

In sum, the dominant style of sixteenth-century Italy, both in the arts and cuisine, favored elaborate, sophisticated presentations offering as many different ingredients as possible, cooked in as many ways as possible. In Messisbugo's recipes dairy products and fish also received increased emphasis. Organ meats such as brains, liver, testicles and various salty cured pork products also suddenly appear with greater frequency than ever before. Again, though sixteenth-century Italian cooking inherited many features from the Middle Ages, the wealth, variety and copiousness of presentation make it something quite new.

Romoli

La Singolare dottrina ... Dell'ufficio dello Scalco (The singular doctrine ... on the office of the *scalco*) by the Florentine Domenico Romoli, known as Panunto, is also among the most important sources for our knowledge of Italian cooking in the sixteenth century. Romoli was a professional banquet manager or *scalco,* and his text describes the various duties of this position, how to manage the staff, when foods are in season, the steps for recipes, and also provides a long catalogue on the qualities of individual foods. But perhaps the most interesting section is where he describes "ordinary meals day by day."

They are probably not the meals average people ate, but they at least give us a good picture of what noble households considered a regular meal. During Lent, when no meat was served, the morning meal consisted of four courses, arranged not by type of food, but rather by cooking method. There was an "antipasto" course, a boiled course, a fried course and then fruit to end. The several dishes served in each course do not exactly follow a pattern we would recognize, but there is a certain logic to them. The appetizers usually included dried fruits, nuts, salads and two or three different fish dishes. The boiled course included more fish and several soups perhaps with a base of chickpeas or almonds. The fried course offered yet more fish and a few vegetable dishes, and then the fruit course consisted of fruits and nuts, more vegetables, usually artichokes or fennel and some sweets. The smaller evening meal or *collation* presented merely one course, usually a salad, vegetables, fish and sweets brought out together.

Throughout these menus there is heavy emphasis on green vegetables, and usually about nine or ten different fish prepared in different ways. It is not exactly the melee of dishes described in Messisbugo's banquets, but a similar procession of variations on a theme is echoed in each separate course. Rather than an orderly unfolding of flavors in each course as we might expect, from pungent to savory to sweet, similar flavors punctuate every course. This too appears to be a mannerist trait. There is no particular focus either, and the cooking methods are not meant to complement or accentuate one item in every course. Instead, there is diversity, profusion and a series of elegant foods that make the diner stop and think about the talent and virtuosity of the chef. Here the art of cooking is the real subject, and practically every single item that appears is cooked in a different way.

The meals that do include meat were structured slightly differently. Usually there were only three courses, the first containing some kind of organ meat, small birds and sometimes pasta, cheese or fruits as well. The second course usually included veal, lamb, kid, salami or perhaps capon, as well as a soup, and the last vegetables like artichokes, fennel or peas, and sometimes cheese and nuts. Only here and there in Romoli's catalogues are there more lavish suppers, which include five courses, separate settings appearing on the table before diners are seated and then another service of sweets at the very end.

Apart from the curious structure of these meals, a modern eater would also be surprised by the flavors in each course. As in Messisbugo's book, practically everything is seasoned with sugar and spices. It might be useful to think of Italian cuisine in this period as the combination of a few standard flavorings to a wealth of basic ingredients, not unlike Chinese food in this respect. But there were simpler dishes too. The following recipe is included as an example of our forebears' willingness to eat recognizable parts of animals, something we shudder with horror at today. It remained a very popular dish in Italy on fashionable tables through the early modern period, though later variations would become far more elaborate. This was probably eaten with a sauce served separately. Presumably it was dissected by a servant and portioned out with perhaps the eyes reserved for an esteemed guest.

Boiled Veal's Head

If you want your boiled veal's head to remain white after it's cooked, you need first to procure a head of suckling veal with red skin, not black and when it's skinned it will stay white. Carefully pull out the tongue, clean the nostrils and ears, and cut the little circle around the eye. Remove all the skin, put it in clear water and let it soak for an hour. Then wash it with hot water, rubbing the inside and out so that no blood remains. Put it in a hefty pot and cover with cold water. Bring it to the boil without salt, and diligently skim it with a wooden spoon, making sure that it never boils. Leave it uncovered and bubbling slowly. When it's cooked put in white salt and above all make sure it doesn't stick to the pot. Touch it and when it feels soft, it's ready. Carefully put it on a plate with flowers and herbs over it.[6]

One also gets the impression from reading Romoli that there has developed a distinctively Italian repertoire of dishes that could be identified as such anywhere. Pasta in countless shapes was probably the most stereotypical of Italian foods, then as now. There is, for example a recipe for *pappardelle,* a broad noodle wider than fettucine, though it was cooked in a way we would hardly recognize today, in a sauce of hare's blood.

Scappi

First published a few years after Romoli, Bartolomeo Scappi's *Opera* (Works) of 1570 is the grandest achievement of Italian culinary literature. It is an encyclopedic tome, the most detailed cookbook written anywhere up to the sixteenth century. The recipes are precise; the procedures described are detailed and easy to follow. It is almost scientific in its organization and presentation. And Scappi goes far beyond the ordinary cookbook. There is advice on how to choose ingredients at their optimal state, the cooking implements needed in a noble kitchen, extensive menus for each season, and something entirely

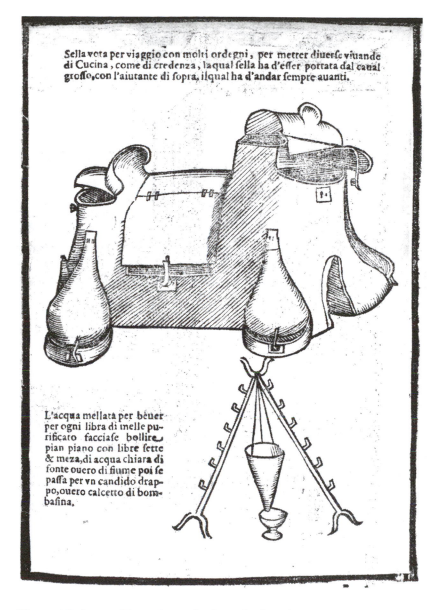

Sella vota per viaggio con molti ordegni, per metter diuerse viuande di Cucina, come di credenza, laqual sella ha d'esser portata dal caual grosso, con l'aiutante di sopra, ilqual ha d'andar sempre auanti.

L'acqua mellata per beuer per ogni libra di melle purificato facciase bollire pian piano con libre sette & meza, di acqua chiara di fonte ouero di fiume poi se passa per vn candido drappo, ouero calcetto di bombasina.

Figure 4.1 A portable credenza for horseback and preparing honey water. *From Scappi, Bartolomeo. Opera/di Bartolomeo Scappi M. dell'arte del cucinare. In Venetia: Presso Alessandro Vecchi, 1610. Recto R4. EPB 5812/B. Courtesy of Wellcome Library, London.*

new: copious illustrations. It may be more than coincidence that similar groundbreaking works appeared in other fields in the same generation: Andreas Vesalius' great book on anatomy, *De humani corporis fabrica* (The fabric of the human body) and Copernicus' work on heliocentricity *De revolutionibus orbium* (On the revolution of the planets). One might hesitate to call Scappi's book revolutionary, but it nonetheless represents a major breakthrough in the science of cooking.

Perhaps what also makes Scappi's work such a landmark in gastronomy is his detailed knowledge of where the best ingredients come from, his appreciation for the quality of regional produce and the season when it is at its prime. Cheese like parmigiano, riviera from Liguria, marzolino from Tuscany are best between March and June. Cacciocavalo from Naples and provatura are best fresh. He also compares the tench and trout from Lake Como with those caught in the Tiber and Po Rivers, and gives extensive information on buying fresh fish. His recipes show no less discernment, highlighting specialties from Lombardy or Milan, from which he probably came, fish dishes from Venice, macaroni from Genoa, an herb tart from Bologna and spinach alla Fiorentina.[7] Rome, his adopted city, is also featured prominently, as the following recipe shows.

The procedure for making these *polpettoni* involves pressing and marinating the meat, and then making a gravy based on the meat juices itself. Scappi's common spice mixture includes 4 ounces of cinnamon, 2 ounces cloves, 1 ounce ginger, 1 ounce mace, 1/2 ounce grains of paradise [meleguetta pepper], 1/2 ounce saffron and 1 ounce of sugar. The finished effect with sweet, sour and spicy flavors would not be unlike a good barbecue sauce.

To Make Meat Rolls Roman Style from Loin of Beef or Cow

Take the leanest part of the loin, without bone, skin or sinews, and cut it across in large pieces of 6 ounces each. Sprinkle them with salt, fennel flowers, or a condiment of pounded common spices. Place four slices of fat-streaked prosciutto for each piece and let it stay pressed down with this composition and a bit of rose vinegar and sapa [concentrated grape juice] for three hours. Then skewer them with a slice of bacon between one and another piece with a sage leaf or bay. Let it cook over a moderate fire. When cooked, serve hot with a sauce over them made from whatever drippings fall from them mixed with the left over from the pressing which will give the sauce a bit of body, and give it the color of saffron.[8]

Scappi was also willing to go further afield for novel recipes. One of his most interesting is an extraordinarily detailed description of how to make couscous, or as he calls it, *succussu* which comes from North Africa. It is essentially semolina flour formed into tiny grain-like bits of pasta, dried and then steamed over a pot of rich broth. The ingredients are not rare or costly, what impresses here is the technical mastery of the chef. One can imagine the effect produced by an intrepid reader who managed to pull off this feat of manual dexterity by him- or herself. It would probably elicit the same response today. He also explains how to make macaroni formed around an iron stiletto, an instrument like a hat pin, which when stuck into the dough and rolled back and forth in the palm, opens it into a hollow tube. He even advises that the dough be lightly floured so it doesn't stick to the metal. It is all about technical precision here.

Above all, Scappi's respect for the ingredients and careful attention to presentation separate his work from most other cookbooks of this era. There is one simple recipe for grilled oysters that specifies how they should be cleaned, and above all not overcooked. This recipe for peas shows more respect for the humble legume than afforded by most today.

A Fricasée of Fresh Peas with the Pod or Without

Wishing to fry peas in the pod, choose the lightest, remove the flower end and stem, and let them boil in a good meat broth, pulling them out just when colored. Then sauté them in lard or bacon grease, and serve with citron and pepper over it. With this you can also fry a clove of garlic, and chopped parsley. These peas can be served with chicken on top, or other fowl roasted on a spit. If you don't want to be bothered with the pods, shell them and cook as above. This way you can also prepare fava beans.[9]

Although Scappi's work is in many ways the culmination of culinary practices originating in the Middle Ages, the precision and thoroughness with which he treats ingredients and procedures make this perhaps the first modern cookbook. Take for example the way he defines various kinds of pies. There is the *pasticcio* inherited from previous centuries with an inedible crust. These are distinct from the *crostate* and *torte* made with flaky pastry that includes butter or lard, the former containing large pieces of meat, vegetables, fruit or fish, the latter with amalgamated ingredients. Further distinctions separate Neapolitan, Lombard and Bolognese pies, as well as pizzas. These are only one example of the level of sophistication baking had attained, and which would not be surpassed for more than another century.

Figure 4.2 Making pasta. *From: Opera/di Bartolomeo Scappi M. dell'arte del cucinare. In Venetia: Presso Alessandro Vecchi, 1610. R7. EPB 5812/B. Courtesy of Wellcome Library, London.*

When we move into the seventeenth century, it is clear that Italian cuisine continued along the same lines first sketched out a century earlier. It became more elaborate, and in keeping with the baroque style, presentations changed significantly, but the ingredients, methods of cooking and favorite dishes remained essentially the same. This is surprising since a major revolution in cooking was taking place in France, but it does not seem to have impacted Italy.

Stefani

Evidence for this is found in one of the most important cookbooks of the century, Bartolomeo Stefani's *L'Arte di ben cucinare* written for the court of the Gonzagas in Mantua and published in 1662. Medieval flavor preferences, abundant use of spice and sugar still prevailed, along with musk, amber and flower waters. Organ meats and veal's head are still featured prominently. Though now the head is deboned and stuffed with herbs, cheeses, marzipan, candied citron, pine nuts, raisins and spices, then reformed and cooked in broth. The complex combinations of flavor and texture are not essentially different from those found in earlier cookbooks, but one gets the distinct impression that like much seventeenth-century Italian art it has now become cloying, too sweet and affected. Italian Baroque painting and architecture at its best is energetic, passionate and has a vitality and energy that is undeniably arresting. But at its worst it descends to the level of kitsch. The same stale subjects are repeated ad nauseam by second rate artists. What had been truly innovative a century earlier has now become cliché. It is doubtful that those who planned and executed these meals thought this; they were certainly very pleased with the results or they would not have gone to great lengths to record the recipes for posterity. But still, one feels that not much new has happened.

The details of banquets Stefani offers vary somewhat in structure from the preceding century, but they are over the top. A banquet for January or February begins with the same sort of sugar sculptures. Starters on the credenza include marzipan pie with pine nut confetti (candies), a boar's head with a pastry serpent trying to eat his eyes, a pastry shaped like a cornucopia with fruit spilling out, a Spanish flan, a marzipan lion's head supporting a chest with four roast pheasants, lemon preserves and candied flowers, gelatines, bread pudding, a custard-like concoction, threads of prosciutto cooked in white wine with sugar and marzipan birds around it, two peacocks in their feathers, and various other cookies. Three more courses follow, each containing meats, fowl,

Figure 4.3 Serving the banquet. *Opera/Bartolomeo Scappi. (Venice: Michele Tromezzino, 1570.) Typ 52570.773, Department of Printing and Graphic Arts, Houghton Library, Harvard College Library.*

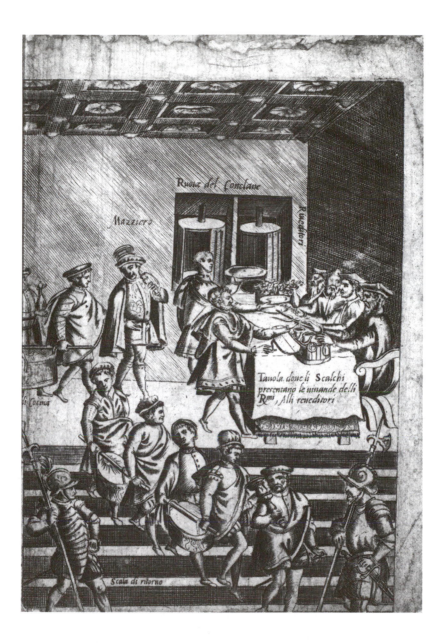

Figure 4.4 Italian banquet scene. *Opera/Bartolomeo Scappi. (Venice: Michele Tromezzino, 1570.) Typ 52570.773, Department of Printing and Graphic Arts, Houghton Library, Harvard College Library.*

pies, as well as seven stuffed veal heads. Meanwhile the credenza too has been changed twice with cold fruits, cheeses and nuts and sweets. The details are perhaps less important than the fact that the intention is still merely to impress with variety and marvels, but now they seem to have become monotonous. What is also conspicuous by its relative absence are the many vegetables and pasta dishes found in earlier cookbooks. It seems as if, because inexpensive, these could no longer be expected to impress.

Not all Stefani's recipes are so overwrought though. Many meats are simply roasted, and fish is afforded several simple preparations. There is also this interesting recipe for butter sauce which apart from the spices much resembles a modern hollandaise and is used in the same way.

Butter Sauce

Take a pound of fresh butter, melt it in a pan. Add to it half a crushed nutmeg, a bit of powdered clove, four ounces of fine sugar, and seven egg yolks. Temper it with three ounces of lemon juice, and if you want it aromatic, a bit of musk or amber will make it pleasant. This can be used for a stew, as long as it's not overcooked, with asparagus, artichokes, little chops and other diverse things.[10]

On the whole, however, Stefani's recipes are complex to the point of obscuring the natural ingredients. Meats stuffed with spices, fruits, truffles, marzipan or crushed *mostaccioli* biscuits, often with mastic or ambergris and covered with sugar are among his favorites. Sausages appear in many guises, one containing pork, cinnamon, cloves and pepper, rosewater, orange flower water, amber, and red sandalwood.[11] Even a simple roast turkey is given the spice treatment. In sum, Italian cuisine remained wedded to the rare and exotic, highly seasoned and vibrantly contrasting flavors. The chef's art, while continuing to produce complex creations, would eventually run out of new ideas following along these same lines.

Latini

The next major cookbook written in Italy, Antonio Latini's *Lo scalco alla moderna* was published in Naples in 1692 and two years later a second smaller volume was added. It is similar to Stefani's in many ways, though betrays the influence of the Spanish court ruling in Naples, especially in terms of etiquette and protocol. Latini's central task was, like Romoli, to describe the duties of the *scalco,* or head banquet manager which included overseeing the staff of the various departments of kitchen and larder. Fortunately, Latini was meticulous about the quantity of ingredients to be used because ultimately, as *scalco,* he would have been responsible for the expenditure. This gives us some idea of not only what was eaten but the precise quantity as well.

In describing a banquet for six people, to start there is set on the credenza a pie of chicken and veal, a turkey, some salads, a *menestrina,* or little thick soup of pigeon, and other ingredients. For the first course from the kitchen there were fried organ meats: brains, sweetbreads and livers, also some artichokes, a boiled capon, a French *pottagio* or stew, little rolled slices of veal called *brasciole, prosciutto* and prunes. There is also another pie of veal, cockscombs and testicles, with pistachios (one of Latini's favorite garnishes). Presumably parts of each animal purchased would go into several different dishes for the sake of economy. There were also various fruits, parmigiano and biscuits laid out. For this entire meal Latini wrote up an ingredient list for the *spenditore,* or professional shopper. For the pie in the first course it included 5 pounds of flour, 6 ounces of sugar, 4 eggs, 1 chicken, 1 pigeon, 1 pound of veal, 4 ounces of prosciutto, 2 ounces of lard and 3 ounces of *sopressata* (a kind of salami). He goes on to enumerate everything in the following courses as well. What is immediately striking is that only 1 1/2 ounces of cinnamon are used, 2 ounces of pepper, 1 ounce of cloves, and 2 ounces of nutmeg for the whole meal. Spices are still used, but they hardly overwhelm the other ingredients. Unlike Stefani, a profusion of garnishes and condiments does not accompany every dish, and most recipes are not laced with sugar. With the exception of the large pie, savory flavors have begun to be segregated from sweet ones, and herbs are used more consistently as flavors to accentuate rather than contrast with the main ingredient.

Clearly this was far more food than six guests could possibly eat, and we should keep in mind that this would also later serve other members of the household and staff. It is apparent though, that the sheer volume of food was not meant to overwhelm the guests. In fact, judging from the number of dishes—four cold and five hot plus a soup—that this was no eating orgy. Most Americans have seen Thanksgiving tables groaning under greater weight than this. In fact, in several places Latini lashes out against gluttony, which he considered a repulsive vice. "I detest those men dedicated to greedy voracity ... I hate gluttony as a cardinal sin, and praise polite eating, made proper with sobriety, because it confers life and our preservation."[12]

One may doubt that his recipes are so simple by modern standards, but they are certainly different than before. Take, for example, the veal's head once again. It is now stuffed with prosciutto, served with herbs and borage flowers on a plate, with a green sauce on the side. The older sugared versions are there too, and Latini seems to have wanted his cookbook to be as comprehensive as possible. But his own tastes, and those of the nobles he served, have become simpler. More recipes allow the ingredient's natural flavors to come through, and fewer are doused with spices and sugar. There is a recipe for filet of beef that is simply marinated in *addobbo* (a word borrowed from Spanish), which includes oregano, garlic and pepper and salt with a bit of vinegar. After seven hours, or overnight, it's roasted on a spit and cut into thin slices.[13]

Latini was also the first anywhere to offer recipes for tomatoes, and his roasted tomato salsa would pass anywhere today. Because it is not cooked beyond charring the skins, this more closely, if not exactly, resembles what we would call a salsa rather than an Italian tomato sauce.

Spanish Tomato Sauce

Take a half dozen tomatoes that are mature and put them over the coals and turn them until they are charred, then carefully peel off the skin. Cut them up finely with a knife, and add onions finely cut up, at your discretion, finely chopped peppers, a small quantity of thyme or pepperwort. Mix everything together and add a bit of salt, oil and vinegar. It will be a very tasty sauce for boiled meats or whatever.[14]

Latini's work is enormous. But apart from these few novel recipes, Latini really offers nothing very new to the art of cooking, and may be considered the last in a long line of Italian cookbooks that use similar ingredients and procedures stretching back to the sixteenth century.

Gaudentio

But there is one more important resource for culinary history in the early eighteenth century: Francesco Gaudentio's *Il Panunto Toscano,* which was discovered in manuscript form in a library in Arezzo and first published in 1974. Gaudentio was a lay brother and chef for a Jesuit college and various other similar institutions. Thus, his cookbook more closely reflects what ordinary people were eating. Take for example this recipe for apple pie, which is unusual in its attention to the quality of the fruit.

Fruit Pie

If you want to make a fruit pie, particularly of apples, make it like this. First peel them and cut them into slices as thin as you can. Place them the day before mixed with a bit of sugar and when you want to make your pie let it simmer on a fire until half cooked. Then take two pastry leaves in a pan first well greased, and place the apples in it with equal amounts of sugar, cinnamon, and candied citron cut in little slices. Cook it and the other things in the way already said above. How much (of the spices used depends) on the quality of the apple, all varieties are good with them, but those that are sweet don't need as much sugar, but for those that are tart and dry put in a bit more. With pears equally follow the same rules, but some need to be cooked longer.[15]

Corrado

By the mid-eighteenth century, the French influence began to be more widely felt, and major changes took place in the organization of cooking as well as the flavors appreciated. But there was one more cookbook in the latter eighteenth century produced in Italy that deserves attention. This was Vincenzo Corrado's *Il Cuoco Galante,* also appearing in Naples in 1778 and then issued in several further editions. Its aim was to glorify and publicize the merits of Italian cooking in a way that French cuisine had been for the past century.

Corrado, of course, opens with requisite recipes for veal's head, but now the sugar and spices have been almost totally replaced with herbs and other typically Italian ingredients like parmigiano, tomato sauce or lemon, anchovies and capers, or interestingly, some versions include cream. Veal received the most extensive coverage among meats, and was clearly still considered the best of foods. Beef was not highly appreciated, and was usually boiled, and lamb was rarely eaten by people of quality, but *castrato* or a young castrated ram was considered tasty and nutritious. Pork also appeared in dozens of recipes. Some, like that for grilled pork chops seasoned with salt, pepper and fennel seeds or another stuffed with ground veal, herbs, truffles, cooked in a casserole with broth and served with prosciutto and tarragon, one would not be surprised to find on an Italian menu today. Many birds and fish are featured and are also given, for the most part, relatively straightforward treatment. This recipe for swordfish or tuna gives a good idea of the flavors appreciated and the simplicity of cooking procedures.

Swordfish or Tuna in Broth

Cut the belly of the fish into large bite-size pieces. Mix these with capers and thin slices of truffle, anchovies and let it cook in a fish broth. When cooked serve it with a puree of tomatoes.[16]

Perhaps the most interesting part of Corrado's book is his section on the "Pythagorean Diet," which offers recipes for fruits and vegetables, which he considered much more healthy than meat. There are creamed spinach recipes, carrot salads, gratins of cauliflower and stuffed tomatoes. We have arrived at a cuisine not very far from that enjoyed by modern Italians, as the following polenta recipe reveals.

Polenta

Corn meal is best to make polenta. Cook it in broth or milk with grated parmigiano, butter and a bit of pepper, stirring constantly until it becomes soft. When cooked, spread it on a baking sheet, and when cold cut it into slices, and serve it returned from the oven with butter and parmigiano. You can also serve it with meat sauce and cervelat sausages. Polenta cut in slices can also be fried, and then served with sugar or without.[17]

The desserts are no less interesting, with several proper cakes, and chocolate finally appears as a flavoring ingredient. Situated in Naples, Corrado could hardly neglect a recipe for canneloni, or cannoli as they are now called. His is simple and similar to those made today.

From the detailed dinners enumerated by Corrado, it is clear that not only has the structure of the meal changed but the presentation, in symmetrical, balanced sets of dishes and plates, has been influenced by French fashion. One thing more is clear, the Italians still hoped to impress with abundance and variety rather than subtlety and complex technique. The average menu, and this does not include antipasti like oysters and olives or closing desserts because they depend on a different staff, included two full courses, the first with 36 dishes and the second with 32. Everything that was brought out also came in balanced sets of two, four or eight. In other words, two different soups, four different terrines, eight hors d'oeuvres (here meaning not a main dish) in triangular plates, eight round entrées, eight small rectangular dishes and so forth. Meat, fowl, vegetables, fish and sweets still appear in every course. So, though the recipes themselves may seem a little more familiar, dining in Italy two centuries ago was still very different and perhaps closer in spirit to the centuries preceding than to our own era.

SPAIN AND PORTUGAL

The Iberian peninsula has been settled or invaded through its long history by a variety of peoples each of whom has had a distinctive impact upon its culture and cuisine. From the original inhabitants including the Basques, there followed Carthaginians and Greeks in ancient times. Later occupants include the Celts, Romans and later Germanic Visigothic tribes from whom the kings of Spain claimed descent, followed by the Moors, who occupied most of the peninsula for centuries. What is today Spain and Portugal have always been beset by invaders. Most of them came to stay. Since Roman times a large and vibrant Jewish community was also present in Spain.

In the Middle Ages the peninsula was ruled by several small kingdoms, some of which had been incorporated into larger regional states through marriage or conquest. The most important of these were Castile in the center which included the kingdom of Leon, Portugal in the west, the Kingdom of Aragon in the east which included Catalonia and Valencia, and the last remnant of the Moorish occupation, the Kingdom of Granada in the south. The geographical setting of these kingdoms to a great extent determined the character and focus of their economies. Facing the Mediterranean, Catalonia had long been a relatively urban and mercantile economy, trading with and eventually controlling Sicily, southern Italy, Sardinia and other Mediterranean islands. Castile, possessing Atlantic ports along its north coast, mainly exported wool raised in its many mountainous regions and brought to graze across the plains. Portugal was also a sea-faring nation facing the Atlantic, which would be crucial in their success as a maritime empire. Lastly, the south and the Kingdom of Granada, comparatively hot and fertile, was a rich agricultural region growing oranges, olives, intensively cultivated vegetables and rice.

During the centuries preceding the early modern period, the Christian kingdoms embarked on the *reconquista* or reconquest of the peninsula from the Moors which was complete in 1492 with the fall of Granada. It was only after the marriage of Isabella of Castile to Ferdinand of Aragon, a decade of civil war and the completion of the reconquest that the nation known as Spain came into existence. Despite the union of crowns, these regions remained culturally, and to a great extent politically, distinct. And despite the fall of Granada and the expulsion of the Jews in the same year, Muslim and Jewish customs and foodways continued to influence Spanish cooking down to the present. This was partly because many Jews converted to Catholicism and remained in

Spain. Agricultural techniques first introduced in the years of Moorish control also remained in place and many Spanish names for vegetables derive from Arabic. The words and usually the plants themselves: *aceituña* (olive), *albaricoque* (apricot), *alcachofa* (artichoke), *arroz* (rice), *azafrán* (saffron), *azúcar* (sugar), *limón* (lemon) and *naranja* (orange) were all introduced during the years of Muslim occupation.

The character of the Spanish court from Ferdinand and Isabella through the entire sixteenth century depended in large measure on the idea of the king as defender of the Catholic faith. The throne took on a certain mystic and religious aura. After the fall of Granada, Ferdinand was busy consolidating his possessions in Italy. But Isabella had by then sent Columbus on several voyages to the New World, which incidentally was held directly by Castile rather than Spain as a whole. In a certain sense the conquest of the New World was merely an extension of the crusading spirit of the *reconquista,* and this assured that Spanish society would always be heavily militarized and dominated by powerful nobles. The conquistadors, by and large, also came from Andalusia in the south, a frontier region, which itself had only been conquered a few generations back. Interestingly, it was also in this region that New World foods were first planted, peppers and tomatoes being ideally suited to the climate. But judging from the cookbooks of the period, they do not seem to have had any impact on the diet of the Spanish court and its nobles.

Cooking in Spain at the start of the early modern period, was like elsewhere, still thoroughly medieval. The influence of Arab cultures, and especially the use of fruits and vegetables native to the Middle East was stronger here than elsewhere. Eggplants and spinach were used extensively in Spain, as were dried fruits, nuts such as almonds, olives, and citrus fruits. We get a sense of the cuisine from a book actually composed in Spanish-ruled Naples in the late fifteenth century and published in Catalan in 1520 and then translated into Castilian Spanish. It is Ruperto da Nola's *Libro di Cucina,* as it was titled in the 1525 Toledo Castilian edition. This recipe for *Broete de Madama* (Madam's Broth) is a good example of the types of dishes included in the book, and the presence of ginger, long pepper and galingale immediately signals that it is a medieval dish.

Madam's Broth

Take almonds that are not peeled, and pine nuts that are clean and white, and pound everything together and when it is all pounded, add a good chicken broth, and strain it through a sieve. After that place it in a clean pot to boil and add these spices: ginger, long pepper, and galingale, all pounded. Put it in the pot with parsley, and oregano, and a bit of pennyroyal, and boil everything together with much saffron. When it is well boiled, you know that it should be lifted from the fire, take a dozen eggs beaten with vinegar and put them in the pot. Make it so that the broth will be a little sour, but not much. When you put them into the broth, be careful that it is not very hot so that the eggs do not cook at once. Stir it constantly with a spoon when the eggs are in the broth, so they don't curdle.[18]

The next king of Spain, Charles, was actually raised in the Netherlands, and just happened to have grandparents who ruled four separate kingdoms. From Ferdinand and Isabella he inherited Spain. From his grandmother came Burgundy (and Burgundian court rituals) and the Netherlands, from his paternal grandfather, a Habsburg, came Austria. He also managed to buy his election as Holy Roman Emperor which made him ruler of what is today Germany. Apart from ruling most of Europe, Mexico also fell into his hands after Cortes' conquest, along with much else in the New World. This fabulous inheritance was a mixed blessing however. At any given time he was called upon to fight Algerian pirates in the Mediterranean, the Turks in the East, rebellious nobles in Spain, the French in northern Italy or Protestant insurgents in Germany. His reign was marked by unmitigated warfare.

Apart from anecdotes about Charles' prodigious appetite, we know little about the cuisine enjoyed at his court. Ruperto's book remained in print through the sixteenth century and seems to have satisfied those who sought out culinary literature, because there were no new cookbooks written in Spanish until the very end of the century. There was one text however, more of a health manual than a cookbook, Luis Lobera de Avila's *Vanquete de nobles caballeros* (Banquet of noble knights: Augsburg 1530) which does give us an impression of what was eaten at the court of Emperor Charles V (Carlos I of Spain). We learn, for example, that it was the custom in Spain to eat the larger meal in the evening, which is unlike the practice in northern Europe. He also reveals the logic behind common cooking methods. Meats that have faults "we amend with art: those that are harmful because of dryness we boil, those that are harmful because too moist, we roast or place in pies with spices."[19] He even explains how to clean snails, and how to roast apples with sugar and anise or with pepper as they do in Vizcaya.[20] But through the early-sixteenth century, it is clear that while Charles has introduced Burgundian form of court etiquette, cooking remained essentially medieval.

This was no less true of his son Philip II's reign. The huge rambling empire of Charles changed shape dramatically as territories were divided up and Philip was left to govern Spain, the New World and the Netherlands which would prove disastrously expensive to hold on to, especially after Protestants had taken control of the northern Netherlands. During his reign the throne of Portugal fell vacant, and as the only available heir, he also ruled that country and its Asian possessions after 1580. Were all this not expensive enough, his armada sent out to conquer England in 1588 foundered, and all the great wealth brought in from the American silver mines could not keep this kingdom financially solvent. Nonetheless, during Philip's reign, Spain was arguably the most powerful nation on earth.

Philip himself was notoriously frugal and had simple tastes. Most travelers to Spain in this period also remarked about how sober and frugal the Spanish were, and in this respect Philip seemed like a quintessentially Spanish ruler. During his reign, protocol and formality still governed court life, but he seemed to have preferred being alone with his paperwork, or brooding in the vast corridors of his palace, the Escorial, laid out in the shape of a grill in remembrance of St. Lawrence who was barbecued for the faith. To a great extent it was faith that informed much of his policy as well. Philip, like his predecessors, considered himself the great defender of the Catholic faith, and in fact reforms initiated by the church in the Catholic Reformation were largely inspired by Spaniards. The most important initiatives for the history of food, as well as all intellectual activity in Spain, were the Inquisition and the Index of forbidden books. They were intended to keep heretical ideas out of Spain, but in practice ended up keeping the country intellectually isolated. No new cookbooks, for example, were published until just after Philip's death in 1598.

Only then did Diego Granado's *Libro del arte de cozina* (Book on the art of cooking) appear. We know practically nothing about the author's life except that he describes himself as "officer of the kitchen in this court," which implies some connection to the king. It is also possible that he lived for some time in Italy because he refers to Italian customs, and includes much of Scappi's work in his own cookbook. Granado actually borrowed much of his work from earlier cookbooks, primarily from Ruperto, whose recipes comprise a good portion of his book. But it contains a lot of original material too and with 763 recipes it is enormous. And there really was no such thing as plagiarism in this era, and even in our own it is usually impossible to credit any given individual with inventing a recipe. Despite all the borrowing, many of Granado's recipes are typically Spanish. For example, he explains how to make *fideos,* a kind of thin pasta made by grating a stiff dough.[21] There are also tortillas made with eggs, *empanadas,* which are little pies, and various *albondiguillas,* little balls of meat or fish. The recipe below appears to reflect the eating habits of ordinary people because the author specifies that anyone can afford to make it.

A Green Mutton Dish

For very little cost and for all people, take a breast of mutton, and cut it in pieces, and place it to cook. Then take lard or salt pork, and heat it up. Add chopped greens, onions and parsley. Fry it all well, and when it is all cooked add it to where the meat is cooking. When you see it is cooked season with a little spice and a clove of garlic. Take it out and let eggs solidify on top, the same number as people you have to serve, tossing in a little vinegar and serve it.[22]

The *capirotada* as it is made in Mexico today is a descendant of this recipe though it has become a sweet bread pudding made with cheese. Granado also offers other versions of this dish which include almonds and sweet wine or veal kidneys, toasted bread and pigeons. The word "lights" in English or *livianos* in Spanish refers to lungs.

A Common Capirotada

Take two pounds of Pinto cheese, and another pound of rich cheese that's not too salty, and mash in a mortar ten cloves of garlic that have been first boiled with the meat from a capon breast that has been roasted. When it is all pounded, you add ten raw egg yolks and a pound of sugar, and infuse everything with cold chicken broth, because if it is hot it can't infuse, nor can you pass the composition as is required through a grinder or sieve, because of the cheese. Being sieved, put it in a tin-lined casserole, and put it on a bed of coals from the fire, and add an ounce of cinnamon, half an ounce of pepper, half of cloves and nutmeg, and a good bit of saffron. While it is cooking, shake it enough to help it take shape. When it is cooked, if you want the best flavor, next take lights (lungs) of veal or kid fried, mix it all together, and serve with sugar and cinnamon on top. In place of the lights you can also put breast of veal cooked and then fried, in the same way you can make a capirotada with any kind of roast.[23]

Fish is also featured prominently in Granado's cookbook. Here he suggests several ways to serve sardines. In sixteenth-century Spain an *escabeche* was a way of marinating and briefly preserving fish or other foods. The green sauce was usually made of pounded garlic, vinegar, bread and parsley or other herbs.

To Fry and Marinate Sardines

Take fresh sardines, scale and wash them and lay them on a table. Mix them with a bit of white salt for a while, then flour them and fry in olive oil, which is always better than fat, and being fried serve with orange juice, or slices of lemon, or fried parsley on top. After they are fried conserve them in bay leaves, or myrtle, and if you want to marinate them place them after they are fried in vinegar, in which sugar helps, or wine cooked with saffron, and conserve in this escaveche until you want to serve it. In summer in place of vinegar you can serve it with verjuice incorporated with egg yolks, or the soft insides of bread, or also after frying you can cover it with green sauce.[24]

Spain in the seventeenth century could not bear the weight of its vast empire. The American colonies grew financially independent, costly wars depleted the royal coffers and a tax structure that supported nobles and the church kept the peasantry in permanent poverty. Although the sixteenth century saw Spain at the height of its power and glory, in the seventeenth century, Spain was comparatively depopulated, which made it quite different from the rest of Europe. Aside from emigration to the New World and expulsions, the economy was to a great extent controlled by powerful Castilian nobles who preferred to live in leisure than invest their savings or innovate. This meant that agriculture stagnated, and Spain was even forced to import grain. The fact that Spanish kings spent their fortunes on far-flung wars also meant that they were forced to lay a significant tax burden on the shoulders of those who could afford it the least. Nobles and clergymen were exempt from taxes, so the rest of the population sank deeper and deeper into poverty. The great arts and literature and even cuisine of the "Golden Age" in Spain were thus created at the expense of the country as a whole.

Ironically, despite economic disaster, the Spanish court blithely went about the business of entertaining itself in grand style, and for a brief time was at the forefront in matters artistic and gastronomic. In the reigns of Philip III and IV great artists and poets were patronized, and Spanish fashions were imitated everywhere. But both kings were poorly advised politically, and in the mid-seventeenth century, Portugal seized the opportunity to win its independence, and Catalonia and other Spanish possessions in Italy also nearly succeeded. These revolts damaged the reputation of the Spanish crown almost fatally. But for a while Spain had the most dazzling court in Europe.

The first cookbook published in this fruitful period was Domingo Hernández de Maceras' *Libro del Arte de Cozina* of 1607. Maceras worked as college chef for the Collegio Mayor de San Salvador de

Oviedo in the University of Salamanca for 40 years. Although the students seem to have been well fed, his recipes are distinct from courtly cuisine and more closely reflect ordinary eating habits. Oddly, it was written in a period of severe food shortage and runaway inflation. It is possible that this cookbook reflects the chef's ideal aspirations rather than the daily fare he hashed up for the college.

This cookbook does give a vivid impression of ordinary meals, and this recipe for rice is typically Spanish. The almond milk suggested as a variant here would have been used during Lent when animal products were forbidden. It was made by pounding, soaking and then straining almonds. In consistency and usage it is not unlike coconut milk, which is made the same way. The *açumbre* was a unit of measurement equaling 2.16 liters or roughly half a gallon.

How to Make Rice with Milk

After washing the rice in four changes of water, you must drain the water, and for 12 bowls of rice, you pour out a pound and a half of rice. After it's drained pour it to cook in an açumbre of water with salt and let it cook until it's well dried. Then add an açumbre of milk, and a pound of sugar and let it cook on a low fire, because you don't stir it, shake it so it doesn't stick, and let it soak up the milk. Cover it and let it rest, and fill the bowls, and pour on top sugar and cinnamon. If you want, make it with almond milk. From one pound of almonds you draw out an açumbre of milk, and to be good you shouldn't draw out more. And add the sugar to be good.[25]

Another recipe that is distinctly Spanish is the following one for eggplant. Few other regions, with the exception of southern Italy made extensive use of them, and practically none offered recipes. They were among the vegetables first introduced by Moorish inhabitants, and in much of Europe they were associated with Jewish communities. Here they are cooked in a covered casserole with hot coals heaped on the lid. The conserve or *arrope* that is offered as another option was much like an Italian *mostarda,* made with sugar, vinegar or grape must and fruits. It is a distant relative of the Indian chutney as well, both possibly derived from Arabic or Persian cuisine. The *maravedi* was a small Spanish coin. Presumably eight maravedis would be an amount of spice of equal weight.

How to Make Eggplants

You must cook the eggplants in water and salt, and being cooked discard the water, you mince them well and put them in a casserole to fry with much oil. Add grated cheese and bread, and 6 or 8 maravedis of spices, and one garlic clove, totally smashed, and cook everything carefully. Add eggs and let them solidify, placing the fire on top. This is called a *caçuela mongil* (monk's casserole) of eggplant, but you can also cook them with fat in a pot, and serve them with fatty salt pork, pepper or parsley. Eggplants can also be kept all year in a conserve having made them in this manner, cook them in the conserve, and adding cloves and cinnamon when you cook it, and put it in a glazed pot, in which you keep it.[26]

Internationally, Spain was most associated with complex stews. One of the most renowned dishes enjoyed all across Europe was the *olla podrida,* which literally translates as "rotten pot," but signified an earthenware pot or *olla* filled with diverse ingredients. Oddly, the French word for sweet smelling dried flowers and spices is the same: "pot pourri." Maceras' recipe basically includes whatever is at hand: lamb, beef, salt pork and pig's feet, sausages, tongue, pigeon, hare, chickpeas, garlic and turnips, all cooked in one pot and served with a mustard made of grape must.[27] Scappi in Italy offered a similar but more detailed recipe which also included various pork parts, along with veal kidneys, beef, capons, pigeons, hare, partridges, pheasants, geese and other wild fowl, as well as peas, chickpeas, garlic, onions, rice, chestnuts and beans.[28] Ironically, Diego Granado translated Scappi's recipe for his own cookbook, letting the Italian be the authority on a typically Spanish dish. The olla podrida in its numerous variations is one of the few recipes one finds in practically all cookbooks across Europe, which itself attests to the influence of Spain, even if few of them could have been considered authentic. Perhaps there was no "authentic" version of this dish in the first place, but rather many local versions of one basic concept, much like chili today.

Francisco Martínez Montiño's, *Arte de Cocina, Pastelería, Vizcochería, y Conservería* (Art of Cooking, and Making Pastry, Biscuits and Conserves) of 1611 is the major monument of Baroque Spanish cooking. Montiño (or Motiño) was chef to King Philip III and arguably had greater resources at his disposal than any other chef in Europe. Yet his recipes show no obscene profusion of ingredients, no bizarre juxtapositions of flavor or wildly extravagant imports. This cookbook was composed from a position of undeniable superiority. There is no threat of social climbing, no emulation of inferiors. In fact, the king and nobility were so infinitely wealthier than the mass of ordinary people, that they did not need to struggle to remain distinct; it was self-evident. At one point Montiño even admitted that "I am not happy about describing fantastic dishes" in a section on how to cook whole fish.[29] Relatively simple recipes will do fine, which ironically made this an extremely popular cookbook for another few centuries, and one that helped to define Spanish cooking.

It is not exactly ordinary fare though, but the book does open with a declaration that harmful pies containing things like chestnuts, mushrooms, carrots and potatoes and a jumble of contrary ingredients and flavors will not appear. It is not entirely clear why the author stressed this—for purely medical reasons or maybe to distance his book from those that use too many strange ingredients. It is certain that he wanted to disassociate himself from Granado, and the first edition actually denounces that book openly. Aesthetically, Montiño appears to be focusing and refining Spanish cuisine, giving it an energy and directness that is not unlike Spanish Baroque painting. One need only think of the gorgeous canvases of Diego Velazquez, though they are painted a few decades later. They are both distinctly Spanish.

The vast majority of Montiño's recipes are for elegant pies, pastries, little meatballs and other foods that can be easily picked up and eaten by hand. He also has an intense affection for stuffing meats and vegetables like eggplants and onions. One can easily imagine a series of simple and elegant little dishes appearing on a table and choosing freely—something like the ancestor of tapas. This recipe for pork *chorizos* seems not only typically Spanish, but also direct, austere and served without fuss or garnish. It can easily stand on its own.

Pork Chorizos

Take pork meat that is more lean than fat, and put it in a marinade of just wine with a touch of vinegar. The meat should be cut into little radish-sized knobs and the marinade should be sparing, no more than to cover. Season with spices and salt and let it sit for 24 hours. Fill up the chorizos. They should be a bit plump. Cook them in water. These can be kept all year. Eating them cooked, there should be so little vinegar that you cannot sense it before eating them.[30]

Like other Spanish cookbooks, Montiño offers a variety of dishes with a base of fish, spinach, garbanzo beans and squash. These were especially important for days of fasting. There are also dozens of egg dishes, many of which use fresh cheese, and recipes for roast lamb, kid, rabbit and game. Nearly all these ingredients can be used either simply roasted, in a pie, as a filling for small turnovers (*empanadas*), ground into meatballs or a stuffing, or finally in a soup. A few basic procedures are used for all available foods. Other typically Spanish foods also appear as accompaniments: grapes, oranges and lemons, almonds, olives and cheese. Fruit preserves also appear to have been used as condiments.

Spain changed considerably in the eighteenth century. This is because the last Habsburg monarch, Philip V, after generations of royal interbreeding, was neither physically or mentally capable of rule. Upon his death without heirs, a major war (the War of Spanish Succession) broke out, involving nearly every European power. Both the Austrian Archduke Leopold and Louis XIV of France had equal claims to the throne through marriage. In the end Spain went to the grandson of Louis, a Bourbon, from whom the kings of Spain to this day are descended. But to Austria went the southern Netherlands and the Italian possessions. The effect of a French court in Spain meant that dining fashions, as well as the arts and sciences were influenced from France through the rest of the eighteenth century. But regionally distinct Spanish cuisine survived among social levels beneath the court.

The best evidence for this is Juan de Altamiras' *Nuevo arte de cocina* of 1758. Altamiras was the pseudonym of the Franciscan monk Raimundo Gómez who was chef for the convent of San Diego in Zaragoza. His book was one of the most frequently printed cookbooks in the eighteenth and nineteenth centuries, and clearly reflects popular taste. The Franciscans were an order committed to poverty, at least in theory. The fact that this was a tiny handbook meant that it was probably bought by ordinary people. It features many hearty stews, stuffed vegetables and bean dishes, and many recipes include the use of tomatoes. What is truly interesting is the inclusion of sugar and cinnamon in so many savory dishes. This fashion had obviously become popular among ordinary people long after it was abandoned by the nobility. In a recipe for sweet artichokes, the author even admits that no one loves sweet flavors as much as monks. This recipe is a fascinating combination of medieval Spanish, New World and Asian ingredients that seems typical of ordinary Spanish food in this era. The spices, here unspecified, in other recipes usually include cinnamon, sugar and cloves. The meat was most likely lamb or mutton; another similar stew recipe says that this is most commonly made with rabbit. The last line implies that smacking your lips, or licking your chops was not considered polite, but was irresistible when served a delicious stew like this.

Stew with Pepper Sauce

Meat from the leg is best for stew; cut it in bits the size of a nut, place it in a pot with salt, bay leaves and bacon between fat and lean cut up as large as dice. Fry it in the pot. Crush some garlic with pepper and loosen it with a bit of water and put it all in the stew, add oil, and place the pot on the embers so that it browns. When it seems right, add enough hot water, season it with salt and all the spices, always get parsley or tomato to throw in, and you can smack your lips if you're not polite.[31]

FRANCE

The geography of France is extremely varied, from the flat plains of the north and fertile Loire Valley to the warm sunny vineyards and olives groves of the south, to the mountainous regions in the center, Alps in the southeast and Pyrennées bordering Spain. The major division to be made is between the relatively cool climate of the north and the Mediterranean south, and this in turn determined the kind of foods that could be grown and animals reared profitably.

The nation we now know as France was put together piece by piece in the course of the early modern period. In the late Middle Ages, there were dukedoms like Burgundy or Anjou that were just as powerful as the kingdom of France, and owed only nominal allegiance to the crown. Brittany in the northwest and Provence in the south were independent kingdoms. And in the course of the Hundred Years' War with England, at times huge parts of the southwest and Normandy were ruled from across the channel. This meant that power and access to it was highly decentralized. Baronial courts set culinary fashions, and in fact Burgundy was in many ways the courtly model of the late Middle Ages.

France emerged at the end of the Hundred Years' War as a tiny wartorn nation with a weak king, dislocated economy and a poor infrastructure. That it could rise in the latter fifteenth century to become one of the most powerful nations in Europe was a minor miracle. The tireless efforts of rulers like Louis XI to make the kingdom financially secure and territorially larger were hugely successful. At the start of the sixteenth century France boasted one of the most extensive tax systems, one of the largest armies and one of the most respected crowns. The key to this success was a centralized administration staffed by men of talent rather than nobles who served because of their lineage. The king for the first time became far more important than his nobles, and from this point to the time of the Revolution in 1789, the royal court would set all culinary standards.

It was in these years that French kings, Charles VIII, Louis XII and Francis I fought in Italy and discovered Renaissance civilization. It was during Francis' reign, and through his direct patronage, that Italian Renaissance culture was imported to France. Artists like Il Rosso and Primaticcio were invited to decorate his magnificent chateaux such as

Chambord and Fontainebleau in the Loire Valley. Leonardo da Vinci became Francis' close friend. But the French Renaissance appeared to be more of a hybrid of native gothic traditions and foreign classical elements, a match that often produced exquisite offspring.

Like his father, Henry II was also a devotee of things Italian, including his wife Catherine de Medici. But he was also an avid warrior and loved chivalric pageantry. In fact it was at a tournament that he died from a lance-point stuck in his eye. It must seem odd that a ruler would be playing with swords in an era when guns and cannons emerged as the decisive weapons on the battlefield. But this was a profoundly nostalgic society. Just as chivalry was becoming totally obsolete and the role of nobles in real war less decisive, the whole pageantry of the chivalric age was revived, or rather dreamed up in an imaginary form. Chivalric epics were among the most popular form of literature. Most full suits of armor that have survived were actually produced in the sixteenth century. It may also be the case that this is why courtly cuisine in the sixteenth century remained firmly within medieval traditions. Huge roasted animals served whole, the great hall with retainers seated by rank, wonderful gilded and heavily spiced foods carried out ceremonially on monstrous platters. It may really have born little resemblance to dining in the Middle Ages, but it was precisely what they thought it should have been. It is no wonder either that medieval cookbooks like *Taillevent* were printed over and over again and enjoyed enormous popularity. This was not an age intent on inventing new dishes, but safeguarding the old and traditional ones, and using them as visible symbols of royal authority.

It was Henry's wife, Catherine de Medici who is said to have introduced Italian dining customs to France, though her influence probably never extended far beyond the court. Her real importance was her role as regent or nagging mother in the reigns of her three sons. In the reigns of Francis II, Charles IX and Henry III France was torn apart in a series of bloody civil wars fought over religion. Although culturally France did not come to a complete standstill, creative energies were obviously hampered, and it is not surprising that France produced no new cookbooks during this time. But they did manage to eat well at court. Henry III and his beloved cronies or *mignons* enjoyed living in style and their effeminate court was later satirized in a book entitled *Description of the Isle of Hermaphrodites,* in which the effete courtiers dine with forks on exotic delicacies ingeniously disguised in perverse ways. Mannerist dining fashions had obviously penetrated France by this time, along with the fashion for drinking wine chilled with snow or ice.

It may seem odd that while Italy was enjoying an efflorescence of cooking literature in the sixteenth century, France produced virtually nothing. There appeared one collection of recipes entitled *Le Grand Cuisinier de toute cuisine* in 1540 which was actually a medieval cookbook with new recipes added. Most culinary historians would agree that major changes really only took place at the start of the seventeenth century, followed by a real culinary revolution mid-century. With little printed evidence, this claim is difficult to refute, but there are hints that dining customs had begun to change, even though actual recipes do seem to still be medieval. For one, food became a more integral part of court festivities, which may have been thanks to Catherine de Medici. The same elaborate classically inspired sugar sculptures we saw in Italy began to proliferate, forks and Italianate tableware began to appear, certain vegetables, like artichokes and asparagus became fashionable at court. The mannerist taste for copious variety, marvels and disguised foods is clearly evident by the latter sixteenth century. Confections, jams and syrups, all the quasi-medicinal flavorings provided by Italian apothecaries also began to appear.

The first vivid impression we get of the food actually eaten in France in the latter half of the century comes from a cookbook published in Liège in what is today Belgium in 1604. Lancelot de Casteau's *Ouverture de cuisine* was the first cookbook to show definite influences from Italy, and since Lancelot worked in the kitchens of the city's prince-bishop for many decades, it is reasonable to assume that he had been influenced long before the book's publication, late in his lifetime. He provides recipes for various Roman dishes, Bologna sausages, mortadella, cervelat and ravioli, or as he calls them "raphioulles." But he also gives German, Spanish, Irish and even Hungarian recipes, so this was really an international cookbook.

This recipe for roasted sturgeon was enjoyed throughout Europe, and as one of the largest and most expensive fish that could be bought, serving it conferred prestige on the host, especially if served whole. Liège is also located at the confluence of several major rivers that in Lancelot's day still provided sturgeon.

Roasted Sturgeon

Take a piece of sturgeon and let it boil strongly to remove the scales. Then stick cloves on top and branches of rosemary inside, and place it to be roasted, always basting it well with butter. Being well cooked, make a sauce with wine, sugar, cinnamon, nutmeg, a salted lemon cut into slices, a bit of butter added, and boil everything together. Toss it over the sturgeons and then serve.[32]

Lancelot also included a banquet menu for the entrance of the prince-bishop of Liège in December 1557. How he managed to recall the details so many years later remains a mystery, but it does give a good idea of what was considered an extremely impressive meal in this period. For the first service there was a boiled turkey with oyster, cardoons and a Spanish salad. There was also a roasted bustard, a "blanc manger" pie, boiled mutton, kid, beef marrow, partridge pies, roasted veal, hare stew, venison pie, roasted crane, boiled partridge and several roasted wildfowl, roasted boar, stuffed breast of veal, stag stew, Hungarian capon stew and roast duck. The second course is pretty much the same, lots of game and not much else. The third continues along the same lines, with hardly a vegetable in sight, though a few fish or mushroom dishes also appear. Only at the very end do sweets appear, such as marzipan, wafers, fruit pies, biscuits and conserves. It is clear that in sixteenth-century France it was still game, sugar and spices that really impressed. All this would change in the middle of the next century.

The change in culinary culture in the seventeenth century has a lot to do with the new Bourbon dynasty and the new form of absolutist government they implemented. Following the assassination of Henry III, the throne passed to the leader of the French Protestant, or Huguenot, party Henry IV, founder of the Bourbon dynasty which lasted until the end of the eighteenth century. Realizing that he could not effectively rule a nation that was predominantly Catholic, Henry converted, but also issued the Edict of Nantes which allowed Protestants to worship in peace. Henry was apparently easy going, with casual manners and breath that reeked of his beloved garlic. His homey demeanor and numerous love affairs nonetheless endeared him to his people, and he became one of the most beloved of French monarchs. Henry also rebuilt France, encouraging agriculture and industry, and building canals. The strong administration he built, governing without the use of the Estates General, the main representative assembly of the nation, also laid the groundwork for the strength of the crown in the seventeenth century.

Henry too was assassinated, by a fanatical teacher, who hated him for "trafficking with heretics" and was succeed by his nine-year-old son Louis XIII. During his reign, his principal minister, Cardinal Richelieu really ran the country. To get an impression of the court in this period, one need only think of the three Musketeers, international espionage and court conspiracies. To his credit, Richelieu managed to keep the nation together and the young king alive. The crown remained strong and wealthy for several reasons, not the least of which was increased taxes and the sale of government offices. Popular wars along the borders in which France grew to roughly the size it is today also added to the prestige of the crown. Richelieu died in 1642 and the king shortly thereafter and were once again succeeded by a boy king, Louis XIV.

It took some time, and a few civil wars known as the Frondes, before the king could break free from the influence of his ministers. But when he did, he emerged as the epitome of a system of government historians call absolutist monarchy. What this means is that all power is derived ultimately from the king. For Louis, "L'etat c'est moi" (I am the state). And Louis was a hard worker, appointing ministers who maintained government finances and stimulated the economy, built up the army to unprecedented levels and codified the laws. It was in this period that France began to build a serious overseas empire and a navy to protect it. Louisiana, then encompassing most of central North America, was named for him. For our purposes, the most significant contribution of Louis XIV was the dazzling court he built at Versailles, the model for all of Europe. More than a palace, it was a virtual city, staffed by literally thousands of chefs, servants and suppliers. Keeping courtiers well-fed and entertained was his way of keeping them pacified, and it worked. Court life was also governed by a complex series of rituals and nearly every daily activity for the king was a carefully orchestrated performance, especially eating. It was in his reign that classical French *haute cuisine* was born.

In the middle of the seventeenth century, as if the flood gates suddenly opened, culinary literature flowed in profusion from French presses. Perhaps earlier chefs were jealous to guard their secrets or guild regulations prevented them from doing so, though why other countries had produced cookbooks earlier remains a mystery. It may be that the urge to systematize, organize and develop rules that so pervades French culture in this period merely spilled over into cooking. Just as new rules for architectural orders, how plays should be constructed, even the French language itself, were set down, so too the method of cooking was rationalized. This period is often referred to as the classical period in French arts and literature, precisely because of this tendency to set down rules. Similarly the culinary style is called classical haute cuisine, for the same reason.

Perhaps another analogy could be made by comparing cooking to science. After all, the scientific revolution was taking place at the same time. Galileo proved that the earth revolves around the sun, and published his finding in an accessible format. William Harvey discovered the circulation of the blood. Chemists and physicists were researching the properties of gases and pneumatic pumps. Renée Descartes and others were perfecting the mathematical language to express science and new scientific instruments promised to change the way data was collected and experiments were undertaken. Though perhaps there was no sudden culinary revolution that totally abandoned old ways, neither in fact was there a sudden scientific one, cookbooks did differ dramatically from those that preceded.

The first cookbook to make the decisive break is *Cuisinier françois* by François Pierre La Varenne published in 1651. The essence of this new cuisine lies in the fact that foods are increasingly cooked in a way that accentuated and intensified the flavor of the main ingredient rather than contrast with it as the sugar, spices and vinegar of older cookbooks had. Sauces were more often bound with a *roux* of flour and fat, rather than bread crumbs and sharp flavorings, and an increasing number of sauces are based on butter. A bundle of herbs or *bouquet garni* is used to add a subtle flavor to a sauce. A consommé is clarified with egg whites. Equally important is the procedural logic of La Varenne's recipes. A few basic preparations, such as a rich stock, can be kept on hand and reduced to make a variety of sauces to accompany many different foods.

Many of the older standbys like exotic birds and game, and large fish and whale, also receive less attention. Although it would take some time, spices were increasingly banished to desserts, and even though many late-seventeenth-century recipes still contain spices, judging from contemporaries' comments the French used spices far more sparingly than elsewhere. Now that the middle classes could afford spices, they no longer served as marks of wealth and sophistication. Pepper began to be used more universally as a seasoning, as it is to this day, and spices like cinnamon were used more rarely, while mace, long pepper, cardamom and saffron disappear entirely. Fresh herbs and aromatics like onions and mushrooms often took their place. This new culinary aesthetic stressed subtlety, simplicity of preparation and a logical order to the foods served. Abundance and huge piles of sugar-coated meat impressed less now than the correct way of organizing a meal. Good taste had replaced what to older generations merely tasted good.

Naturally it took many years to totally break from ingrained culinary habits. In La Varenne there were as many medieval descendants lingering around as there were new ideas. But the following recipe gives some idea of how procedures have changed. Salt and pepper (as well as cloves) season along with aromatics. The meat is floured and seared, and the sauce is reduced. This all presages things to come. The following translation was made for the 1653 English edition. The whitening procedure, blanching or soaking, was done in cold water to remove any blood or impurities from the meat. Seam is rendered pork fat, while the lard would have been drippings from bacon.

Legs or Knuckles of Veal Epigramme Way

After they are well whitened in fresh water, flowre them and pass them in the pan with melted Lard or fresh Seam. Then break them and put them in a pot well seasoned with Salt, Pepper, Cloves, and a bundle of Herbs. Put an onion with it, a little Broth and a few Capers, then flowre them with some paste, and smother them with the Pot lid; seeth them leasurely thus covered for the space of three houres, after which you shall uncover them, and shall reduce your Sauce untill all be the better thereby. Put some Mushrums to it, if you have any, then serve.[33]

The following simple recipe for stewed salmon, although it appears immediately after a ragoût of salmon that includes sugar, is a good example of how salty flavors have begun to replace sweet ones. It also shows how a reduced wine and butter sauce that accentuates the main ingredient has replaced a sour one that was in previous years thought to cut through the "gluey humors" of the fish. The next translations are rendered into modern English. Incidentally, as La Varenne points out, salmon goes equally well with red or white wine.

Stewed Salmon

Cut it into slices the thickness of two or three fingers. Then stick them with cloves, the way stews are done, in a pot with white or red wine, well seasoned with butter, salt, and chopped onion. Cook it with capers if you have any. Let the sauce reduce and thicken, and serve garnished with whatever you like.[34]

An absolutely simple, straightforward recipe, this one for fried artichokes reflects La Varenne's respect for the clarity and pureness of flavors. In earlier generations they would have been sprinkled with cinnamon and sugar or probably swathed with some kind of sauce.

Fried Artichokes

Trim them as you do for a poivrade (pepper sauce), and also remove the sharp points. Blanch them in hot water. After that dry them, and flour them to fry when you need them. Serve them garnished with fried parsley.[35]

Le Cuisinier by Pierre de Lune appeared shortly after La Varenne in 1656. De Lune is credited with introducing several further technical innovations: the modern *bouquet garni,* a bundle of herbs used for flavoring stocks and stews, and one of the earliest set of directions for making a roux with flour, which he called "fried flour." De Lune was chef to the duke of Rohan, and so his recipes reflect the best that money could buy, which now meant refinement and elegant procedures rather than rare and exotic ingredients, variety and abundance. Take for example this mushroom stock in which a simple ingredient is raised to a higher level as it becomes the base or garnish for other recipes, such as the one that follows.

Method for Extracting True Mushroom Juice to Use in Meat and Vegetable Dishes

Clean the mushrooms well, put them in a pan with a bit of bacon; let them brown on the embers just until they stick to the bottom of the pan; being brown, put in a bit of flour, then let it brown. Being done, put in good bouillon and remove the mushrooms from the fire, and place the juice in another pot seasoned with a bit of lemon and salt. You can also make the same juice without meat by placing butter in the bottom of the pan in place of bacon. The mushrooms you can serve finely chopped, cut or whole, in soups, in entrées or in side dishes.[36]

This recipe for crayfish soup is another good example of how chefs sought to intensify and concentrate the flavor of the main ingredient and garnish it with other foods that complement it as well as decorate the plate. Here it is roe or fish eggs and mushrooms. Presentation and pleasing the eye was clearly just as important to de Lune as subtly matching flavors. Consider how different an approach this is than the spiced, sugar and vinegar-laden sauces added to fish in the previous century. While the logic of combining contrasting flavors in medieval and Renaissance cuisine may have had some medicinal or corrective logic to it, clearly pleasing the eye and palate is the only consideration here.

Crayfish Soup

Wash the crayfish well, cook them in water with a bundle of herbs, a bit of salt and butter. Then draw out the tails and the legs, and pound the shells which you strain with the crayfish bouillon and place in a pot. Then you put the tail and leg meat in a pan with a bit of butter and fine herbs well chopped, and you place them in a pot or plate with the bouillon, the reddest you can strain. After, simmer bread crusts with the bouillon, three or four finely chopped mushrooms, arrange your crayfish and garnish the soup with roe and mushrooms, lemon juice and mushroom juice.[37]

Among late-seventeenth-century French cookbooks, *L'Art de bien traiter* of 1674 was the largest and perhaps the most innovative and important. Its author was also a professional chef working for the noblest of patrons. But apart from his initials—L.S.R.—we know practically nothing about him. He is usually remembered today for his scathing remarks about the vulgarity of earlier cookbooks, especially that of La Varenne, whose teal soup a l'hypocras, larks in sweet sauce, fried calf's head and turkey stuffed with raspberries, struck L.S.R. as the most backward and revolting things imaginable. He also ridicules the veal epigramme dish cited above. Far more interesting though are the ways that L.S.R. anticipates developments in haute cuisine yet to come: his detailed interest in sensory perceptions, the way food looks and feels in the mouth, the subtle perfumes evoked by perfect cooking. The aim here was delicacy, refinement and discernment, and L.S.R. instructed his readers exactly how to achieve the effects desired. Moreover, foods should taste of themselves, and not an infinity of flavors competing in the mouth. Perhaps more than any other chef of this generation, L.S.R. achieves the cool refinement, balance and proportion sought after by architects and garden designers who designed Louis XIV's Versailles and the playwrights who entertained his guests. As he himself said, it is not abundance, strange meats or a jumble of spices, but "the exquisite choice of meats, the refinement of their seasoning, the politeness and propriety of their service, their quantity proportionate to the number of guests, and finally the general order of things that are essential to the goodness and ornament of a meal .... "[38]

The refinement of L.S.R.'s cookbook was, of course, achieved in large measure by distancing himself from the culinary fashions of the common rabble and especially from those of previous generations. These brief obnoxious comments should serve to illustrate how he achieved this. They are on the first page of his section on roasting. The petit-bourgeois roughly means lower middle class, but implies the recent acquisition of wealth and a desire to fit into their new social class by imitating others—like parrots in this case.

Fat Lamb

When it is nearly cooked, place on it only fine salt, and do not bind yourself to those base maxims of the petit-bourgeois with their bread crumbs which only suck up the substance and juice of the meat. And regarding the infinite quantity of chopped parsley that is customarily put on, even on veal and mutton, I counsel you to leave this useless ornament on this occasion for mister parrot, to whom it is given as food, and which makes the most delicate part of his daily nourishment.[39]

One of the most sensational stories in the history of food dates from this period, and gives some idea of the importance attached to cooking. It involves a professional chef who had worked for some of the leading nobles in France and finally for the king's brother. The chef's name was Vatel. The story is told by Madame de Sevigne in a letter of 1671. King Louis had come to visit the Prince de Condé and of course had to be entertained in style. And as it turned out one night there were not enough roasts to go on all the tables because some unexpected guests showed up. The 25th table down and one other had no roast. And Vatel was completely humiliated; beside himself.87 Condé assured him that everything was fine. The next day at 4 o'clock in the morning, Vatel was running around preparing for the next day, and met a fish supplier who had only two loads of fish. He asked him if that was all there was. The man responded yes, not knowing that tons of fish had been ordered, but Vatel assumed that this was the entire supply to feed dozens of people. So he went up to his room, steadied a sword against a door and ran it through his heart. It took three tries. He was found dead in a puddle of blood, just as all the cartloads of fish he ordered started arriving.

The most popular cookbook of the latter seventeenth century was Massialot's *Le Cuisinier roïal et bourgeois* of 1691. Massialot probably worked as a freelance caterer for the royal household, and whomever could pay for his services, and his connections at court and the descriptions of meals served there made his cookbook a continual success. Its popularity probably also has a lot to do with the broad audience it addressed. It is at once royal but would also appeal to up and coming city dwellers, merchants and other wealthy members of the middle class who could make many of the recipes, though perhaps on a simpler scale. It was reissued several times and in an expanded version well into the eighteenth century. Although in many ways it was not as modern as L.S.R. and even borrowed recipes from de Lune, it marks a significant advance in culinary literature. To start with it is arranged alphabetically, and thus can be used easily in a working kitchen. The following turkey recipe is one example of a recipe that might appear on both royal and bourgeois tables. The fact that he suggests ways to use up the leftovers the next day is indicative of his audience.

Turkey Stuffed with Fine Herbs

Take the turkeys and truss them for roasting, but do not blanch them at all. You must separate the skin above the stomach so you can stuff it. The stuffing is made with chopped raw bacon, parsley, onion and all sorts of fine herbs, all well chopped, or pounded a bit in a mortar and well seasoned. You stuff the turkeys between the skin and flesh and put a bit inside the body. You must next skewer them well and let them roast. Being roasted, dress them in the plate, and place a good ragout over it, and arrange all sorts of garnishes, and serve it hot. You can do the same with chickens, pigeons and other birds. And to dress them up to serve the next day, you can braise them being stuffed as above, being cooked, drain them and serve with a good ragout of truffles and sweetbreads, all well strained, defatted and garnished with little croquettes.[40]

The next recipe is a good example of the technical precision employed by Massialot. Although the ingredients are not particularly expensive and the procedures not very complicated, they do require previous preparation of a fish stock. In planning an entire dinner several of these *fonds,* or flavor bases, would have been prepared ahead by a large kitchen staff and could be used in dozens of different sauces, ragoûts or braises. In this case the *coulis* would have been a rich, strained and thickened fish base. This is one of the most important organizing principles of French cuisine from this period to the present. Note, however, that he offers another simpler version as well, and even here he seems to be improvising rather than presenting rigid rules that cannot be altered. Note also the use of a proper stove rather than using pots arranged in the fire.

Pike with Sauce Robert

Scale and clean your pikes; slash them and cut them into quarters; trim them and place them to marinate in pepper, salt, onions, slices of lemon, basil, bay leaves and vinegar. After an hour take your pikes out of the marinade, and place them on a white cloth to dry them. Flour them and fry them. Next make the Robert sauce. Take a bit of butter in a casserole that you place on the stove. Have onions cut in a dice that you fry in the casserole, just until they begin to color, and moisten them with fish bouillon. When cooked, degrease them well and thicken them with a good coulis. Place your pikes in your sauce to simmer on the hot cinders. When it is ready to serve, dress them properly on a plate. Before pouring the sauce on top, put it back on the fire a bit, and add a bit of mustard and a dash of vinegar. Be sure that it tastes good. Put it on your pike and serve it hot. Those who do not have the means to make a coulis, can serve it by adding a bit of flour when the onions color, before moistening it, so that the flour has a little time to cook. The marinade can also be used for all sorts of sweet fresh water fish that are fried.[41]

At the turn of the eighteenth century, the glorious reign of the Sun King began to cloud over. Louis had grown old and toothless. His wars were no longer so glamorous, and still cost a fortune. Louis also believed that France had to be uniform in religion. Revoking the edict of Nantes, which granted Protestants full civil rights, caused a mass exodus of talented and industrious Huguenots, many of whom fled to the New World. This was only one of the setbacks that began to become apparent toward the end of Louis' reign. Serious food shortages and crop failures became more frequent in the early eighteenth century, and there was even a brief economic recession. When Louis died he was succeeded by a king who did not seem to have been much interested in governing. Louis XV was an avid hunter and liked to chase women. His favorite mistress, Madame Pompadour, was even suspected of making important decisions of state herself. As in any highly centralized state, lack of a strong leader spells disaster. It is perhaps surprising that expensive wars and lavish court entertainments did not precipitate a revolution earlier than it did. Rather, the nation continued to focus on the court and imitate its latest fashions.

But something else odd had happened. The bold, assertive and self-confident style of the Sun King gave way to a sweet, affected, overwrought and, some might say, nauseating style called *rococo*. The word rococo comes from *rocaille* which refers to the ornate mock stone grottos so popular in this period. Conjure images of men in starched white wigs, women with mounds of hair intricately piled on their heads, everyone tightly bound by constrictive clothing. Picture the curved lines of gilt furniture, so light and ornate that it seems to defy use. Picture little sweet ceramic figurines of harlequins and animals, pure frou-frou. Now imagine what these people wanted to eat. We have moved once again into a period of culinary excess, over refinement, the exotic and artificial outweighing the homegrown and traditional.

There were no new cookbooks for the first three decades of the eighteenth century until Vincent La Chapelle's *Cuisinier moderne* of 1735 which first appeared in English in 1733 as *The modern cook*. This work and those of this decade were essentially a reaction against the overly-refined and excessive style that dominated in the previous decades, and this new simplicity caught on in the highest social circles. La Chapelle was chef to Lord Chesterfield, and then went to Holland to work for the Prince of Orange. Fully one third of his book is taken from Massialot, but it does show some culinary novelties. Here the coulis is a meat stock which is strained and thickened with a roux of cooked flour and butter rather than bread crumbs. La Chapelle was the forerunner of a group of chefs who sought to redefine elegant dining by simplifying recipes and streamlining procedures.

Probably the most novel of this generation of chefs of the "modern cuisine" movement was François Marin whose *Les Dons de Comus: ou L'Art de cuisine,* first appeared in 1739. It is difficult to determine exactly why Marin wanted to invent a simpler and more elegant cuisine. Many food historians have assumed that this was an effort to further distance elite cooking from the aspiring middle classes who could now afford to imitate their lavish style. But if we trust Marin's introduction actually written by two Jesuit priests, it seems like the motivation was concern with health. He also makes open concessions to his bourgeois readers by offering simplified versions of more difficult recipes. His work should be "useful to everyone. The professional chef ... the bourgeois with more ordinary dishes ... and those who for amusement wish to know a bit about cooking."[42]

The introduction, although not necessarily Marin's own views, claims that his new cooking accords with the precepts of physicians, is easy to digest, more nutritious and can help diners avoid such maladies as gout and kidney stones. To accomplish this he uses animals and vegetables at the point of maturity, smaller rather than large animals, and those that are dry rather than oily or fatty. He also prefers animals from their natural habitat rather than those artificially fattened in coops and stables, or vegetables raised in hot beds. Most importantly, abandoning the strange jumbles of ingredients and contrary flavors and textures, he prefers reduced essences, smooth sauces that accompany the main ingredient, and cooking methods that make foods more digestible and nutritious. He even compares cooking to chemistry. "The science of cooking consists in refining, breaking down, and reducing meats to their essence; drawing nourishing juices, and yet remaining light, and mixing them together so that nothing dominates, and everything can be tasted."[43]

Consequently sauces become more refined (literally), cuts of meat become smaller and more tender, and the storm of garnishes give way to subtle flavors enmeshed in the whole ensemble creating a harmony that Marin compares to music. Now whether Marin carries these ideals into all his recipes is debatable, but this veal cutlet recipe certainly is something quite different than what was served in previous decades.

Veal Cutlets

Marinate the cutlets in oil with two cloves of garlic and two bay leaves for two hours. Place in a casserole with the oil two glasses of Champagne, two glasses of veal essence and two truffles cut into dice. Simmer it all over hot cinders. When the cutlets are cooked, drain them and degrease the sauce well. Add to it a pat of butter combined with flour, a pinch of chervil blanched and crushed. Stir everything and sprinkle on some lemon juice. The sauce should be a little thick.[44]

The last of the "modern" cookbooks of this decade was Menon's *Nouveau traité de la cuisine* of 1739. It was followed shortly thereafter by his *La cuisinère bourgeoise* in 1746 which was the most popular cookbook of the latter eighteenth century and is clear proof that professional chefs were trying to appeal to middle class audiences rather than stay aloof from them. But Menon also composed works for professional chefs that included recipes and long detailed procedures that were well beyond the capability of most households *La science du Maître d'Hôtel Confiseur* of 1750 is a good example of this type. This recipe for chocolate ice cream, is a typical example of the magnificent courtly creations that could translate into a more humble milieu.

Chocolate Ice Cream

Take 3 half sétiers (12 pints) of cream and 4 pints of milk and let it boil with 3/4 pound of sugar. Take 1/2 pound of chocolate that you melt in a pan of water set in the fire, which you stir with a spatula or wooden spoon, and let it simmer just to the point of boiling. You must add three egg yolks that you have tempered well with the milk and cream. Pour it all into the pan with the chocolate and mix together. Then you must place it in a terrine until you are ready to place it on ice.[45]

ENGLAND

As an island nation, England had always maintained its own distinctive culinary traditions, but there was a constant battle between native and continental fashions. This had a lot to do with their religious situation, being Protestant but with both Puritan and Catholic minorities, and their political development as a constitutional monarchy with a powerful landed nobility and gentry. At times courtly and continental fashions dominated, at others simple country tastes.

The sixteenth century opened with a rich and secure kingdom emerging from the aftermath of the Wars of the Roses with Henry VII on the throne. By arranging careful marriages, his own as well as those of his children, he was able to secure both domestic and international peace. In 1509 the throne was inherited by his son Henry VIII who was married to the Spanish Princess Catherine of Aragon, daughter of Ferdinand and Isabella. Contrary to the image we have of Henry as the obscenely overweight and grotesquely ill-mannered glutton, when he came to the throne he was young, deemed attractive by his contemporaries and the very model of tact and courtesy. For nearly half his long reign he and his Spanish queen lived happily in a prosperous kingdom.

Eventually it became clear that two separate problems demanded attention: how to make the kingdom financially secure after squandering much of his inheritance on war, and how to procure an heir to the throne. Having spawned several bastards by this point, Henry was convinced that his wife was barren and proceeded to request an annulment of the marriage from Pope Clement VII. His attractive (and pregnant) young mistress Anne Boleyn only spurred on his ambition to dump Catherine.

As fate would have it, the Pope's hands were at this very moment tied. In 1527 the troops of Emperor and King of Spain Charles V had surrounded Rome and were ready to descend upon and plunder the city. And Catherine was, after all, Charles' aunt. It would have been a gross breach of diplomacy to grant Henry his annulment, although this was something Popes routinely did. Without further recourse, and with the aid of his advisors, Henry declared himself Head of the Church in England, thus disposing of papal authority altogether. Significantly, this was enacted in Parliament, thus given official sanction by the nation through its representative body. This break with Rome was, however, merely a political move, and doctrinally nothing had changed. In fact Henry had been awarded the title "Defender of the Faith" for a tract he had written denouncing Martin Luther who began the Protestant Reformation. But this situation opened opportunities and advisors saw a way to kill two birds with one stone. As Head of the Church, the vast and wealthy monastic properties scattered across England were now technically the king's, and he wasted little time in claiming them, dissolving the monasteries and spending the proceedings. Many of the activities undertaken by monks—growing wine grapes, raising bees for honey and wax and tending medicinal herb gardens were now suspended. Former monastic lands were also quickly bought up from the crown and made to turn a profit, either by renting them to tenant farmers or exploiting them directly.

Henry was now able to dispose of his first wife, technically not a divorce since the union was declared illegitimate from the outset. Catherine and their young daughter Mary, still loyal to the Catholic Church, remained in England. Henry quickly married Anne, who later bore him a daughter—the future Elizabeth I. Without dwelling on the details of the next four marriages, he was also given a son by his third wife. The fate of his wives is as gruesome as legendary and the little jingle "divorced, beheaded, died, divorced, beheaded, survived" at least tells you what became of them. More important however was the move toward and away from true doctrinal Protestantism in the latter half of Henry's reign.

We know something about the cuisine of Henry's reign partly through the accounts of banquets thrown by his principal minister Cardinal Wolsey. A witness to one of these lavish affairs, George Cavendish remarked principally about the "subtleties and curious devices" depicting castles, beasts, men sword fighting, jousting or dancing with ladies. These were presumably made of sugar, though not necessarily edible. What they do show is that as in France, the court was still obsessed with chivalric themes, even a cardinal. The other impression one gets from sumptuary laws designed to limit the number of courses each rank could serve at a feast, is that the food was still thoroughly medieval as well—huge wild animals served with spicy sauces.

There are a few cookbooks from this period too. As early as 1500 a small anonymous book titled *This is the Boke of Cokery* appeared, and shortly after in 1508 a carving manual called *Here Begynneth the Boke of Kervynge,* printed by Wynkyn de Worde, the most influential printer of his generation. Most of the book is about carving and serving various kinds of food, but it does reveal what kinds of food were eaten too. A list of sauces, for example, reveals that eating habits in England were no different than they had been in previous centuries. There is verjuice made from unripe grapes, a gamelyn or cameline sauce made of cinnamon, cloves, ginger, bread crumbs, nuts, raisins and vinegar. It also mentions chawdon made with liver and other entrails, blood, bread, wine, vinegar, pepper, cloves and ginger. All these are standard medieval sauces.[46]

About 1545, at the very end of Henry's reign, there appeared another anonymous and undated cookbook titled *A proper newe Booke of Cokerye,* although it may actually have been printed around 1557 or 1558. This work begins to depart from earlier medieval texts, particularly in the appearance of fruit tarts and other pies with crusts that were meant to be eaten. It directs that "To make a short paest for tarte" one should "Take fyne floure and a cursey of fayre water and a dyshe of swete butter and a lyttel saffron, and the yolckes of two egges and make it thynne and as tender as ye maye."[47] With this crust one could make various tarts of gooseberries, medlars, damson plums, cherries and even flowers like borage or marigolds. There is also evidence of continental influence, as a tart in the French fashion and a recipe "To make a stewe after the guyse of beyonde the sea" reveals. It is basically just a mutton stew with wine and spices, but for some reason struck this author as foreign. Perhaps even more convincing is this recipe (which is also found in Scappi and other continental cookbooks), which was apparently very popular across Europe. Although these directions are not very clear, it seems as if the egg whites are beaten first and then all the ingredients further beaten with a makeshift whisk cut from a stick. The mixture then seems to be passed through a colander over the rosemary bush, creating a little winter scene.

To Make a Dyschefull of Snowe

Take a pottell of swete thycke creame and the whytes of eyghte egges, and beate them together wyth a spone, then putte them in youre creame and a saucerfull of Rosewater, and a dyshe full of Suger wyth all, then take a styke and make it cleane, and than cutte it in the end foure square, and therwith beate all the aforesayde thynges together, and ever as it ryseth take it of and put it into a Collaunder, this done take one apple and set it in the myddes of it, and a thycke bush of Rosemary, and set it in the myddes of the platter, then cast your snowe uppon the Rosemarye and fyll your platter therwith. And yf you have wafers caste some in wyth all and thus seve them forthe.[48]

When Henry died in 1547 and his young and sickly son Edward took the throne, his advisors initiated a full and thorough Protestant reform through the country. This is significant for several reasons. First, abandoning the mass and adopting a reformed prayer book meant that the central miraculous food ritual of the Mass in England had been replaced by a memorial service. Secondly, a Puritanical spirit was unleashed, one that looked with derision upon the supposedly sacred festivals that dotted the Christian calendar, and one that took a harsh attitude toward food and pleasures of the body. This attitude would resurface in succeeding reigns, but at this point it was not at all clear that Puritanism would prevail. In fact, when young Edward died, the nation without hesitation proclaimed Mary Queen of England. In a moment, England reverted to full obedience to the Pope and the Catholic Church in Rome. Many of the leading prelates associated with the Protestant reform were burned, thus giving Mary the perhaps not totally undeserved nickname "Bloody." In all fairness, she was no better or worse than her predecessors or successors who did their own fair share of killing in the name of God. Mary was not a very successful ruler, having made an unpopular marriage to Philip II of Spain— who of course had his own kingdom to run.

When Mary died the nation seemed relieved, and they proclaimed the last daughter of Henry VIII, Elizabeth, queen. Elizabeth unlike her sister grew into a skillful and respected monarch. Politically, Elizabeth was manipulative but extremely successful in earning the love of her subjects by ruling through Parliament, the supreme legislative and judiciary body in the kingdom. Prevailing against conspiracies, intrigues, as well as a huge Armada sent from Spain only enhanced her reputation as "Good Queen Bess." On the topic of religion she was also careful to steer a middle course between Protestantism and Catholicism, the so-called "via media" which while officially Protestant would accommodate both more traditionally minded subjects and the "hotter sort" of Protestant or Puritan. This compromise lasted throughout her reign, but would also conceal the fact that a religious rift was widening within the country as well as two opposed attitudes toward food and festivity. But the reign of Elizabeth would long be remembered for the dazzling court festivities and sugar-laden banquets over which she presided. Reputedly, Elizabeth's fondness for sugar made her teeth black.

Toward the end of her reign, in the 1580s and 1590s a spate of cookbooks began to be published, most of which freely borrowed from each other, which makes it impossible to sort out when any given recipe first appeared. Many were published anonymously and without dates. The first of these was *The Good Huswifes Handmaide for the Kitchen* which appeared in 1588. What makes this book so interesting is that it is addressed to a woman cooking for or managing a household, presumably a wealthy one located in the country because many of the recipes call for wild game. Red deer were especially associated with the aristocracy who could maintain forests and had the leisure to hunt. The coffin in which it is made is a huge free standing pastry crust made of flour, egg yolks, butter and water. We know that it was actually eaten because the author specifies that "too many yolks of Egges ... will make it drie and not pleasant in eating," but obviously it could not be sliced because the deer still contained bones. This was a standard practice, and there is even a recipe for a pie with oyster shells inside. The recipe below appears in nearly exactly the same form in later cookbooks.

To Bake a Red Deare

You must take a handful of Fennell, a handfull of winter Savorie, a handfull of Rosemarrie, a handfull of Time, and a handfull of Baie leaves, and when your liquor seethes that you perboyle your Venison till it be half ynough, then take it out, and lay it upon a faire boord that the water may run fro it, then take a knife and prick it ful of holes and while it is warme, have a faire traie with Vineger therein, and so put your Venison therein from morning untill night, and ever now and then turne it upside downe, and then at night have your coffin readie, and this done, season it with Synamon, Nutmeg and Ginger, Pepper and salt, and when you have seasoned it, put it into your coffin, and put a good quantity of sweet Butter into it, and in the morning draw it foorth, and put in a sawcer full of Vinegar into your pie at a hole above in the top of it, so that the Vinegar may run into every place of it, and then stop the hole againe, and turne the bottom upward, and so serve it in.[49]

The next important cookbook produced in England first appeared around 1596, but there may have been earlier editions. Thomas Dawson's *The Good huswifes jewell* like *The Good huswifes handmaid,* reflects new ideas in cookery as old medieval standbys. It contains, for example, the first recipe for sweet potatoes, even before they appear in Gerard's *Herbal*. It includes directions for making various marzipan figures, which were so beloved on the Elizabethan banquetting table. Although many of the recipes call for boiling ingredients, they also show a fairly simple and direct way of dealing with them, and many like the one below, seem quite modern in the flavors and textures achieved. This one also contains no spices. The *sippets* over which the chicken and grapes are placed in this recipe are slices of bread that soak up the gravy, much like one used to see with "chicken à la king" in the twentieth century. A *pipkin* was a small pot with a handle and usually three legs, made of either ceramic or metal that could be placed over hot coals.

To Boil Chickens

First you must take chickens and boil them with grapes and with a rack of mutton together. Let the rack of mutton boil before the chickens one hour and a half. Then make a bunch of herbs with rosemary, thyme, savory and hyssop and also marjoram. Bind them fast together. Put them in the pot and when you see your time put in your chickens with parsley in their bellies and a little sweet butter, verjuice and pepper. When you have so done, boil your grapes in a little pipkin by themselves with some of the broth of the chickens. But take heed not to boil them too much nor yet too little. Then take the yolks of five eggs and strain them with a little broth of the pot, and when they are strained put them in the pipkin to the grapes and stir them. When they begin to boil take them from the fire and stir them a good while after you have taken them up. Then have your sippets ready in a platter and lays your meat upon it. And take your pipkins and grapes and all that is in them and pour it upon the meat. After this sort serve it in.[50]

One unique feature of English cooking was the pudding, which Dawson offered several recipes for, including haggis, typically associated with the Scots, which was basically organ meats, fat and a starch binder boiled in sheep's stomach. This recipe is fairly standard, though some versions include sugar and more sweet ingredients. It is only in the United States that a pudding has come to mean exclusively a sweet dessert.

To Make a Pudding

Take parsley and thyme and chop it small. Then take the kidney of veal, and parboil it, and when it is parboiled, take all the fat off it, and lay it that it may cool. When it is cold shred it like as you do suet for puddings. Then take marrow and mince it by itself. Then take grated bread and small raisins the quantity of your stuff, and dates minced small. Then take the eggs and roast them hard and take the yolks of them and chop them small, and then take your stuff aforehearsed, and mingle altogether. Then take pepper, cloves and mace, saffron and salt, and put it together with the said stuff, as much as you think by casting shall suffice. Then take six eggs and break them into a vessel, whites and all. Put your dry stuff into the same eggs, and temper them all well together. So fill your haggis or gut, and seethe it well and it will be good.[51]

Cookery in the early seventeenth century did not differ dramatically from that of the previous century. There was a new king on the throne, James I, first of the Stuart dynasty. He tried to maintain the dazzling court of Elizabeth, though was perceived by the English as a foreigner. His bookish habits and pomposity were also found distasteful. James even composed an angry diatribe against the latest fashion for smoking, which he found vile.

The first cookbook of this century was John Murrell's *A New Book of Cookerie* which appeared in 1615. It too contains recipes taken from earlier works, and also a fair number of new French ones as the title advertises. This pudding recipe he offers more closely approximates the dessert pudding known to later generations. It is also boiled in a cloth rather than a stomach bag. There was a distinct trend in this period toward the greater use of butter, which this recipe includes.

A Cambridge Pudding

Searce grated Bread through a Cullinder, mince it with Flower, minst Dates, Currins, Nutmeg, Sinamon, and Pepper, minst Suit, new Milke warme, fine Sugar, and Egges: take away some of their whites, worke all together. Take halfe the Pudding on the one side, and the other on the other side, and make it round like a loafe. Then take Butter, and put it in the middest of the Pudding, and the other halfe aloft. Let your liquour boyle, and throw your Pudding in, being tyed in a faire cloth: when it is boyled enough cut it in the middest, and so serue it in.[52]

Although recipes for vegetables are rare in English cookbooks of this period, the following adaptable salad recipe at least shows the variety of greens that were common to Stuart households. Vegetables such as spinach, endive and chicory were often parboiled to rid them of their supposedly noxious cold qualities. Most of the vegetables listed are still familiar, though their names have changed slightly. Rocket is the British name for arugula, alexanders (*Smyrnium olustratum*) is a celery-like plant, of which the thin stems and leaves were probably used here. Coleflowers probably refers to flowering cabbage or broccoli rabe rather than cauliflower.

Diuers Sallets Boyled

Parboyle Spinage, and chop it fine, with the edges of two hard Trenchers vpon a boord, or the backe of two chopping Kniues: then set them on a Chafingdish of coales with Butter and Uinegar. Season it with Sinamon, Ginger, Sugar, and a few parboyld Currins. Then cut hard Egges into quarters to garnish it withall, and serue it vpon sippets. So may you serue Burrage, Buglosse, Endiffe, Suckory, Coleflowers, Sorrel, Marigold leaues, water-Cresses, Leekes boyled, Onions, Sparragus, Rocket, Alexanders. Parboyle them, and season them all alike: whether it be with Oyle and Uinegar, or Butter and Uinegar, Sinamon, Ginger, Sugar, and Butter: Egges are necessary, or at least very good for all boyld Sallets.[53]

Gervase Markham was one of the most prolific author/compilers of this generation, writing about a variety of topics that would appeal to the owner or steward and housekeeper of a typical country house. With titles covering agriculture, husbandry, medicine for people and animals and cooking he provided readers, probably landed gentry, with practically everything they would need to know. *The English Housewife* of 1615 and then appearing in expanded editions for the next two decades, is his foray into cookery, but it also contains sections on distillation, brewing beer, making cloth, curing ailments and even the virtues requisite for the ideal housewife. It is clear from some of his recipes that the household was wealthy enough to afford fashionable and exotic Mediterranean ingredients worthy of royal tables. For example, a compound *sallat* recipe includes layers of almonds, capers, raisins, spinach, sugar, oranges and lemons, and spinach, sage and cabbage hearts as well as red cauliflower leaves. This was eaten raw, like a modern salad, with a dressing of oil and vinegar. Markham describes the dish as typical at great feasts, and upon princes' tables. The following recipe for *quelquechose* ("something" in French) also shows that jumbled, spiced and sugar dishes remained popular well into the seventeenth century in England, and clearly conjured up continental associations. The recipe also concludes by adding that one can use either pig's petittoes (feet) or flesh, birds, shellfish, fruits, beans or whatever. The marigold flowers would have made the dish bright yellow. Technically this dish is an omelet rather than a fricassee.

To Make Any Quelquechose

To make a quelquechose, which is a mixture of many things together; take eggs and break them, and do away with half the whites, and after they are beaten put to them a good quantity of sweet cream, currants, cinnamon, cloves, mace, salt, and a little ginger, spinach, endive, and marigold flowers grossly chopped, and beat them all very well together; then take pig's pettitoes sliced, and grossly chopped, and mix them with the eggs, and with your hand stir them exceeding well together; then put sweet butter in your frying pan, and, being melted, put in all the rest, and fry it brown without burning, ever and anon turning till it be fried enough; then dish it upon a flat plate, and cover it with sugar, and so serve it forth. Only herein is to be observed that your pettitoes must be very well boiled before you put them into the fricassee.[54]

When James died his son Charles I inherited the throne. Immediately people began to notice changes at court. First a new style of clothes and architecture, modeled closely for the first time in England on classical precedents. Then there were artists like Van Dyck who painted some of the most remarkable portraits of Charles and his Catholic queen. This all seemed foreign to Englishmen, and when Charles decided to reign without Parliament through the 1630s it seemed evident that he wanted to remodel England along continental lines and rule as an absolutist monarch. It was actually his attempt to modify the broadly defined church of Elizabeth and force the episcopacy on Scotland that brought about his ruin. The Scots invaded and short on cash he was forced to summon Parliament, which immediately demanded that he address their grievances. Their anger was fueled partly by Charles' innovative ways of raising revenue, which it seemed to them was being spent on his lavish new building projects and court painters. After a series of political blunders, a bloody civil war erupted that succeeded not only in removing Charles' head and abolishing the monarchy, but in instituting a godly republic led by Oliver Cromwell and a host of puritanically minded parliamentarians. These people were, incidentally, cut out of exactly the same mold as the Puritans in Massachusetts who left a decade or so earlier.

The significance of this episode for the history of food, is that among many people the pleasures of the palate became suspect. All sensory indulgence was deemed sinful. The theaters were closed, village festivals banned. Anything redolent of paganism was purified following strict biblical authority. Christmas was actually formally abolished in these years. Without a royal court, one might think the arts of the table languished, but Cromwell maintained a fairly lavish court, which only became more magnificent with the restoration of Charles II in 1660 as king. For the rest of the seventeenth century the full splendor of the royal court returned, but the power of parliament also remained strong, leaving England with a government called a constitutional monarchy. This meant that power was not concentrated in the hands of the king and his immediate advisors, but was rather spread among a broad aristocracy whose power was based on their landed estates. England, in contrast to the continent, developed its dining traditions closely tied to the stately manor and its produce. Cookbooks reflect this difference, the ingredients and procedures are simpler, and dishes tend to be more traditional. England was still profoundly influenced by dining customs abroad, but the constant pull between native and foreign, simple and complex, royal and bourgeois, would continue to give English cookery two different faces. The fact that many cookbooks address a middle class audience also makes them quite different from other European works.

The first crop of cookbooks published after the Restoration were thoroughly courtly though. The first of these, *The Accomplisht Cook* by Robert May is one of the longest and most detailed of seventeenth-century cookbooks. May was a professional cook working for several Catholic noble households before, during and after the civil wars. The work was first published in 1660 immediately after the king returned, and then appeared in an expanded version fifteen years later. May's cooking procedures and ingredients are at once traditionally English, and he speaks wistfully about the good old days "before hospitality left this nation," but it also reflects the latest continental fashions. Like his patrons, he looked to Catholic Europe for aesthetic inspiration, but still remained thoroughly English. This can be seen throughout his recipes. Most of them make use of fairly ordinary butcher's meat like mutton, pork and beef, often simply boiled or stewed, but garnished with rare or elegant ingredients he associated with southern Europe: oranges and lemons, artichoke bottoms, asparagus, currants and dates. There is also extensive use of spices, pistachios and almonds, grapes and gooseberries, and the rarer musk and ambergris. In many respects this cookbook is similar to Stefani's produced in Mantua about the same time, except that the procedures and staples are English. Take, for example this pie dressed up with all manner of odd embellishments. The peepers are baby chicks. Marrow bones are one of the most frequently used garnishes in his book and along with grated bread and eggs were probably used in enormous quantities in his kitchen.

To Bake Chickens or Pigeons

Take either six pigeon peepers or six chicken peepers, if big cut them in quarters, then take sweetbreads of veal slic't very thin, three sheeps tongues boil'd
tender, blanched and slic't, with as much veal, as much mutton, six larks, twelve
cocks combs, a pint of great oysters parboiled and bearded, calves udder cut in
pieces, and three marrow bones, season these foresaid materials with pepper,
salt and nutmeg, then fill them in pies ... and put on the top some chestnuts,
marrow, large mace, grapes, or gooseberries; then have a little piece of veal and
mince it with as much marrow, some grated bread, yolks of eggs, minced dates,
salt, nutmeg and some sweet marjoram, work up all with a little cream, make it
up in little balls or rouls, put them in the pie, and put in a little mutton-gravy,
some artichoke bottoms, or the tops of boild sparagus, and a little butter; close
up the pie and bake it, being baked liquor it with juyce of oranges, one lemon,
and some claret wine, shake it well together and so serve it.[55]

It is only toward the end of his mammoth cookbook that May offers
some simpler recipes for Lent, probably intended for his Catholic patrons who still observed its restrictions. Here we find pease pottage,
furmenty (boiled wheat grains), oatmeal caudle made with ale and
cooked oatmeal, which was reportedly Oliver Cromwell's typical
breakfast. The panoply of exotic garnishes also recedes somewhat, as
this soup shows, even though it can be made with New World root
vegetables which were fairly quickly adopted in England. The seasoning he mentioned in the previous recipe included sliced dates, salt,
sugar, cinnamon and currants. Virginia artichokes were what we now
call Jerusalem artichokes. In fact, May had the origin correct, our
term is a corruption of the Italian *girasole,* meaning to turn toward the
sun which the flowers do.

Soops of Carrots

Being boil'd, cleanse, stamp and season them all in points as before; thus also
potatoes, skirrets, parsnips, turnips, Virginia artichoks, onions, or beets, or fry
any of the foresaid roots being boiled and cleansed, or peeled, and floured, and
serve them with beaten butter and sugar.[56]

A cookbook similar to May's was published in 1661 called *The
Whole Body of Cookery Dissected* by William Rabisha. A Catholic exile
during the interregnum, working for much the same sort of patrons as
May, Rabisha's recipes are also liberally spiced, seasoned with Mediterranean garnishes, especially oranges, and often claim to be of foreign
provenience. In fact, they are more traditional English dishes doc-
tored up with some regal-sounding names and exotic ingredients. It is
clear that with the restoration of the monarchy, Rabisha hoped that a

full court culture would return to England. What shape it would take at this point he could only guess. A few sample menus he offered show that he hoped the new court would be lavish. A bill of fare for a flesh dinner in autumn includes two courses with 22 dishes in each. In the first course there are boiled and roasted meats, salad, pudding, pheasants, turkey, geese and a chicken fricassee, a pie, hares, pork, venison pasty, a leg of veal. In the second are smaller birds and rabbits, an omelet, salads, some sweet pies, stewed fruit and custard. Along with the lack of much order or organization, this is still basically traditional English fare, mostly meat and game birds. He has picked up a few novelties during his travels in Europe, but they seem to be taken entirely out of context. This recipe is a good example.

A Made Dish of Parmyzant [Parmigiano]

Take a Grater, and grate half a pound of Parmyzant, then grate as much manchet, and mince some Tarragon together with Horse Raddish; season this with almost a handful of Caraway Comfits; put to it a little brisk Claret-wine to moisten it over, then dish it in a small dish, from the middle to the brim, in parcells as broad as your knife; garnish it with Carraway Comfits, Horse-Raddish and Tarragon; send it up the last dish of your mess or messes, with Mustard and Sugar; because at a Feast it is not common to send up a whole Cheese.[57]

This next recipe is a good example of how new ingredients were appropriated in traditional, and in this case seemingly medieval, recipes and garnished with a strange mixture of local and exotic items. The spices, dates, raisins and orange as well as the "sack" or sherry wine were expensive imports, the latter used in the "lear" or sauce. Eryngoes are the roots of the sea holly that were often candied. Cittern is Rabisha's odd way of spelling citron, in this case candied peel, as is the orangado.

To Make a Potato Pie

Boyl your Spanish Potatoes (not overmuch) cut them forth in slices as thick as your thumb, season them with Nutmeg, Cinamon, Ginger, and Sugar; your Coffin being ready, put them in, over the bottom; add to them the Marrow of about three Marrow-bones, seasoned as aforesaid, a handful of stoned Raisons of the Sun, some quartered Dates, Orangado, Cittern, with Ringo-roots sliced, put butter over it, and bake them: let their lear be a little Vinegar, Sack and Sugar, beaten up with the yolk of an Egg, and a little drawn butter; when your pie is enough, pour it in, shake it together, scrape on Sugar, garnish it, and serve it up.[58]

Among the most colorful and eccentric of figures of the seventeenth century is Sir Kenelm Digby who was astrologer and alchemist to the late King Charles. His life is a brilliant reflection of the fate of courtiers, in this case Catholic, during this period. He was educated at Oxford, traveled throughout Europe, was secretly married and according to rumor later poisoned his wife, did some privateering in the Mediterranean, and was banished several times during the interregnum. *The Closet of the Eminently Learned Sir Kenelme Digbie Opened,* published posthumously in 1669, was his contribution to culinary literature, assembled from his notebooks containing recipes collected from throughout his life and travels. "Closet" in the title refers to a private space rather than a place to keep clothes. A good portion of the work contains recipes for mead and metheglin, spiced alcoholic drinks made from honey. Many of the recipes are also medicinal, and usually attributed to some noble personality, which would have lent them credibility or at least clout. An ingenious recipe from Italy for boiled capon shows not only his continental taste but also his alchemical understanding of cooking procedures. The slow cooking of the flesh is likened to distillation and fermentation, which scientists were just then suggesting as part of the digestive process. The capon would have then been pre-digested in a sense, making it more nourishing. It can either be cooked sealed in a bladder or in a covered flagon or pitcher set in a boiling water bath, which is basically a *bain-marie,* itself an alchemical procedure.[59]

The next major cookbook author in England was Hannah Wolley (or Woolley, as it was spelled in the book discussed below), apparently the first female to earn a living writing cookbooks in England. With such titles as *The Cooks Guide* and *The Queen-like Closet,* she was one of the most prolific authors in this genre of ladies household manuals. Her books also targeted gentry and merchant households rather than the professional cook like May's, so they offer a glimpse of life among social aspirants rather than the old nobility. *Gentlewoman's Companion, or, A Guide to the Female Sex* appeared in 1673, and although her authorship is disputed, it is a conduct book that describes more explicitly than most, exactly what the duties and character of the ideal woman should be. These included cooking, distilling, preparing medicines, making clothes—obviously all domestic tasks associated with the family. The sections on cookery, seem to be largely paraphrased from Robert May which suggests that her readers wanted to imitate their social superiors, and had the means to do it. The author did not automatically approve of courtly fashions, but here the appearance of rare ingredients and lengthy procedures implies that these did not seem incongruous in a book for households of middling wealth.

Though it is also possible that this book was merely thrown together by a publisher who happened to take whatever recipes he had at hand rather than those particularly suited for its audience.

This simple stew recipe would certainly be within the means of most households, but does contain expensive spices. "A la Mode" implies that this dish is fashionably French, the larding, use of wine and absence of sugar being imported techniques.

Beef a-la-Mode

Cut some Buttock-beef a quarter of an inch thick, and lard it with Bacon, having hackt it before a little with the back of you Knife, then stew it in a Pipkin with some gravy, Claret-wine, and strong Broth. Cloves, Mace, Pepper, Cinnamon and Salt; being tender stewed, serve it on French-bread sippets.[60]

Marmalades and jellies such as this one are found in cookbooks across Europe and throughout the entire early modern period. Wolley's version is fairly simple, and knowing how to make it would certainly have been required of any self-respecting woman running a household, although aristocratic women would probably have had servants do the dirty work.

Quince Marmelade

Take of the fairest Quinces, wash them very clean, grate them very small, and wring out as much juice as you can; then take other Quinces and cut them into six pieces, put them into a pot, let them be evapoured with hot water, until they be thoroughly mellow; then take half a pot full of the former juice, and pour it on the former, stew'd and cut to pieces; break it well together, and put the rest of the juice amongst it, then wring through a clean cloth; seeth no more of this juice at once than will fill a box therewith, and put white sugar to it, as much as you please.[61]

No discussion of cuisine in England would be complete without mentioning *Acetaria, A Discourse on Sallets* written by John Evelyn and published in 1699. Evelyn, best known for his diary and treatises on gardening and architecture, wrote this work after years of practical experience growing and preparing vegetables. But as a scholar and fellow of the Royal Society, Evelyn felt obligated to compose a learned discourse replete with classical quotations. This description of beets gives an impression of the broad range of his knowledge as well as a flavor of what scholars were writing about humble vegetables in the late seventeenth century. The Epigrammatist is the ancient Roman Pliny, Diphilus (of Siphnis) a Greek nutritional theorist, and Martial a Roman poet. *Oluscula* refers to tiny salad greens; the Pliny quote means "less harmful than other vegetables and *fabrorum prandia* means a workingman's meal. Note that in his description of how to serve beets there is no sugar. It had by this time been increasingly relegated to sweet desserts at the end of the meal, just as in France.

Beets

Beet, Beta; of which there is both red, black, and white: the costa or rib of the white beet (by the French call'd the chard) being boil'd melts, and eats like marrow. And the roots (epecially of the red) cut into thin slices, boil'd, when cold, is of itself a grateful winter sallet; or being mingl'd with other *oluscula*, oyl, vinegar, salt, &c. 'Tis of quality cold and moist, and naturally somewhat laxative: but by the Epigrammatist stil'd foolish and insipid, as *innocentior quam olus* (for so the learned Harduin reads the place) 'tis by Diphilus of old, and others since, preferr'd before cabbage as of better nourishment: Martial (not unlearn'd in the art of sallet) commends it with wine and pepper: he names it indeed—*fabrorum prandia*, for its being so vulgar. But eaten with oyl and vinegar, as usually, it is no despicable sallet. There is a beet growing near the sea, which is the most delicate of all. The roots of the red beet, pared into thin slices and circles are by the French and Italians contriv'd into curious figures to adorn their sallets.[62]

During the latter seventeenth century England was ruled by the descendants of Charles. There was however one major succession crisis over his son James, a Catholic, who although he was crowned was soon deposed in an episode known as the Glorious Revolution in 1688. His Protestant daughter, Mary, and her husband William of Orange, ruler of the Netherlands, then became joint rulers, and it was made completely clear that they were invited by Parliament, which was increasingly becoming the sovereign body of the nation. At the very end of the seventeenth century James' other daughter Anne became queen. Despite the fact that England was becoming a constitutional monarchy, the allure of the court was nonetheless still very strong in this period. As chef to each of these rulers in succession, Patrick Lamb is better qualified than anyone to tell us how these monarchs dined. His *Royal-Cookery: Or, the Compleat Court–Cook* of 1710, reissued in an expanded version in 1716, records recipes served at court during the preceding 50 years. More than merely a lavish, illustrated courtly cookbook, Lamb also testifies to the impact French culinary techniques and tastes had on England. Most importantly, Lamb used stocks and *fonds,* or cooking bases, that took hours to prepare and would require a huge staff. His recipe for an Olio, a descendant of the Spanish Olla Podrida, begins with making a beef broth at 6:00 in the morning. In an incredibly complex, four-page recipe, Lamb reveals exactly how this giant cone of veal, mutton, pork, vegetables and fowl is arranged. Clearly the emphasis on ostentatious presentation and complex procedures has come into fashion just as it had in early-eighteenth-century France.

The following recipe illustrates exactly how much time and effort went into composing a single dish, which would have been just one of a few dozen prepared for a state dinner. It is also a good example of how elegant little units of food that can be easily served have replaced large whole animals carved up at the table. Note that a fork and knife have now become indispensable, and the chef is no longer working before an open hearth but a stovetop. The recipe also requires the previous preparation of two others, a *ragoo,* which is vegetables or meat cooked in a *cullis,* which is basically a thick rich stock made of roasted meat and vegetables pounded in mortar, cooked in broth and then passed through a sieve. A farce means a stuffing here. Sweetbreads are the thymus gland or pancreas, usually of a calf.

Beef-Steakes Rowl'd

Take, for Example, three or four large Steaks of Beef, according to the size of your Dish, and flat them on a Table with your Cleaver. Make a Farce with Capon's Flesh, a Piece of a Filet of Veal, some of the Fat and Lean of a boil'd Gammon of Bacon, and the Fat of a Loin of Veal, Parsly and young Onions, Sweet-breads, Truffles and Mushrooms, the Yolks of four Eggs, and a little Cream; when all this is well season'd with Spice and Herbs and hash'd very small, lay it on your slices of Beef, which you must then rowl up very handsomely, so that they may be firm and good Size. Then put them a stewing, and let them stew a good while. When you think they are enough, take them up, drain off the Fat, slit them in two, and lay them in the Dish, the cut Side uppermost. You may put to them some Ragoo or other; or only a good Cullis if you think fit.[63]

There were a few more courtly cookbooks produced in the early eighteenth century. Charles Carter's *The Complete Practical Cook: Or, A New System of the Whole Art and Mystery of Cookery* published in 1730 is the last of these. Although it does reflect some of the latest technical innovations imported from the continent such as reduced stocks, one can not help but feel that this way of cooking has become over-refined, too fussy and garnished with all sort of incongruous ingredients. Many of the dishes are disguised or colored with saffron or cochineal. Many of them have preposterous names badly translated from French like Rockampuff with Capon, Attletoon of Livers. A few really are foreign dishes like Kibbob of Lamb. But as in France, this style had worn itself out and lost the original focus and direction. Instead of preparations meant to intensify the main ingredient, we have lemons and spinach strewn everywhere, odd concoctions of starch, vegetable and meat set in what must have been very elegant-looking presentations but ultimately confusing to the palate. Like all styles, this type of cooking was beginning to burn out. This recipe is a good example of Carter's desperate attempt to present something new and exotic. Sago is a starch extracted from palm trees in southeast Asia, and would have been used in Europe in the form of small starch pellets like tapioca. It was considered quite elegant because of its origin. Another version of this recipe uses "Vermajelly" (vermicelli noodles). The end product is a strange thick soup with manchet bread beneath and common English birds along with exotic garnishes.

Pottage of Sagoe with Squabs

First take some Spinach, Sorrel, Lettice, Purslane, and green Onions; mince them, and pass them in brown Butter thicken'd; put to it half Broth and half Gravy; stove in it three Ounces of Sagoe, and stove in it likewise your Squab-Pigeons; you may put in Eight, or a Dozen if small; dice in a Sweetbread or two, and a few small Forc'd-meat Balls; then stove up an Ounce of Sagoe in good gravy till thick; stove French manchet dry'd in Gravy, and put in the Bottom of your dish; put in your Pottage, lay in your squabs, and lay the thick Sagoe up and down in Spoonfulls; garnish with scalded Spinach, Forc'd-meat, and sliced Lemon, and serve it away hot.[64]

This kind of courtly cooking did not ultimately prevail in England after the 1730s, and this is partly due to the lack of a proper court. For the rest of the eighteenth century England was ruled by German kings of the Hanover dynasty. The first of these, George I was largely absent from the kingdom and in these years the country was mainly run by ministers, particularly of the Whig party. This meant that the court virtually disappeared, and this may partially explain why eighteenth-century culinary literature is heavily geared toward the country house and the city town house, rather than the palace. These were the new centers of power and cookbooks were increasingly written for aristocratic and gentry women managing their country estates. Significantly, recipes become simpler and homier, and French fashions are looked upon with disdain.

The cookbooks produced in eighteenth-century England all borrowed from each other extensively, and sorting out where a recipe first appeared has become a minor sleuthing industry. Without trying to recount such things, a few examples of what this cooking looked like should suffice. E. Smith's *The Compleat Housewife* of 1727 was one of the more popular and successful of this generation of cookbooks. It is also eminently practical, explaining procedures assuming no prior knowledge. It also contains an extensive section on home remedies. It is clear that Smith herself had abundant experience, and hoped to pass it on to her female readers, perhaps new brides first managing a household. Her cookbook is sort of like *The Joy of Cooking* of the eighteenth century. It also contains most of the quintessential eighteenth-century favorites: dozens of fruit preserves, bizarre creamy alcohol drinks like syllabubs, possets, caudles and flummery, puddings and pies and countless pickles. The recipes offered by Smith are also straightforward, simple and use mostly local ingredients prepared without a lot of fuss. Incidentally, hers was the first cookbook printed in the American colonies, in Williamsburg in 1742. This goose recipe is a good example of her attitude toward food.

To Roast a Goose

Take a little sage, and a small onion chopt small, some pepper and salt, and a bit of butter; mix these together, and put it into the belly of the goose. Then spit it, singe it with a bit of white paper, drudge it with a little flour, and baste it with butter. When it is done, which may be known by the leg being tender, take it up, and pour thro' it two glasses of red wine, and serve it up in the same dish, and apple sauce in a bason.[65]

The eighteenth-century fascination with creamy drinks can perhaps only be explained by reference to the ingredients themselves. They are not rare or exotic, but are often either colonial or betray some important British trade connection. In other words, they seem to embody the growing power of the British Empire, especially now that ordinary housewives can purchase sugar from the West Indies, nutmeg from the Spice Islands, lemons and sherry from Spain. The British housewife is apparently no longer aware that these were once rare and costly ingredients available to only the wealthiest consumers. This syllabub recipe, one of dozens, is something like a cross between an eggnog and a creamy dessert floating on wine, in this case German white wine mixed with Spanish Sherry.

To Make Very Fine Syllabubs

Take a quart and a half a pint of cream, a pint of rhenish, half a pint of sack, three lemons, and near a pound of double refined sugar; beat and sift the sugar, and put it to your cream; grate off the yellow rind of your three lemons, and put that in; squeeze the juice of your three lemons into your wine, and put that to your cream, then beat all together with a whisk just half an hour; then take it up all together with a spoon, and fill your glasses; it will keep good nine or ten days, and is best three or four days old; these are call'd everlasting Syllabubs.[66]

Without doubt the most popular cookbook of the mid-eighteenth century, in Britain as well as the American colonies, was Hannah Glasse's *The Art of Cookery Made Plain and Easy* which first appeared in London in 1747 and remained in print through the following century. Glasse is notorious for her denunciation of fancy French kickshaws (a corruption of quelquechoses, mentioned above), but in fact does betray some continental influence. Her advice is, moreover, much like Smith's, honest, straightforward and eminently practical, though like the former making use of new American ingredients like chocolate and even tomatoes. One is tempted to think that this recipe was inspired by the cooking of India, which was also just then being brought into the Empire, and she does have a recipe for curry but this one probably came from Morocco. In either case, appreciation for such flavors was on the rise.

To Pickle Lemons

Take twelve lemons, scrape them with a piece of broken glass, then cut them across in two, four parts downright, but none quite through, but that they will hang together; put in as much salt as they will hold, rub them well, and strew them over with salt. Let them lie in an earthen dish three days, and turn them everyday; slit an ounce of ginger very thin, and salted for three days a small handful of mustard seeds bruised and searced through a hair sieve, and some red Indian pepper; take your lemons out of the salt, squeeze them very gently, put them into a jar with the spice and ingredients and cover them with the best white wine vinegar. Stop them up very close, and in a month's time they will be fit to eat.[67]

The British Housewife, a massive compilation of recipes and household advice by Martha Bradley, appeared in 1756, probably first in serial format in magazines before being sold bound in two volumes. Like Smith and Glasse, this book purports to be a complete guide to the duties of a country housewife, including a veritable cooking course progressing from simple basics to more elegant and complicated dishes. But here the text implies that many of these tasks would be delegated to household servants. Presumably the wealthy housewife now has other more diverting activities to spend her day pursuing while the servants put up pickles and fix dinner. This is more a guide to increasing household efficiency by properly instructing servants, than a how-to manual for hardworking housewives. By the end it is also clear that the targeted reader may well be the aspiring servant herself who hopes to make it as a professional chef.

The recipes themselves are for the most part unoriginal, and most have been traced back to earlier sources. But Bradley apparently liberally

Figure 4.5 Frontispiece from Martha Bradley's *The British housewife: or the cook, housekeeper's, and gardiner's companion. Calculated for the service both of London and the country: and directing what is necessary to be done in the providing for, conducting, and managing a family throughout the year.* London: Printed for S. Crowder and H. Woodgate, [1770?]. EPB 15140/B. Courtesy of Wellcome Library, London.

changed the recipes she included, clarifying the language, or substituting ingredients or procedures. Her changes usually reflect her own preference for simpler dishes without elaborate garnishes or soaked with ragoos, which in fact reflects the "nouvelle cuisine" of French authors of the 1730s. If we are to judge from the lack of commercial success of this book, the English never enthusiastically adopted the new style. The mutton recipe is certainly a concession to basic English tastes, but does, interestingly, encourage innovation and experimentation. It is also only slightly fancied up with garnishes.

To Hash Mutton

There is not any thing in which the Cook may so much indulge her Fancy as in a Hash; for almost any Thing may be put into it: But we shall lay down an easy and rich Method. Make a half Pint of good Gravy, put this into a Sauce-pan, and cut the Meat into very thin slices and put into it, first strewing over it a little Flour, and at the same time put in a piece of Butter rolled in Flour, set this upon a slow Fire, then cut a Shallot fine, and chop a few Capers and a couple of Girkin Cucumbers, and one blade of Mace; when the Flesh has stewed a little, put in these, shake them about, and let it do a little more; then put in a spoonful of Walnut Liquor and Half a glass of red Port Wine, shake all together over the Fire, and let it stew a very little longer: When it is done lay some toasted Sippets in a Dish and pour it in.[68]

THE NETHERLANDS

At the start of the early modern period the Netherlands encompassed what is today the nations of Belgium in the south and the Republic of the Netherlands in the north, which includes the province of Holland. This had long been a wealthy, heavily urbanized area facing the sea, from which it drew sustenance and on which it traded extensively with the rest of Europe. The Rhine River, as well as numerous waterways cross the region allowing internal and international trade. Because land was relatively scarce, and at a premium, the Dutch were required to practice intensive agriculture, both market gardening and dairy farming to feed their large population. They even went so far as to reclaim land from the sea by draining flat marshes and holding back the water with extensive systems of dikes. The Netherlands also never had a powerful landed nobility, so buying and selling land was comparatively free, which meant that innovations were more easily adopted than elsewhere. It is not surprising that farmers chose to grow expensive fruits and vegetables rather than cheap grain which was largely imported from the Baltic region.

Antwerp, the most important city in the south, was also one of the major financial capitals of Europe, taking over that role from Bruges and Ghent after the Schelt River silted up in the late Middle Ages. One could borrow money there, buy wines made in Portugal, wool from Spain, spices brought by the Venetians from Asia, as well as products from throughout Germany. In other words, Antwerp was the great *entrepôt,* or storage hub, for goods traded across most of Europe.

In the late Middle Ages, the region, although enjoying relative autonomy, was officially ruled by the Dukes of Burgundy. But when Burgundy was engulfed by the kingdom of France, and then Charles V, heir to the dukedom became king of Spain, the Netherlands became a possession of the Spanish crown. This was no problem, especially because Charles, being born in the Netherlands, never attempted to impose Spanish administrators or burdensome taxes on the people. It was, nonetheless, financially extremely rewarding for Spain to control the region. Its own products were sold there, and it could levy customs on the products of every other nation. It is no surprise then, that when this region rose in revolt, the Spanish did everything they could to hold on to it.

But they also had motives other than financial. The Netherlands by the mid-sixteenth century had a large proportion of Protestants, specifically following Calvinist doctrines. When Philip II of Spain attempted to enforce religious orthodoxy on the people, they reacted with violence. The revolt was thus partially religiously motivated, as much as it was a war of independence. Interestingly, it was circumstances similar to our own War of Independence that the Dutch faced: arbitrary taxation by a faraway king and lack of a representative body in which to express their grievances.

In the latter 1560s full-scale war broke out, even though Philip was chronically short of money to pay his troops. In 1576 the situation became so grave that Spanish troops mutinied and pillaged Antwerp, an attack from which it never recovered. Although the conflict continued, dragging in the English and French, in the end the region was divided between a Catholic Spanish Netherlands in the south and the Protestant United Provinces of the Netherlands in the north. The war actually continued well into the next century, and the north was not officially recognized by the Spanish until 1648.

In the mean time, Amsterdam in the north took over the role formerly enjoyed by Antwerp. By the latter seventeenth century it had grown to be the wealthiest city in Europe. There are several reasons for this. Without a king or formal court, the Dutch were basically ruled by rich merchants. This meant that the extravagant royal lifestyle, funded by exorbitant taxes, was absent here. The merchants were more inclined to make laws favoring their own mercantile interests. Which made them extremely wealthy, embarrassingly so for a people whose religion favored simplicity and the Protestant work ethic. They were therefore, more inclined to invest rather than spend their savings on superfluous luxuries. The result is that Dutch cuisine is very simple.

It was also in this period that the Dutch embarked on their efforts to build an overseas empire, in which they succeeded by forcefully stealing colonies from other nations following the principles of mercantilism. Their most important acquisitions were the spice islands in what is now Indonesia, South Africa, a nice chunk of North America around New York and New Jersey, and a few islands in the Caribbean, and some of the mainland.

Though they held on to most of these regions into the eighteenth century and maintained their monopoly of the spice trade, the Netherlands witnessed a period of relative decline after the golden age of the seventeenth century. While the decline in the popularity of spices among the elite probably had little to do with this, ordinary people continued to use them, the great volume being imported probably brought their cost down significantly. Probably more important was the refocusing of the global economy toward cheap manufactured goods, which the English began to produce in great quantities. In other words, as England was gearing up for the industrial revolution, the great mercantile ways of doing business were gradually becoming outdated.

The cuisine of the Netherlands remained simple and straightforward, despite their enormous wealth. The earliest cookbook was published in Brussels around 1508. It is called *Een notabel Boecxhen van Cokeryen* (Notable Book of Cookery. Brussels: Thomas van der Noot, n.d. but c. 1508 or later). It is, just like most cookbooks of this time, still largely medieval with recipes for *bruwets* (broths) and *blancmangers,* jellies, pastries and various spiced and colored dishes. But there is also, as might be expected, an unusual emphasis on fish. This blancmanger, which is usually made with capon, may be an adaptation for Netherlandish cooks.

Blancmange of Fish

To make blancmange all fish like snoek (pike) or trout or other fish there will serve if you need blancmange. Put these fish to bake or fry in lard or butter.

Then take almonds and take off the shells and mix them with puree of peas and with white wine and pass it through a sieve. Then take white ginger and mix that with verjuice and sugar enough so that it's not sour in taste. Then set the blancmange alone in its own clean pot until you serve the fish, then after you pour this over the fish.[69]

The most popular and exemplary Dutch cookbook of this era is *De Verstandige Kock* (The Sensible Cook) first published in 1667. Its author is not known, though it was part of a larger work called *The Pleasurable Country Life* which included sections on gardening, medicine, bee-keeping and related topics, all by identified authors. Its readers appear to have been wealthy city folk who either tended their own small gardens at their country getaways or those who liked to read about farming. The book reveals that even at this level of wealth, the Dutch diet was quite frugal and consisted primarily of bread (rye or wheat), cheese and butter supplemented with a wide variety of vegetables, fish (especially pickled and green herring) and some meat as in the famous *hutspot,* a slowly simmered stew. Baked goods like cookies (itself a Dutch word, *koekjes*), waffles, pancakes and *olie-koecken* (a kind of donut) are also prominently featured. The Dutch also held on longer to spices, which is not surprising since they had monopolized the spice trade by this time. Sugar also, most of it refined in Amsterdam, remained a prominent ingredient.

This recipe uses a vegetable that was commonly cultivated on intensively sown Dutch farms and justly praises dairy butter as well as spices brought by Dutch merchants.

To Stew Cauliflower and Savoy Cabbage

One takes Cauliflower or Savoy cabbage after it has been cleaned and cooked until well done and stew it with Mutton-broth, whole Pepper, Nutmeg, Salt, without forgetting the excellent Butter of Holland. A hardboiled egg yolk which has been rubbed fine is sometimes placed underneath.[70]

Pancakes were a food enjoyed at all levels of society and this simple recipe shows the care tendered them by the Dutch. They were also always eaten on Shrove Tuesday or Pancake Day.

To Fry the Best Kind of Pancakes

Take 5 or 6 Eggs beaten with clean, running water, add to it Cloves, Cinnamon, Mace, and Nutmeg with some salt, beat it with some wheat flour as thick as you like, fry them and sprinkle them with Sugar; these are prepared with running water because [when prepared] with Milk or Cream they would be tough.[71]

GERMANY

The regions which now comprise Germany are geographically extremely varied. To the north and facing the Baltic fish played a prominent role in the diet, as well as dairy farming and cultivation of rye. In the center there were many forests and hills, and consequently pork was more important, as pigs were often let loose to forage in the wild. In the south the terrain becomes Alpine. Despite these differences, a number of foods were common to the entire region and uniquely German: sauerkraut, smoked hams and sausages, roast meats (*braten*), goose and duck. Dumplings were also very important, but extensive use of potatoes in these and other dishes dates only to the end of the early modern period. The principal beverage was of course beer, and in fact the purity laws of the early sixteenth century are still in effect. Almost all foreign visitors remarked on two things: the large amount of meat in the diet, and the German's inordinate fondness for beer. For reasons that are not entirely clear Germany held on to medieval sweet and sour flavor combinations and cooking fruit with meat, longer than any other people.

Speaking of Germany in the early modern period is however a misnomer. There was no nation of Germany until 1871. Instead the entire area was gathered into a loose federation of autonomous political units known as the Holy Roman Empire. Through the early modern period the emperors were always drawn from the Habsburg family, whose inherited seat of power was Austria. The emperor was also an elected position. The leading powers, either cities, dukedoms, or even bishoprics acted as electors. These were the real powers in Germany: the duke of Saxony, the margrave of Brandenburg and the count palatine of the Rhine, the bishops of Mainz, Trier and Cologne and the king of Bohemia. Later Bavaria was added and after that Hanover. After the religious wars in the sixteenth century, each ruler was also free to choose the religion of his domains, the north and east being mostly Lutheran and the south and west largely Catholic. The religious question was not settled though until after a devastating series of wars (Thirty Years' War from 1614–1648) that involved nearly all of Europe and wrought havoc on the German economy and its people.

Through the early modern period the smaller courts, as well as the emperor in Vienna, and later the king of Prussia, presided over courts resembling those elsewhere in Europe. In the late seventeenth century they willingly imitated the French, building their own copies of the palace at Versailles, using the French language and adopting the

French absolutist system of government. Not surprisingly they also hired French chefs. So to get a glimpse of native German cuisine, one must look to the thriving and independent cities. It was here that a prosperous burgher culture, literate and proud of its cuisine, patronized German cookbooks.

Germany, after all, was the birthplace of the printing press, and since Lutheranism stressed reading the Bible in the vernacular, the literacy rate was exceptionally high. It is not surprising then to find cookbooks catering to this sophisticated urban audience. The earliest of these was the *Kuchenmeisterei* first published in 1485, which was reprinted many times up into the sixteenth century. There also appeared other early anonymous cookbooks: *Ain nützlichs Buchlin von der Speis der Menschen* c. 1500; *Koch und Kellerey, von allen Speisen unnd Getrancken*, Frankfurt 1545; *Ain sehr Künstlichs und Fürtrefflichs Kochbuch von allerlay Speysen*, Augsburg 1559.

Among these early works is also the manuscript cookbook of Sabina (or Sabrina) Welserin, written in Augsburg in 1553. It is the first cookbook written by a woman, and gives a good impression of ordinary middle class and distinctively German cooking, although the author did include some foreign dishes like ravioli. This recipe for pickled tongue, however, involves a typically German way of curing meats.

Pickled Tongue

If you would make good pickled tongue. They are best made in January, then they will keep the whole year. First take twenty five tongues or as many as you will and take them one after the other and pound them back and front on a chopping block, then they will be long. After that pound salt small and coat the tongues in salt. Take then a good small tub and put salt in the bottom, after that lay a layer of tongues as close together as possible, put more salt on them so that it is entirely white from salt. In this manner always place a layer of tongues, after that a layer of salt, until they are all laid out. Then weigh them down well so that they are covered by the brine and allow them to remain for fifty days, afterwards hang them for four days in smoke. When they have smoked enough, hang them next in the air, then you have good smoked tongue.[72]

Marx Rumpolt's *Ein New Kochbuch* which was published in Frankfurt in 1581 is the most extensive German cookbook of the century. Rumpolt eventually became chef to the queen of Denmark. His book contains thousands of recipes, many of them international, and in format and scope is much like Scappi's work of a few decades before. For most ingredients Rumpolt offers a few dozen recipes, some simple and others more complex. This recipe for stuffed turkey parts in a broth is one of 20 recipes for the bird.

Stuffed Turkey

Disjoint the Turkey, removing the thighs and wings. Stuff each one carefully, and once filled put it in a pot, and let it simmer. Place it on the coals and let them brown, and make a broth with it. It can be sour or sweet. It's good both ways.[73]

German cooking in the seventeenth century began to reflect more regional foodways. The first Austrian cookbook was published, as well as works from other German-speaking regions. Gradually, the Germans fell under the sway of foreign cuisine. Some of the English cookbooks were translated, but at court it was French fashions that dominated. Rulers in Vienna and Berlin came to speak French, modeled their palaces after Versailles, and of course hired French chefs. Among ordinary people German cuisine naturally survived and finally blossomed in the era of national revival in the nineteenth century when German culture in general was once again highly valued.

NOTES

1. Antonio Cocchi, *Del vitto pitagorico* (Florence: Francesco Moücke, 1743), 723.

2. Petronio, 57 and 196.

3. Christoforo di Messisbugo, *Banchetti* (Ferrara, Italy: Giovanni de Buglhat and Antonio Hucher, 1549), 40v.

4. Messisbugo, 107.

5. Messisbugo, 71v.

6. Romoli, 133.

7. Alberto Cappatti and Massimo Montanari, *La cucina italiana* (Rome and Bari: Laterza, 1999), 16–20.

8. Bartolomeo Scappi, *Opera* (Venice: Alessandro Vecchi, 1610), 14v (mispaginated).

9. Scappi, 53v.

10. Stefani, 54.

11. Stefani, 32.

12. Latini, 27.

13. Latini, 135.

14. Latini, 444.

15. Francesco Gaudentio, *Il Panunto Toscano,* ed. Guido Gianni (Rome: Trevi Editore, 1974), 60.

16. Vincenzo Corrado, *Il cuoco galante*, facsimile (Bologna, Italy: Arnaldo Forni Editore, 1990), 75.

17. Corrado, 146.

18. Rupert of Nola, *Lybre de doctrina pera ben servir*, #63. Online at http://www.cervantesvirtual.com/servlet/SirveObras/bc/168080675986 732751765222.

19. Lobera, xli.

20. Lobera, lxviii.

21. Diego Granado, *Libro del arte de cocina*, reprint (Madrid: Sociedad de Bibliófilos Espanoles, 1971), 87.

22. Granado, 44.

23. Granado, 77–78.

24. Granado, 184–185.

25. Domingo Hernández de Maceras, *Libro del arte de cozina*, facsimile (Salamanca, Spain: Ediciones Universidad de Salamanca, 1999), 73. See also Manuel Martínez Llopis, *Historia de la gastronomia Española* (Madrid: Editoria Nacional, 1981).

26. Maceras, 85–86.

27. Maceras, 55.

28. Scappi, 46.

29. Francisco Martínez Montiño, *Arte de cocina* (Barcelona: Juan Fransisco Piferrer for Juan Sellent, n.d.), 276.

30. Montiño, 202.

31. Juan Altamiras, *Nuevo arte de cocina* (Barcelona: Maria Angela Martí Viuda, 1767), 12.

32. Lancelot de Casteau, *Ouverture de Cuisine*, reprint (Antwerp: De Schutter, 1983), 84 (mispaginated 94).

33. François Pierre La Varenne, *The French Cook*, tr. I.D.G. (Lewes, England: Southover Press, 2001), 42.

34. François Pierre La Varenne, *Le cuisinier françois*, ed. Jean-Louis Flandrin and Philip and Mary Hyman (Paris: Montalba, 1983), 236.

35. La Varenne, 272.

36. Pierre de Lune, *Le cuisinier*, in *L'art de la cuisine française au XVIIe siècle* (Paris: Payot and Rivages, 1995), 249.

37. de Lune, 293.

38. L.S.R., *L'art de bien traiter*, in *L'art de la cuisine française au XVIIe siècle* (Paris: Payot and Rivages, 1995), 21.

39. L.S.R., 46.

40. Massialot, *Le nouveau cuisinier royal et bourgeois* (Paris: Claude Prudhomme, 1708), 232. Available online at http://www.bib.ub.es/grewe/show book.pl?gw037.

41. Massialot, 177.

42. François Marin, *Les Dons de Comus* (Paris: Pissot, 1758), v.

43. Marin, xxii; see also Rachel Laudan, "A Kind of Chemistry," in *Petits Propos Culinaires*, 1999.

44. Marin, 257–258.

45. Menon, 171.

46. *Boke of Kervynge* in *Early English Meals and Manners,* ed. Frederick J. Furnivall (London: Early English Text Society, 1868), 36.

47. *A proper Newe Booke of Cokerye,* ed. Jane Hugget (Bristol, England: Stuart Press, 1995), 10.

48. *A proper Newe,* 8.

49. *The Good Huswifes Handmaide for the Kitchin,* ed. Stuart Peachy (Bristol, England: Stuart Press, 1992), 27.

50. Dawson, 10.

51. Dawson, 45.

52. John Murrell, *A Newe Booke of Cookery* (London: John Brown, 1615). Online at http://staff-www.uni-marburg.de/~gloning/1615murr.htm.

53. Murrell.

54. Markham, *The English Housewife,* reprint ed. Michael R. Best (Montreal and Kingston: McGill-Queen's University Press, 1986), 70.

55. Robert May, *The Accomplisht Cook,* facsimile (Totnes, Devon: Prospect Books, 2000), 212.

56. May, 426.

57. William Rabisha, *The Whole Body of Cookery Dissected* (London: R.W. for Giles Calvert, 1661), 97.

58. Rabisha, 150.

59. Digby, 127.

60. Hannah Woolley, *The Gentlewomans Companion,* reprint with introduction by Caterina Albano (Totnes, Devon: Prospect Books, 2001), 146.

61. Woolley, 194.

62. Evelyn, 19.

63. Patrick Lamb, *Royal-Cookery: or the Compleat Court-Cook* (London: J. Nutt and A. Roper, 1716), 16. See also Ragoo, 220, and Cullis for Ragoo, 59.

64. Charles Carter, *The Complete Practical Cook : Or a New System of the Whole Art and Mystery of Cookery,* facsimile (London: Prospect Books, 1984), 19.

65. E. Smith, 22.

66. E. Smith, 198.

67. Glasse, 152.

68. Martha Bradley, *The British Housewife,* facsimile with introduction by Gilly Lehmann (Totnes, Devon: Prospect Books, 1996), 57.

69. Van der Noot, translated by Andrew Martin from http://www.davidfriedman.com/Medieval/For_Translation/Het_Eerste_Nederlandsche/Het_Eerste_Nederlandsche02.html.

70. *The Sensible Cook,* 48.

71. *The Sensible Cook,* 76.

72. Sabina Welserin, tr. Valoise Armstrong, #27. Available online at http://www.best.com/~ddfr/Medieval/Cookbooks/Sabrina_Welserin.html.

73. Marx Rumpolt, *Ein new Kochbuch* (Frankfurt a.M., 1581) R66A Online at http://staff-www.uni-marburg.de/~gloning/kobu.htm.

CHAPTER 5

RELIGION AND FOOD

THE MEDIEVAL INHERITANCE

At the start of the early modern period there was one universal Catholic Church to whom all faithful Christians in western Europe looked for guidance. At the head of the church, the pope claimed absolute authority over a huge ecclesiastical hierarchy that extended down through the bishops to every last parish priest. Only in matters of holy doctrine did the pope call ecumenical councils before promulgating dogma. What this meant is that all western Europeans were expected to observe the same food strictures dictated by the church, partake in the same sacraments and observe the same holy feasts.

The Pope's claim to absolute authority was mitigated by the fact that many kings appointed their own bishops and many holy orders operated in virtual autonomy. The power and prestige of the papacy had also waned considerably in late medieval times. Nonetheless the pope could claim to preside over a huge Christian community of believers, and he had the power to see that those who strayed from the prescribed form of worship and orthodox belief would be punished.

Regarding religious food customs and attitudes toward food, there were several important features that early modern Europeans inherited from their medieval forebears. The most important of these was the Mass in which the Eucharist was celebrated, or the taking of bread and wine as commanded by Jesus during the Last Supper. Although Jesus' intentions were not entirely clear, later Christians interpreted his comments that when eating the bread "this is my body" and when drinking the wine "this is my blood" in a very literal sense. At the Fourth Lateran Council of 1215 it was decided that the real presence of Christ in the bread and wine could be understood by reference to a doctrine known as transubstantiation. In the miracle, they contended, the host, or at least its "substance" actually transforms into the body of Christ even though its "accidents" or external form still appears to be bread. By tradition wine was only consumed by the priests during the ritual rather than the whole congregation.

By consuming the body of Christ, it was believed that the communicant would gain merit and would be infused with grace, which is essentially the power of pardon given by Jesus to parishioners absolving them of their sins and ultimately contributing to their salvation. Thus participating in the Mass earned one credit and ultimately access to everlasting life. Apart from the self-sacrifice of Jesus himself, no other ritual was considered more instrumental for achieving forgiveness of sins.

There were also other sacraments, or holy rituals, which signaled passages in life from one state of being to another. Baptism initiated the infant into the community of believers and insured that he or she could be saved. Marriage officially recognized passage from single status to that of inseparably bonded. Two other sacraments were ordination, marking the final transition from layman to ritually pure and celibate priest, and extreme unction, the last rites of the dead. Surrounding each of these important life events, there was naturally a celebratory feast. These could range from the raucous peasant affairs depicted in the paintings of Peter Breughel the elder replete with bagpipe players, endless drink and a steady supply of plates brimming with some sort of custard to grand stately ceremonies with dozens of courses, as with the marriage of kings. Although not explicitly religious in nature, it is important to remember that such feasts almost always followed a ritual of great religious significance.

The other occasions at which the average European had a chance to feast were ostensibly religious "holi-days" but they could involve a great deal of irreverence and even violence. Bearing in mind that there were no regular weekends off from work, these holidays, sprinkled throughout the calendar were really the only way Europeans could let off some steam. In most cities, there was an official holiday on the feast of the patron saint of the city or entire nation. For example, Florentines celebrated the feast of St. John the Baptist on June 24, and the Spanish celebrated the Feast of Santiago on July 25. There were also special feast days celebrated everywhere in Europe: All Saint's Day

(November 1), Candlemas (February 2) as well as the moveable feasts like Easter and Whitsuntide which was celebrated on the seventh Sunday after Easter, usually in late May. This was also known as Pentecost, from the Greek word denoting 50 days after Easter. A Whitsun Ale, not a drink but rather a country fair in England with competitions and performances, was another feast day.

Easter, then and now, was associated with eggs, partly as a symbol of the resurrection and rebirth, but also because one was allowed to eat them again following Lent. Lamb was also served at Easter, partly as a commemoration of Jesus, known as the "Lamb of God" sacrificed on the cross, but also coincidentally because this was lambing season. Certain festivals were also associated with particular foods that come into season at that time, like goose on St. Martin's Day (November 11) or the roast pig enjoyed at Bartholomew Fair in England.

Christmas, following the fast of Advent (which means "coming"), was one of the most important feasts, though the customs associated with it varied greatly from country to country. It is nearly impossible to determine when the many food customs associated with Christmas originated: the first Christmas goose or plum pudding in England, black and white *boudins* (sausages) and the *bûche de Noël* or Christmas log cake in France, or the lavish fish dishes served on Christmas Eve in the south of France and Italy. It would not be unreasonable to assume that these are all surviving remnants of premodern practices. We do know that boar's head was a frequent feature, not only from the Christmas carol, but because the hunting season ended at this time, and the last boar was thus accorded special status. On the Feast of the Epiphany (January 6) celebrating the visit of the three Magi to the infant Jesus, a "King Cake" was served, often containing a coin or some bauble that would make the recipient king for the day.

The wildest of the feasts in the Christian calendar was Carnival, whose name derives from *carne* or meat, and was celebrated on Shrove Tuesday or Mardi Gras (Fat Tuesday) and often for several days before as well. This was a riotous orgy of indulgence during which any remaining meat and animal products like butter and cheese had to be consumed prior to the 40-day fast of Lent stretching from Ash Wednesday to Easter. Lent itself commemorated the 40-day fast of Jesus in the desert. Naturally before the fast was a time of incredible indulgence in meat and drink, as well as certain treats like waffles and pancakes doused in butter.

During Carnival all the normal rules of order and subordination were subverted. Women got to boss their husbands around, men got to mock the village priest or lawyers with mock weddings and mock trials. At one point the lowliest person would be crowned king for the day, often the village idiot, and would preside over a Feast of Fools. This was also a time to indulge in other pleasures of the flesh. The revelries usually culminated with a great mock battle between the personification of Carnival, a fat man armed with phallic sausages, charging against Lent, a scrawny woman armed only with a herring, some vegetables and dry bread. Naturally Lent always wins after which the community was reminded that their meaty celebration has come to an end, and the normal modes of behavior are once again in force.

Historians have explained Carnival as a ritual that provides a safety valve for a community that must normally hold in their pent up frustrations against those in power. During this one celebration they need not bow in deference to the lord of the manor or village priest. In fact, exactly the opposite and since the revelers were often masked or disguised they were afforded some anonymity in their mockery. Returning to the normal order of things after the celebrations also reinforced the fact that this is an unusual and one-time occasion, and during the rest of the year everyone has to obey their superiors. In the end, Carnival strengthens the social order and usual patterns of subordination. Unless, of course, the whole occasion passed from mere fun into violent uprising, which is always a possibility in times of great distress.

The other side of the picture, the fast, is an equally important food custom inherited from the Middle Ages. Although not a total fast, all healthy individuals were expected to abstain from all animal flesh and products obtained from animals such as milk, butter or eggs, for the entire period of Lent. They were also technically supposed to eat only one meal a day during Lent. Minor fasts were also scattered throughout the Christian calendar, such as Advent, as well as fasts every Friday, as was instituted by the apostles in commemoration of the day of Jesus' death. In some periods every Wednesday was observed as well. About 150 days of the year in total were set aside as fasting days. People were allowed to eat fish, if they could afford it, and most people could only obtain dry or pickled fish such as stockfish or herring. Beans were also firmly associated with Lent and periods of fast. Vegetables and fruits, and the starchy staples formed the bulk of the Lenten diet. Though this may not seem terribly austere, it was deemed a real sacrifice by most people, especially considering how many fast days were observed.

What began to upset many people was that dispensations could be bought from the church that would allow an individual or even a whole city to disregard some particular detail of the fast. In other words, you could pay the church for the right to eat butter. This of course was a major consideration in northern Europe where they were forced to import olive oil to use as a cooking medium during Lent. Other patent absurdities, such as declaring beaver's tail to be a species of fish and therefore edible during Lent, caused a considerable amount of rancor against the church. This garden variety anticlericalism would be fused to a more substantive theological attack on the church at the start of the Reformation.

Before that, however, there are a few more features of medieval foodways that bear upon this story. Most important is the Christian tradition of asceticism. Unlike the Lenten fasts, these could involve intense austerity, deprivation of all food and drink as well as sleep. The intention was to shed off the distractions of the body, to "mortify the flesh" in an effort to strengthen the soul. To destroy one's body totally was naturally considered suicide, a mortal sin, but to chasten it to the point of death was considered a positive virtue. Historians have speculated that many extremely austere holy men and women actually starved themselves to death after years of abstinence. For young women in holy orders especially, assertion of control over the body and conquering the appetites, was probably the only type of power they were able to exercise in an entirely male dominated world. Their rigorous self-denial has been classified as a species of "holy anorexia" not essentially different from the disorder we know by the name anorexia nervosa today.

Apart from these acts of heroic asceticism, there was also a long tradition of including gluttony among the Seven Deadly Sins along with wrath, pride, avarice, lust, sloth, and envy. Eating too much not only ruins your health, but will earn you eternal damnation, and the punishments meted out to gluttons in hell usually involved some gruesome torture like being stuffed by demons, or being dismembered and eaten. Thus, a religiously inspired type of food guilt was indelibly imprinted on the European consciousness and would manifest itself in later forms of Christianity long after asceticism had fallen from fashion.

Monasticism itself also provided another opportunity for individuals to live and eat in a unique way. In an effort to live as Jesus did in comparative simplicity among brethren and devote one's life to prayer, many men and women turned their backs on the world. Monks and nuns often lived in relatively isolated communities, eating communal meals, and in the most austere of orders, such as the

Carthusians, abstaining from meat altogether. Most monastic orders, sometimes ironically because of vows of personal poverty, became quite wealthy collectively. Individuals could not own expensive baubles, but the monastery as a whole could certainly purchase them. Monasteries and nunneries were also often a refuge for younger sons and daughters of noble families who would not inherit the family estate, or for whom a dowry could not be provided. As pious benefactors, these families often left money to the monastic orders so that the monks could pray for their souls and get them a speedy exit from purgatory, a kind of waiting station for the less than totally devout before entering heaven. This meant that monasteries were often very wealthy, even extensive landowners. They could thus furnish themselves with lavish meals if the occasion required it, and the image of the fat fun-loving monk was firmly imprinted on the popular consciousness. It is not surprising that most religious orders experienced periodic waves of reform in which members would break away and take more austere vows.

One need not become a fully ordained priest to become involved in a monastery, and frequently people would take lay orders or become a minor brother in an order, perhaps serving as a gardener or chef for a monastery. There were also a number of lay confraternities, which operated like holy orders in that they were devoted to prayer and provided communal support for the members, but they included married men. There was also a wide variety of practices among the monastic orders themselves. Some demanded total poverty, such as the Franciscans, while others were more closely connected with learning and the universities, such as the Dominicans.

Last among the features of medieval food culture inherited by the early moderns is heresy. The most dangerous and widespread heresy in the minds of church leaders were the Cathars, centered around Albi in the south of France and spread sporadically throughout Europe. These people were important for the history of food because they believed that the entire universe is divided into the forces of good and evil. The soul, angels and God are of course good forces, while the earth and everything it contains, including food, are evil. The Cathars literally starved themselves to death in hope of being saved. Despite a vicious crusade against the Albigensians, as they were also called, in the reign of Pope Innocent III, pockets of similar beliefs lingered on among heretical cells up to the start of the early modern period, especially among peasants, but sometimes in more organized movements such as the Waldensians.

At the start of the early modern period there was mounting a considerable reaction to what were considered abuses of the medieval church. The failure of priests to live up to their vows of chastity, the sale of church offices, clerical ignorance, and a general failure of the church to meet the spiritual needs of the populace which was largely alienated by rituals in Latin, a language they could not understand. It did not help that a number of questionable individuals occupied the papal throne: the fun-loving Leo X and the warrior Pope Julius II. They may have been great patrons of the arts, but as spiritual leaders they were considered failures. Humanist scholars were also concerned that the church had lost sight of the original intentions of Jesus and his followers, which was moral reform, and had instead begun to focus on the hollow rituals and the letter of the law. But this picture of the church is somewhat simplistic, because on the eve of the Reformation, ordinary people were still making pious benefactions to their local churches, venerating the many relics scattered across Europe and going on pilgrimages. All these were ways to gain merit and earn salvation. So it would be a mistake to see the medieval church and its practices as totally corrupt and doomed to failure.

But the first major break from Roman Catholicism occurred at the start of the early modern period, and is in fact one of the major justifications for considering this a period distinct from the medieval era. It is no less important for the history of food, because along with criticism of the dogma and rituals of the church, its food strictures also came under attack.

THE REFORMATIONS

The Reformation was, first and foremost, an attempt to return to the original doctrines of Paul that stated that an individual can in no way earn his own salvation. The rituals, donations of money and even observing all the moral laws do not somehow gain you points of merit with God that will compel Him to grant you salvation. Justification is by "faith alone" and despite our own personal and inevitable failings, grace is given even to the worst of sinners if there is true faith. These ideas were forcefully articulated by Martin Luther in his 95 theses, which were basically topics posted on the door of the cathedral at Wittenberg University for discussion among theology students. Luther himself had taken holy orders, and found the ascetic rigors he underwent extremely frustrating because he could never be sure when God might be satisfied and when he had done enough to merit salvation.

Paul's doctrines offered him comfort, because they assured him that without any merit whatsoever on his part, he could be saved by faith alone. It was this single idea that hastened the permanent rift in western Christendom. Because if the rituals were not crucial, then of what use are the sacraments, the priesthood, and all the tithes (a tax) paid to the church?

Significantly, Luther was not very concerned with the rituals themselves, nor did he care much about overhauling the entire church government. But his challenge drew the attention of masses of peasants resentful of the power of the church, as well as temporal rulers who would have welcomed any increase in their own power. Ultimately, placing Luther under the protection of German rulers like the elector of Saxony, meant that the Reformation would be carried out by the state, rather than as a grassroots movement. In the end the German Lutheran states broke away from the Roman Catholic Church and abolished monasticism and clerical celibacy. The Mass was also held in German, and the congregation participated directly by singing hymns, many of which Luther composed. But the church government and its rituals remained relatively unchanged. Lutherans retained bishops, and even the Lutheran understanding of the mass retained the idea of the real presence, although Luther himself made a compromise stating that the flesh was really substantively present, but so is bread, a doctrine called consubstantiation.

On the topic of fasting, Luther believed that an individual might choose to fast, and just like all spiritual exercises it can be of use as long as the individual understands that it does not gain you any merit. But the idea that the pope could sell dispensations from fasting, and other "indulgences" was plainly erroneous. Especially since most people could not afford such dispensation and were forced to use oil during Lent with which people in Rome "would not grease their shoes. But they sell us permission to eat butter and other things in spite of the holy apostle who says that the gospel gives us complete freedom to do everything."[1] Luther was right, early Christians had no food prohibitions at all, considering that it is not what goes into the mouth but what comes out, that is evil words, that defiles a man. But in his mind "They think that eating butter is a greater sin than lying, swearing or committing fornication." In the end fasting among Lutherans was no longer officially enforced, but individuals were nonetheless still encouraged to fast privately, much as the apostle Matthew suggested when he criticized hypocrites for fasting in public and pulling faces to show off how much they were suffering.[2] And like the apostles, voluntary fasts were still practiced among Lutherans.

With the possibility of abolishing all dietary restrictions looming on the horizon, the humanist Desiderius Erasmus composed a satirical dialogue in 1526 (still in the early years of the Reformation) between a fish monger and a butcher, wondering which would fare better if everyone were freed from observing Lent.[3] The fishmonger thinks that meat would no longer be valued so much if not forbidden. The butcher is sure that if the Church allowed meat it would be in conformity with basic nutritional principles which state that cold and moist fish can only cause diseases in cold months. They go on accusing each other, one claiming fish stinks, the other that butchers pass off cats and dogs for rabbits and hares. Eventually, however, the discussion blossoms into a theological discourse on how the laws and fasts of the Old Testament were abrogated by the New Testament. Yet a multitude of new food restrictions somehow arose. Erasmus was the last of a breed of humanist thinkers who could be critical of the Catholic Church's rules, and yet remain loyal to the church. In the ensuing decades, it became clear that as Protestants abolished practices like fasting, Catholics would cling ever more tightly to them.

In the wake of Luther's first decisive break with Rome, a number of other Reformation movements sprang up. One of the most important of these occurred in Switzerland in cities like Zurich, where men like Ulrich Zwingli were preaching a variety of reform distinct from Luther's. First, these men understood the Mass as a mere memorial, pointing out that Jesus' words were to be taken in a metaphorical sense when he said "This is my body." Eating the bread is still an important ritual, through which communicants gain grace, but there is no miracle of bread turning into flesh, which seemed to them some kind of cannibalism. This theological quibble was actually the principal reason that the Swiss Reformed Churches never joined with the Lutheran, but there were actually greater cultural differences as well. To start, the Swiss were biblical literalists, and believed that all practices should ultimately find sanction in the Bible or should be abolished. Thus they went much further in abolishing the veneration of relics and images, considering it a kind of idolatry. They were also much more interested in the government of the church itself in a way that would promote moral purity in the congregation.

The most influential thinker among the Swiss was Jean Calvin, who eventually settled in and practically governed the town of Geneva. His importance is primarily the formulation of a system of church government known as Presbyterianism in which the hierarchical structure of Rome is replaced with a more democratic system of elders who decide on doctrine at Synods, or councils of church elders. This, Calvin believed, was more in keeping with the simplicity of the early church. This system would also be adopted by the Dutch, Scots, French Huguenots as well as the English Puritans on both sides of the Atlantic. Regarding their attitude toward food, it is clear that the Calvinists favored an austerity and rigorously guilt-ridden attitude toward pleasures of the flesh. It is also significant that while asceticism of the sort practiced by medieval monastics disappeared in countries that espoused Calvin's ideas, a new kind of personal simplicity and basic distrust of elegant food flourished among the populace at large. Just as they considered all righteous people to be "saints" they also expected them to act as such, and enforced morality by any means necessary. Arguably puritanical thought more than any other factor quelled the spread of culinary refinement in Calvinist countries.

It is also interesting that most Calvinist countries reinstated public fasting as a way to atone for sins, avert plague or somehow garner divine favor. In England these were called "political fasts" intended purely pragmatically to keep a good supply of meat at a low price. During the interregnum however, when Puritans came into power, they made no such excuses, and often declared public fasts to gain God's favor in times of political crisis. Despite the return of the fast though, the Carnival celebrations that preceded it were definitively banned in the course of the sixteenth and seventeenth centuries. They smacked too much of paganism, and their violence and license could not be tolerated within a morally righteous nation. The cycle of feast and fast was definitively broken as ordinary people were expected to maintain simple habits throughout the year, and austere ones on certain occasions.

Another important distinction to be made separating Calvinist from Lutheran thought is the doctrine of predestination. This posits that since God is omniscient and omnipotent, he already knows who will be saved and who will be damned. Every individual's fate is already inscribed in the book of fate. This is a logical corollary to the idea that we cannot participate in our own salvation. But if this is the case, how is one to know whether they rank among the elect or the damned? It became common, although never officially sanctioned, to seek for "signs" of divine favor. Material success might be one, and it has been argued that the Puritans became such successful capitalists down the road because of a work ethic that encouraged investment, frugality and conscious attempts to appear among the elect.[4] In other words, the value that the medieval church had placed on poverty was completely erased from the Protestant consciousness, and in a society that values simplicity and sobriety, conspicuous consumption becomes embarrassing. The only thing to do with wealth is reinvest it. Obviously this is a caricature of the work ethic, and people did indeed spend their money. But compared to Catholic elites in southern Europe, they were models of restraint.

Beneath these official or "magisterial" reform movements, implemented by temporal rulers, there were also a broad variety of popular movements, most of which can be categorized as Anabaptists. Anabaptist was considered a term of abuse given to those who believed that, since in the Bible baptism was only performed on adult believers who willingly entered the congregation after mature deliberation, the practice of infant baptism is totally unwarranted. Ana-baptism means re-baptism, since these individuals were all baptized already. Their understanding of the Bible was a natural consequence of placing the translated text in ordinary people's hands, who could see that the accretions of tradition after a millennium and a half of Christianity often had little to do with Jesus' original intentions. Hoping to return to the pristine roots of the religion, these people are also appropriately called "radical" reformers, *radix* being the Latin term for root.

Like the apostles, they believed that a formal priesthood and a physical structure or church building for each congregation is unnecessary. All the rituals and sacraments could also not be explicitly defended with the text, and began to be questioned. For example, the consecrated wafer used in communion was replaced with ordinary bread. Changes were made in haste because most of these groups believed that the end of the world was imminent, and upon final judgement they wanted to be counted among the elect. This intense apocalyptic strain in early Anabaptist thought motivated many communities to waste no time in "separating themselves from the abomination" by living in strict accordance with the Bible. Wanting no contact with the corrupt world they avoided the law and refused to take oaths, would not serve as civil magistrates and even took the biblical injunction not to kill literally. That is, they became strict pacifists. In one of their most radical experiments they took over the town of Münster, abolished private property and celebrated communal love feasts.

Needless to say, this defiance of established church and state unleashed a swift and violent reaction. The Anabaptists were severely persecuted in Protestant and Catholic countries alike. They did manage to survive though, and their descendants are known as the Amish and Mennonites in the United States and Canada. The Hutterites are similar descendants of an Anabaptist movement of the sixteenth century, who were pushed eastward in the seventeenth century during the Thirty Years' War and eventually settled in the Dakotas in the United States and Canada in the nineteenth century. These groups are all of particular interest for food history because in separating themselves they also adopted unique food customs. The Hutterites, for example, lived communally in large buildings called the *bruderhof* or brother house in which meals were prepared and shared together. Among the Amish followers of Jacob Amman who split from the Swiss Mennonite Brethren in 1693, there was a conscious rejection of modern technology, and their foodways became a virtual time capsule of past practices.

THE CATHOLIC REFORMATION

It was not until the mid-sixteenth century that the Catholic Church mounted a concerted effort to reform their own practices in a way that would attract the lost fold of sheep. Earlier in the sixteenth century, the reaction of the church was primarily to hunt down and burn heretics. The Inquisition was the major institution employed in Spain and Italy. Eventually it appeared that unless a major rethinking of Catholic rituals took place more countries would break away. The Catholic Reformation was fully underway by the late 1540s and 1550s with the Council of Trent.

In a nutshell, the council decided that instead of abandoning the ritual aspects of Christianity as had many Protestant sects, they would strengthen them. The Mass would become the central part of worship and it would be elevated to a glittering, majestic, even theatrical event stressing once again the miracle of transubstantiation. The role of the priests as celibates, and now increasingly learned, coterie acting as intermediaries to God was also stressed. New churches were built with dazzling ornamentation, and by the seventeenth century a new style of architecture would become the perfect vehicle for expressing this new vibrant energetic religiosity: the baroque. But in the course of strengthening doctrine and ritual, the church was also forced to crack down on any heterodox practices, local festivals that still retained pagan elements, odd customs that did not fit the exacting definition of the sacraments. So in reforming Catholic practices, they also more narrowly defined them. It is not surprising that just as in Protestant countries carnival celebrations were among the first to go, particularly because they lacked the decorum not deemed fitting for religious celebrations. This emphasis on decorum is a feature of Catholic reform in general—approaching the church and celebrating holy feasts could no longer be the casual familiar affair defined by generations of odd customs. It now had to be a solemn, rigorously prescribed and sacrosanct rite, one that was indeed extremely stimulating with all the dazzling sights, music and incense burning, but also an imposed ritual.

Among Catholic Reformation thinkers there was also a new attitude toward food, one that can be gleaned indirectly through the writings of St. Francis de Sales in the early seventeenth century. Although actually discussing sex, he disguises his comments by talking about food. First he maintains that eating is necessary to maintain life, and therefore a duty. It also serves a social function, and thus like reproduction is a virtuous act. Eating only to satisfy our appetite is tolerated, but not in itself praiseworthy. Eating to excess is of course dangerous and "It is an infallible mark of a wayward, infamous, base, abject and degraded mind to think about food and drink before meal time, much more so to delight ourselves later with the pleasure we had in eating."[5] Of course these are the greatest pleasures associated with food! In any case, this straightforward and methodical approach to eating (and sex) appears to be an effort to offer a new kind of religiosity to ordinary people without alienating them, which presumably stories of heroic fasting did. Actually, de Sales' book *Introduction to the Devout Life* is basically a "how to" book of spiritual exercises to help ordinary people get in spiritual shape.

The greatest effect of the Catholic Reformation on the eating habits of ordinary people was that the periods of fasting were rigorously maintained. Monastic orders flourished in southern Europe, and a slew of new miracle-working saints, some still performing incredible feats of self-denial, suddenly appeared. The church also retained its fabulous wealth and high-ranking churchmen and wealthy monasteries remained significant patrons of the arts and refined cuisine. In Catholic countries, Spain, Italy, France, parts of Switzerland and southern Germany, the fast and feast mentality remained firmly entrenched, especially in regions of the south that were particularly poverty-stricken.

The struggle between Catholic and Protestant continued throughout the sixteenth century and prompted disastrous Wars of Religion in France, the Revolt of the Netherlands and various other conflicts extending into the next century and culminating in the Thirty Years' War (1614–1648) which began in Bohemia but spread through much of Europe and was particularly devastating for Germany. In the long run, many regions were re-Catholicized, particularly in central and eastern Europe. By the mid-seventeenth century, however, the religious division of Europe into two opposing camps was complete.

At the end of the fracas, Europe was left with a few entirely new religious movements as well. The English Civil Wars produced the churches now known as Congregationalists, as well as the Baptists and the Quakers or Society of Friends. The latter, grew out of a sect known as the Ranters who believed that humans are born without sin, and therefore every human action is allowed. Their worship consisted of swearing in the pulpit, smoking and eating to excess and engaging in all manner of sexual liberties, or at least this is what they were accused of doing. It is ironic that from among these types emerged the very simple Quakers, who were models of sober industriousness. Their ideas bear a great resemblance to the Anabaptists, the only major difference being that Quakers believe that beyond the Bible true believers can receive direct revelations from God through the inner spirit. It is not coincidental that both groups escaped to Pennsylvania at about the same time—in the late seventeenth and early eighteenth century.

In this flurry of religious experimentation and speculation emerged one of the most interesting figures in the history of food: Thomas Tryon. Influenced by the German mystic Jacob Boehme, Tryon became a fervent pacifist and even extended his nonviolent position toward animals. Believing that oppressing any fellow creature was against God's intentions, he became a vegetarian. He was also a prolific writer, churning out title after title in the late seventeenth century on a variety of topics: health, diet, longevity and wealth, and even a vegetarian cookbook. In his most popular book, *The Way to Health, Long Life and Happiness,* he stresses how humans become violent when they get used to killing animals and eating them. "For there is greater Evil and Misery attends mankind, by killing, hurrying, and oppressing his Fellow-creatures, and eating their Flesh, and that without distinction, than is generally apprehended or imagin'd."[6] In other words, by getting used to killing animals we have become all the more willing to hate and kill each other. He even amends the biblical injunction, the "Law of *doing unto all Creatures, as a man would be done unto;* which cannot therefore admit, that any *Violences* or *Injuries* should be done unto God's Creatures .... "[7]

Tryon's vegetarianism had some followers in the coming years. Even Ben Franklin briefly tried it. But Tryon himself seems to have understood that few would be willing to give up meat "since there is no *stemming the Tide of popular Opinion and Custom,* and people will still gorge themselves with the Flesh of their *Fellow-Animals.*"[8] As a concession he included a whole section on how to cook meat. He would not, however, make any concessions to common pleasures he found loathsome such as drinking brandy and smoking. Godliness for Tryon meant strict sobriety, simplicity of food and especially abstaining from junk food. "Observe the composition of *Cakes,* which are frequently eaten, and given especially to Children as *Food?*"[9] In them is such a jumble of ingredients that they make us sick, especially when eaten all the time.

THE ENLIGHTENMENT AND THE GREAT AWAKENING

By the eighteenth century a spirit of secular rationalism began to spread among European intellectuals, as if finally fed up with the hatred and intolerance of their predecessors. Largely inspired by the scientific discoveries of men like Sir Isaac Newton, they believed the human condition could be improved without recourse to religious solutions, which had, after all led to bloody wars. These ideas eventually blossomed into the movement known as the Enlightenment.

Perhaps the most important contribution of the Enlightenment to the history of food was a new critical reexamination of all the strange food customs still rigorously dictated by the Catholic Church. Most notorious was the French *philosophe* who wrote under the pen name Voltaire. Although not an atheist, he certainly did not hesitate to attack what he considered to be ridiculous and irrational doctrines such as transubstantiation and the whole idea of a fast. He asks, "Why does the Roman church consider it a crime to eat terrestrial animals during the days of abstinence, and a good action to be served soles and salmon? The rich papist who has five hundred *francs'* worth of fish on his table will be saved; and the poor man dying of hunger who ate four *sous'* worth of pork, will be damned."[10]

The Enlightenment was not entirely critical though. In fact, the great *Encyclopedie* of Diderot and D'Alembert was an effort to disseminate as much knowledge as possible to the widest variety of readers. Much of the information they included was devoted entirely to what might be called the food trades, agriculture, milling techniques, baking and the like.

Another important Enlightenment figure, Jean Jacques Rousseau, can be credited with devising an entirely new attitude toward food which had long-lasting consequences down to the present. Rousseau was technically a deist, a believer in a God of nature rather than of the church and its man-made customs. As such he also believed that humans, as created, are essentially good creatures and it is only civilization, property and all the other trappings that we usually associate with progress that have corrupted us. This not only directly contradicted Christian teachings on the moral depravity of humans, but scoffed at the philosophes' great faith in progress. Rousseau's brand of nature worship also inverted the traditional value placed on man-made and improved products of nature, now giving a negative spin on the term "artificial." Indirectly Rousseau spawned what we now know as the health food movement. Now simpler foods, unprocessed, unrefined, and unspoiled at the hands of over-zealous chefs, were to be sought out. In his guide to natural education, *Emile,* Rousseau's opening lines are "Everything is good as it leaves the hands of the Author of things; everything degenerates in the hands of man."[11] And this includes food. He has his young student romping through the fields, eating coarse ordinary foods rather than dainty delicacies. He quips "it is only the French who do not know how to eat, since so special an art is required to make dishes edible for them."[12]

Rousseau also favors vegetable foods, believing that eating meat makes humans more cruel and ferocious. He scorns his readers, and quotes the ancient Roman author Plutarch who said that if you eat meat you should be willing to "Kill the animals yourself—I mean with your own hands, without iron tools, without knives .... Bite this cow and rip him to pieces."[13] Most people of course need butchers, cooks and others to hide the horror of murder. Rousseau's ideas were especially influential on the Romantics of the nineteenth century, such as the poet Percy Bysshe Shelley, who was a vegetarian, as well as on religious/health movements that sought spiritual and bodily perfection.

But there was another strain of thought originating in the eighteenth century of a decidedly religious nature that promoted natural foods and simple tastes. In conscious reaction to the Enlightenment, the early eighteenth century also witnessed a religious revival called the Great Awakening. It was felt most strongly in Protestant England, Scotland and Germany as well as in the American colonies. Although actually a series of separate movements, most were characterized by an emotional and ecstatic form of worship. The first of these movements were the Pietists in Lutheran Germany in the late seventeenth century. Their most influential writer was Philipp Jakob Spener who stressed greater use of the Bible and the practical applications of faith rather than scholarly disputation. John Wesley, the founder of Methodism, was also part of this movement.

Methodism sprung up in Oxford in the 1720s among a group of scholars who sought to define their religiosity through methodical study and daily exercises, including frequent communion and fasting twice a week. They also tended to have very sober daily habits. Although they were not yet teetotalers as they would become in the next century, the revivalist sects assured that piety and sobriety would go hand in hand.

THE JEWS

The Jews had always held a unique position in European society. Not only were their customs and the foods they ate immediately recognizable and different from the Christian majority, but they were frequently subject to persecution, and were considered a stubborn race who had refused Christianity. Fuelling this antisemitism were vicious stories of Jews using the blood of Christian babies for making their Passover matzoh. Among other absurd fabrications were the accusations that they poisoned wells and intentionally spread plague. These stories were used as a pretext for unofficial and sometimes official persecution.

Jews were officially forbidden to live in some countries. In England they were expelled by King John in the thirteenth century, and then invited back by Oliver Cromwell in the seventeenth century. Since the conversion of the Jews was considered to be a necessary prerequisite to the Second Coming of Christ, his invitation was not entirely altruistic. The Jews were also expelled from Spain in 1492, and shortly thereafter from Spanish possessions in southern Italy, and from Portugal. Most cities in northern Italy officially tolerated the presence of Jews, as in Venice, though they forced them to live in restricted areas or "ghettos," many of which welcomed the Spanish exiles.

Most of these people however sought refuge under the relatively tolerant protection of Muslims within the Ottoman Empire, in places such as Greece, Turkey and northern Africa. These Spanish Jews, or Sephardim, retained much of the culture of their Golden Age in Spain, their language (Ladino, a fifteenth-century Spanish dialect mixed with some Hebrew) and their cooking for centuries after the expulsion.

Many Jews also stayed behind in Spain through the early modern period, having officially converted, though perhaps willingly or unknowingly carrying on many of their earlier foodways. In fact, one of the principal tasks of the Spanish Inquisition was to hunt down and punish with death if necessary "New Christians" who were relapsing into former Jewish practices. This, of course, would have been considered heresy, and for the unrepentant there awaited torture and public burning. In an atmosphere such as this, it is not surprising that an individual's unwillingness to eat pork, or lighting candles on Friday evening, became immediately suspect.

Certain dishes associated with the Spanish Jews in medieval times have remained in their repertoire. Eggplants, fried artichokes and chickpeas were readily associated with the Jews by Christian writers, as was a long-cooked stew prepared on Friday before the Sabbath when lighting fires was forbidden. So too was their practice of smoking goose and serving it like a prosciutto ham, which is of course forbidden to Orthodox Jews. Carp roe was another typically Jewish food, as caviar from sturgeons, a scaleless fish, is considered unkosher.

Most openly practicing Jews lived in central and eastern Europe, and cities such as Vienna and Prague boasted large and vibrant communities of Jews. These people were called Ashkenazi, and they spoke Yiddish, a dialect of German mixed with Hebrew; their food customs were entirely different from the Jews of Spain. Their cooking was the direct ancestor of the food we associate with American Jewish cookery: bagels, gefilte fish and matzoh ball soup. In the seventeenth and eighteenth centuries the Jews of eastern Europe also experienced a religious revival, not unlike the Great Awakening among Protestant sects. Partly messianic and partly an effort to observe a more strict form of worship, the movement known as Chasidism swept through Jewish communities in Poland and much of eastern Europe.

Regardless of their geographical origin, all Jews through the early modern period were expected to follow a series of food laws originating in Leviticus, the third book of the Old Testament, purportedly given to Moses by God. Although much of this book of the Bible gives a precise description of how to ritually sacrifice animals in the temple at Jerusalem, these practices ceased with the destruction of the temple by the Romans in 70 A.D. and the subsequent dispersal of the Jews throughout the Empire or Diaspora. The food restrictions, or laws that separate clean (kosher) animals from unclean, however, remained in force, and they can be summarized as follows.

First, animals must be slaughtered painlessly and their blood thoroughly drained from the body and discarded. Even in Genesis, Noah was commanded to pour the blood on the ground because it contains the life, which belongs to God. Next, clean animals are defined as only those that chew their cud and have a cloven hoof. This essentially means ruminants, such as goats, sheep and cows. Animals that have only one or the other are unclean, such as the camel that chews its cud but has toes, or the pig that has cloven hooves but does not chew its cud. These qualifications were essentially a shorthand way for Levitical priests to categorize animals they believed to be vegetarians. Predatory animals were also forbidden, as it was of course God's original intention in Eden that there would be no killing involved in gaining sustenance. It was only after the fall in Eden that concessions were made to man's brutal nature. But clean animals were still expected to be herbivores. Other animals were classified as unclean essentially because they did not fit neatly into any category, such as animals that move without legs like snakes, or fish without fins, like shellfish. Both are taxonomic aberrations.[14] To disabuse anyone of the idea that this concept of clean animals had to do with hygiene in the modern sense of the word, or with avoiding animal-borne pathogens, one must merely consider that Jews are allowed to eat locusts.

Lastly, there was a prohibition of seething the flesh of an animal in its mother's milk, which was interpreted to mean that milk and meat products should never be mixed in one meal.

Rituals involving food have also been central to the Jewish faith. Following the Jewish New Year or Rosh Hashana, Jews are commanded to fast, abstain from work and atone for their sins for an entire day, a holiday called Yom Kippur. During Succoth they build a small hut decorated with autumn fruits to celebrate the harvest. But no Jewish holiday is as laden with food symbolism as Passover. To commemorate the bondage in Egypt, a *seder* plate is laid out containing *charoseth,* a spiced fruit and nut mixture resembling the mortar used by the slaves to make bricks, bitter herbs, a neck bone, egg and salt water. Each of these acts as a reminder of some aspect of enslavement. Most distinctive is the *matzoh,* or unleavened bread, meant to commemorate the actual escape from Egypt when there was no time to let the bread rise. During the seven-day holiday, no leavened bread is to be consumed, nor, later Jewish scholars decided, could one eat legumes or rice because they too rise somewhat in cooking.

The passover seder, the ritual itself, also includes some curious features which were additions in Hellenistic times, perhaps a concession to Greek fashion in an attempt to keep young Jews observant. These include drinking four glasses of wine, reclining while eating and hiding a piece of the matzoh called the *afikomen* until the end of the meal. All these are essentially elements taken from the Greek symposium, the afikomen being only a vaguely disguised version of the epicomium, or desserts.[15]

The most frequently observed holiday, however, was the Sabbath itself, celebrated from sundown Friday night to sundown Saturday evening. During this time no work could be done, nor fire lit, which meant that food had to be cooked the day before.

NOTES

1. Martin Luther, *Selections from His Writings,* ed. John Dillenberger (Garden City, NY: Anchor, 1961), 456.

2. Matthew, 6:16.

3. Desiderius Erasmus, *Concerning the Eating of Fish* in *The Essential Erasmus,* tr. John P. Dolan (New York: Penguin, 1964), 271–326.

4. Max Weber, *The Protestant Ethic and the Spirit of Capitalism* (New York: Charles Scribner's Sons, 1958).

5. St. Francis de Sales, *Introduction to the Devout Life,* tr. John K. Ryan (Garden City, NY: Image, 1972), 227–228.

6. Thomas Tryon, *The Way to Health, Long Life and Happiness* (London: H. Newman, 1697), 232.

7. Tryon, 235.

8. Tryon, 55.

9. Tryon, 159.

10. François-Marie Arouet (Voltaire), *Philosophical Dictionary* (Harmondsworth: Penguin, 1972), 77.

11. Jean-Jacques Rousseau, *Emile,* tr. Alan Bloom (New York: Basic Books, 1979), 37.

12. *Emile,* 152.

13. *Emile,* 155.

14. Jan Soler, "The Semiotics of Food in the Bible" in *Food and Culture, A Reader,* ed. Carole Counihan and Penny Van Esterik (New York and London: Routledge, 1997), 55–66.

15. Michael Ashkenazi, "Food in the Passover Seder" in *The Meal, Oxford Symposium on Food and Cookery 2001* (Totnes, Devon: Prospect Books, 2002), 42–49.

CHAPTER 6
DIET AND NUTRITION

Along with religious ideas about food, early modern Europeans also had elaborate theories about how foods affect the human body and what combinations of food would foster optimal health. These theories were inherited from physicians of ancient Greece recorded in the body of writings attributed to Hippocrates, and above all from Galen of Pergamum (died c. 200 A.D.) whose prolific works overshadowed those of all his predecessors. These medical texts were largely lost or forgotten in Europe after the fall of Rome, but were preserved by Byzantine and Arabic scholars such as Avicenna and Averroës, from whom Europeans gradually relearned their basic principles. Through the Middle Ages and at the start of the early modern period most nutritional texts were based on translations or interpretations of Arabic authors. This began to change in the course of the Renaissance as more scholars could read Greek and more ancient medical texts were recovered. This was part of a larger intellectual movement called Humanism, which sought to restore the body of classical learning and place it at the core of their own educational curriculum. As a result, physicians increasingly abandoned the Arabic authorities and relied on the original Greek texts, which they believed were closer to the original source of wisdom. In the early sixteenth century, therefore, nutritional ideas adhered more strictly to the theories of Galen than ever before or since.

HUMORAL PATHOLOGY

These theories were based on a few basic physiological principles that remained more or less intact through most of the early modern period. First, physicians believed that the human body is regulated by four basic fluids or humors. These are blood, phlegm, yellow bile or choler and black bile or melancholy. Health was defined as the proportional balance of these four fluids, though all humans are born with a predominance of one particular humor, or at least a tendency for that humor to be produced in excess. This meant that individuals could be classified as sanguine, in which case blood dominates, phlegmatic, choleric or melancholic. An individual's humoral makeup or complexion determined the diseases they would be subject to, their character and emotional state and most importantly what diet they should follow. Thus unlike our own nutritional theory, there could be no universal set of prescribed nutritional guidelines or even an idea of good foods or bad foods that would apply to all people. Accurate diagnosis and a tailor-made regimen for each individual was therefore considered crucial in this system.

Another central idea in this system was that each humor has qualitative properties that can be described as hot and moist (blood), cold and moist (phlegm), hot and dry (choler) and cold and dry (melancholy). These properties are not so much actual tactile measurements of temperature and humidity as they are the effect each humor has on the body. Thus an excess, or plethora, of blood will make the body excessively hot and moist. This explains why blood-letting was such a popular therapy; opening a vein or applying leeches would restore the patient to the proper humoral balance. Equally, medicines that were classified as cold and dry in action could be administered to counteract the excessively hot and moist body. This system is thus defined as allopathic; it corrects ailments by applying remedies opposite to the patient's distemperature or imbalance.

Just as human bodies were said to be regulated by four humors, so all organic matter, including animals and plants, and even inorganic minerals, were thought to be composed of elements that gave them their own humoral properties. Thus a person could be described as phlegmatic, and a cucumber could be described as cold and moist. Matching the proper foods to the individual was the key to this entire system. Hot and moist people needed cold and dry foods when imbalanced; cold and moist people needed hot and dry foods. The assumption here, and one that was adhered to through most of the early modern period, is that few people are ever well-balanced and usually need some form of correction. Theoretically, however, healthy people should maintain their particular humor by eating foods similar in qualities to their own humoral makeup. This rule was largely de-emphasized after the mid-sixteenth century.

Another crucial consideration when determining the ideal diet for an individual was the texture and consistency of a given food. How quickly something would pass through the body and how easily it could be digested was just as important as its humoral qualities. Those who receive a lot of exercise, laborers especially, were advised to eat more solid and sustaining foods like beef and beans. More sedentary people were told to eat lighter foods that are easily digested, and offer less nourishment like chicken or eggs. Occupation was therefore one of the major factors in prescribing a diet.

Along with the effect of exercise, physicians also took into account a variety of other factors that came to be known as the "non-naturals" or external factors that influence the human body, as opposed to natural or internal processes. The non-naturals, unlike internal processes, could be regulated at will, and so were usually included in a prescribed regimen or diet. The term diet originally denoted food intake as well as exercise, air quality, sleep patterns and evacuations such as bowel movements and perspiration and even sexual activity. Each of these had its own ability to heat, cool, moisten or dry the body. For example, to correct an excessively cold person, brisk running, warming foods and sleeping well bundled could all be prescribed as a therapeutic regimen. Even managing one's emotions could play an integral part, excessive anger makes a person choleric, and an abundance of cold and dry humors makes one melancholic. We still use these humoral terms to describe mood and character types. A sanguine person is cheery and optimistic, phlegmatics are lazy and slothful, cholerics are prone to violent outbursts of anger and melancholics are, of course, sad.

Renaissance nutritionists also believed that a person's age and gender had an important influence on the humoral makeup. Young people tend to be hotter and more sanguine. As they age, the body's vital fluid and heat is expended, and they become increasingly colder and drier. Younger people were thus allowed to eat colder foods while the elderly were given warmer and more easily digested foods as their digestive capacity gradually diminished. As a rule women were considered colder and moister than men, which was used to explain why women were generally believed to be softer, weaker and less intelligent than men. Obviously medical theory was used here as a tool of subjugation, but it also meant that a woman's diet should be different from a man's. Diet should also vary by season. Weather conditions will naturally affect a person's internal temperature and humidity, and therefore heating foods are more appropriate for winter and cooling foods for summer. People were also advised to eat more food in colder months and both less and lighter foods in the summer when the digestive "heat" of the stomach is withdrawn into the surrounding air.

In practical terms it seems unlikely that in any given household an entire family could be served different foods to suit each individual's unique complexion. But for those with the wealth to serve many different foods in each course or for individuals who could freely choose what they ate, these medical theories did offer a powerful system for categorizing foods and deciding what is best to eat. Judging from the fact that many nutritional handbooks were published in the vernacular languages and were offered in relatively cheap format, we can only conclude that there was a good proportion of the literate population that took an avid interest in nutrition. In the first half of the early modern period alone over 100 separate titles were published all across Europe.

What must have been truly confusing though is that rival ways of thinking about food often made different claims. For example, while an elegant meat pie might have been considered fashionable in elite social circles, the Catholic Church may have banned it during Lent, and a physician might have forbade it because it contained a jumble of too many ingredients of contrary qualities making it impossible for the body to digest efficiently. What was a person to do? Like today, there were a variety of different food ideologies that made eating, if anything, a confusing and hazardous enterprise. Even for nutritional writers themselves, their own native customs and habits often flavored their recommendations. Galen may have thought beef too difficult to digest, but why then can Englishmen eat it without harm? Fish may be dangerously cold and moist, but who has ever caught a cold from eating too much fish? Questions such as these were indications that physicians were anything but united in their opinions about food and, like today, readers had a variety of opinions to choose from as nutritional writers argued among themselves.

These arguments make generalization difficult, and over time certain foods that found favor among nutritional writers were later banned. Sugar is a good example of this, considered an ideal aliment in the early sixteenth century, by the seventeenth-century physicians

THE HAVEN
OF HEALTH:

*Chiefly made for the comfort of Students, and con-
sequently for all those that haue a care of their health,
amplified vppon fiue wordes of Hippocrates , written
Epid.6.* Labour, Meate, Drinke, Sleepe, Venus:
By *Thomas Cogan* Maister of Artes , and Bacheler of
Phisicke : And now of late corrected
and augmented.

*Hereunto is added a Preseruation from the Pestilence:
With a short Censure of the late sicknesse at Oxford.*

*Ecclesiasticus, Cap.*37.30.
By surfet haue many perished : but he that dieteth
himselfe prolongeth his life.

Imprinted at London by Thomas Orwin,
for William Norton. 1 5 8 9.

Figure 6.1 English health manual by Thomas Logan. *Courtesy of the New York Academy of Medicine Library.*

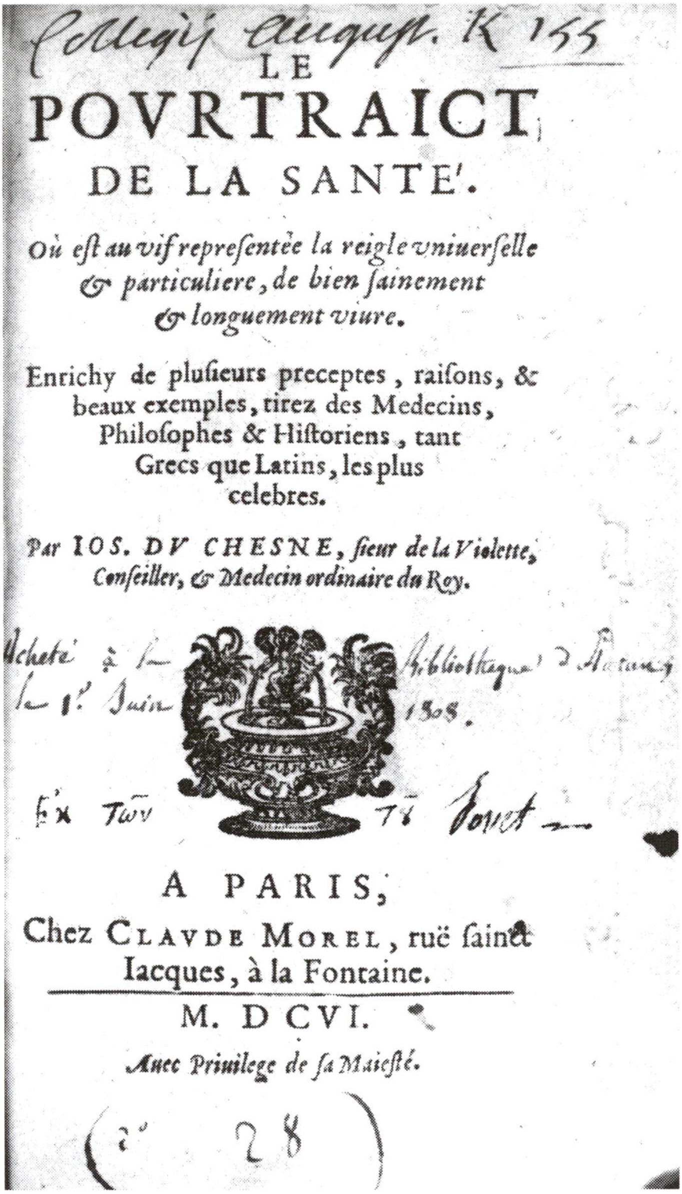

Collegij Augusp. K 155

LE
POVRTRAICT
DE LA SANTE'.

Où est au vif representée la reigle vniuerselle
& particuliere, de bien sainement
& longuement viure.

Enrichy de plusieurs preceptes, raisons, &
beaux exemples, tirez des Medecins,
Philosophes & Historiens, tant
Grecs que Latins, les plus
celebres.

Par IOS. DV CHESNE, *sieur de la Violette,*
Conseiller, & Medecin ordinaire du Roy.

Acheté à ... le 1. Iuin *Bibliothaque d'Auxancy* *1808.*

Ἐκ τῶν *τῦ Iouet*

A PARIS,

Chez CLAVDE MOREL, ruë sainct
Iacques, à la Fontaine.

M. DCVI.

Auec Priuilege de sa Maiesté.

(28)

Figure 6.2 French health manual by Joseph Duchesne. *Courtesy of the New York Academy of Medicine Library.*

claimed it makes the teeth black and burns in the digestive system, causing clogs. Wine also was theoretically among the substances most analogous to human blood, and therefore, it was believed, is most easily transformed into blood. Yet in the hands of a puritanically minded author alcohol could be seen as a debilitating vice. Beyond these variations though, certain basic nutritional ideas about food would have been held by all writers, at least up until the mid-seventeenth century.

First, bread was considered absolutely essential for proper nutrition. It was thought to be a kind of glue that kept all the other foods in place, and in fact the ability for food to "stick to the ribs" was called agglutination. Meat was considered equally important. Since nutrition itself was defined as the ability for a food to be converted into the substance of the human body, those substances most similar to our body were also considered most nutritious. Providing the body could digest meat, it was the perfect aliment; weaker and less exercised people require lighter meats. There was absolutely no question that the human body needed some form of meat to maintain health; vegetarianism was practically unthinkable. Fish was problematic for most authors. Although it qualified as a nutritious form of flesh, its cold and moist properties and excessively gluey texture meant that it could provoke an abundance of phlegm, or worse get stuck in some stage of the digestive process. Clogs were considered one of the major causes of disease, leading to gout, scabies, fevers and elephantiasis. To counteract these harmful effects, proper condiments should always accompany fish, flavorings that would cut through their gluey humors and balance their coldness. Lemons and heating spices and sugar would do just that. Condiments were thus thought of as medicinal foods rather than just flavor enhancers.

The use of condiments meant that any potentially harmful food could be corrected. Thus nutritional theory incorporated a culinary system as well, and in fact some culinary historians have seen medicine at the root of European cooking practices. The abundant use of spices, particularly on foods classified as cold or difficult to digest, may then have a medicinal origin. Even the very idea that moist foods like pork or lamb, should be roasted to dry them out, and dry foods should be boiled has a certain medical logic to it. Each makes the dish a more humorally balanced whole, more easily assimilated and more appropriate to nourish the human body. Condiments were defined not only as spices and sauces, but any food that is served with or used to correct another one. This is why vegetables like lettuce, considered excessively cold and moist, were believed to be more of a corrective rather than a food per se. It is one of the greatest misconceptions held today that people in the past were told not to eat vegetables. To be accurate, phlegmatic people were warned against them. In fact for hot people, or in summer, or to counterbalance hot foods, vegetables were a fine condiment.

The same is true of fruits. Although they were always believed safer when eaten cooked and corrected with spices, in choleric bodies or for the brawny laborer, fruits are perfectly fine. They can also be corrected by drying. Raisins and dates have less noxious moisture, and their sweetness is concentrated, making them hotter.

One may well ask, how did physicians originally assign these foods to their respective categories? Of course they relied on the authority of the ancients often aided by their own observations and experience. But the most important criterion for assigning foods qualities in the first place was taste. Sweet and savory or meaty flavors were usually classified as hot and moist foods, and because heat and moisture were the two fundamental requisites for life, they were also considered the most nutritious. Milder flavors, like chicken or light-fleshed fish were considered more temperate, with moderate heating and warming qualities. Foods that have bite that we can feel heat the body were thought to be hot and dry. Into this category go most spices and hot herbs as well as salt. Our use of the term "hot" to describe pepper or chilies is a remnant of humoral theory. Foods that constrict the body's passages and make the tongue pucker were categorized as cold and dry. Sour and bitter flavors and those with tannins dry the tongue (like tea). We still refer to "dry" wines or a "dry" martini in this sense. Lastly, insipid flavors and watery foods were placed in the cold and moist category which included most leafy vegetables and fruits.

So a "balanced" meal meant combining hot and moist staples with cold and dry condiments like vinegar; cold and moist foods could be corrected with hot and dry spices. Foods that are thick and crass equally are improved with cutting and sharp flavors that will help them pass through the body, mustard on pork for example. And very light foods like small birds can be given some body and substance by serving them with a thickened sauce made with bread crumbs or ground almonds.

This is not to say that behind every recipe there is some kind of medicinal logic though. Physicians' incessant tirades against dining practices at court are enough to show that all cooking practices did not qualify as acceptable. They were especially incensed against the practice of eating too many different kinds of food in one sitting, mixing meat and fish in one meal and heaping on all sorts of sweet confections. This causes a disruption in the stomach since each food required a different amount of time to be properly digested. Some foods pass out of the stomach still half raw, while others burn up, offering little valuable nutritional content. They also believed that a strict order of foods was crucial. Fruit, for example, should never be eaten at the end of a meal because it would float on top of the stomach contents and eventually putrefy, sending noxious vapors into the brain and disrupting the entire system. They knew very well that no such order was followed at courtly banquets.

There were few foods condemned outright according to this theory. But the few positively harmful foods were usually those difficult to categorize as flesh, fish or fruit. Mushrooms and truffles, for example, were thought to be excrements of the earth, and the fact that so many are poisonous meant that clearly all varieties are dangerous. Snails also were problematic for many writers, though Galen recommended a restorative broth based on snails. Frogs were another almost universally condemned food, again partly because they were so difficult to categorize. It was also thought that some creatures generate spontaneously, like maggots on meat, or eels which were thought to reproduce asexually from rotting organic matter. Any food raised in an unwholesome atmosphere was equally suspect: waterfowl that feed on muck in stagnant pools, vegetables grown in marshy malarial fens or cooped unhappy animals wallowing in their own filth. The defects of the environment, fodder and even mood, would eventually be passed on to whomever ate such foods, a principle we seem to have largely forgotten today.

These ideas inherited from classical antiquity were complemented with a number of home-grown ideas about the effect of food on the body. While it would be a mistake to label these systems "folk or old wives' tales" because many learned physicians also made use of them, it is clear that they more closely represent popular beliefs. By the latter sixteenth and seventeenth centuries they also consistently came under attack by medical professionals as "popular errors." The doctrine of signatures is the name given to the first of these systems which contends that the shape or color of any given substance, including food, will offer hints about its therapeutic or dietary value. The outward form of an object is laden with "signs" left by the beneficent creator for the use of humans who must only read them correctly. For example, a walnut, because it is shaped like a brain, must be good for the intellect. Similarly, a red flower might be good for the blood, or a yellow one for jaundice (a sickness in which the eyes turn yellow). A food that is yellow like the sun, saffron perhaps, would increase the memory because the sun embodies the power of enlightenment and eating saffron was said to tap into that astral power. Both sympathetic magic and astrology were involved in these theories as well. This system was not always consistently applied though, because sometimes a certain colored food would treat an ailment of the same color, but other times it could foster or promote a similar part of the body. The doctrine of signatures was generally regarded as nonsense by most physicians in the early modern period, but it would be revived in a different form by Paracelsus, whom we will turn to shortly.

Another simpler way of thinking about food might be called the doctrine of similarities. Following its logic, the characteristics of any given food, usually an animal, are directly transferred into the consumer. You literally become what you eat. Eating rabbit would make you timid, just as fox would give you cunning. Apparently people believed that deer live many years, and so eating deer confers longevity. Similarly, eating testicles promotes virility. Ideas like these were held by some physicians at the start of the early modern period, but they were usually ridiculed by the latter sixteenth century. This itself suggests that many people continued to believe in them.

For those properties of a given food that could not be explained by reference to its humoral makeup, or one of these other systems, dietary writers often referred to a food's "occult" qualities. The word occult was not meant to imply anything sinister; it merely refers to "unseen" powers that could not be rationally explained through sensory perception. The attraction of magnets was explained this way. So too were drugs like poppies, or opium derived from them, which have a narcotic effect. Whenever the properties of a food could not be explained, writers often claimed that some occult virtue was in effect. For example, cabbage was said to prevent inebriation and fennel was thought to be good for the eyes. How exactly this worked remained a mystery, and hence an occult virtue.

At times astrology could also play a major role in assessing a particular food. It was most often herbalists who prescribed cures with a plant's astral powers in mind, but this is more properly therapeutic medicine than nutritional theory per se. Most nutritional writers did not discuss astrology, and despite a resurgence of interest in this and magic in the seventeenth century, by the latter seventeenth century it had gone out of fashion among scientists.

When one uses the term science in connection with nutritional theory, it can only be in a very loose sense. Nutritional science as we know it today and detailed knowledge of vitamins, protein and carbohydrates, etc., dates only from the past century or so. But there were scientists running experiments following systematic methodology, using sophisticated instruments and even quantifying their results and framing them into grander theories. These are all characteristic of the so-called scientific revolution of the mid-seventeenth century. But unlike astrology, physics, and other scientific fields, there was no revolution of understanding regarding physiology or diet. Older humoral ideas often shorn of explicit reference to the humors themselves, nonetheless persisted right into the nineteenth century. But they were now accompanied by and often curiously mixed with some new theories that sought to explain the effect of food on the human body in very different terms.

PARACELSIAN CHEMISTRY

The first new theory is very difficult to assess fairly. On the one hand it represents the first major leap toward pharmaceutical chemistry, on the other, its founder was often considered a religious mystic, showman and quack. Theophrastus Bombastus von Hohenheim, who took the name Paracelsus, was indeed the first person to reject humoral physiology outright. He replaced it with a chemical, or more properly alchemical, system which considered three basic elements, sulfur, mercury and salt, to be the basic constituents of life. All food could thus be assessed in terms of its chemical components. This indeed sounds scientific. And Paracelsus was alone in suggesting that physicians abandon the ancient authorities like Galen and Avicenna and instead rely on direct observation, trial and error and curing diseases with concentrated doses of a plant or mineral's chemical essence, rather than herbal concoctions. Again, these theories sound modern, but Paracelsus was also a firm believer in astrology, hermetic and folk magic, and harnessing divine forces to cure his patients. To understand the power of a given food or drug he would try to "overhear" its virtues by looking for signs or by directly perceiving its therapeutic value through a kind of mystical trance. Clearly he was not running clinical trials on his patients or quantifying his results and forming more general laws. Paracelsus is in fact an excellent illustration of the way that genuine progress is usually not made by brilliant theories that suddenly find pure truth, but rather strange combinations of old and new ideas that grope however tentatively toward scientific understanding.

Of course Paracelsus could not have believed that his theories were tainted with backwardness. In fact, he was trying to create a system that was wholly integrated with Christianity, of the radical reformed variety, and that would be accessible to common folk the way that learned medicine never was. His was a grassroots movement rather than some erudite speculation undertaken in university halls, and published in Latin. Significantly, his works were published in German. Equally significant is the fact that he was scorned by professionals and chased out of universities all his life. He was also apparently extremely obnoxious and quarrelsome. It is perhaps not surprising that his theories really only gained wide attention a generation after his death. Only in the latter sixteenth and seventeenth centuries did a recognizable school of Paracelsians or *iatrochemists* (healing chemists) come into being as a rival to the Galenic system.

The iatrochemical school, refining Paracelsus' ideas and dropping some of his stranger mysticism, described the three fundamental chemicals not so much as elements or building blocks, the way we think of hydrogen, carbon and helium, but rather as transformative processes. That is sulfur is key to all combustion, flammability and change inside the human body. Mercury is the volatile principle, and explains how things move through the body, and salt provides structure and solidity. Thus digestion can be considered a process which both transforms food, transports it through our body and becomes our solid parts. Similarly, when wood burns, the sulphurous principle is the flame, the smoke that rises is the mercurial and the ashes left over are the salts. What the alchemist sought to do was speed up these transformative processes by means of burning, distilling, precipitating and evaporating substances into their chemical essences. It was alchemists who invented alcohol, the concentrated "spirits" of wine. Other intensely concentrated drugs also became bestsellers, such as the opiate laudanum.

Apart from its therapeutic applications, the iatrochemists also began to think about the human body in very different terms. Paying close attention to processes like fermentation and the effect of acids and alkalis, a Paracelsian of the seventeenth century, Jan-Baptista van Helmont discovered that digestion is a breaking down of food particles by means of acid in the stomach, rather than heat as the Galenists believed. Others began to note that when chemical processes are faulty, they leave behind residues or tartars (just like the tartar that builds up on the inside of wine barrels during fermentation or the tartar that accumulates on the teeth). These calcified deposits can also build up in the arterial walls or in the muscles, which is the cause of gout. Kidney stones too, believed to be the result of improper diet, were another form of tartar. The significance of these ideas is that real research into the chemical reactions taking place in the human body were finally underway, and it would not be long before the chemical constituents of food would also be analyzed. But despite all this, Paracelsians did not construct a new dietary system. Nor did they suggest radically new ways of assessing foods. So the humoral system tended to be blended with Paracelsian ideas, humors giving way to chemicals, but the old concept of heating, drying, cooling foods remained firmly in place. Instead of foods that are excessively heating, it was now foods that are excessively sulphurous in the new school of thought.

IATROMECHANICS AND OTHER SCHOOLS OF THOUGHT

The other new school of thought to arise was called the iatromechanics or iatrophysicists. They believed that human life can be explained entirely in terms of physics, and cures really only need to restore the proper functioning of the human machine by tightening or loosening or tinkering with the mechanism. This school saw one particular individual, an Italian working in the early seventeenth century named Santorio Santorio as their forerunner. Santorio was important for being the first person who believed that quantification of physiological functions is the key to understanding them. For example, he weighed himself on a huge scale every day. By comparing the weight of food he ate each day with what he expelled, and noting a discrepancy in the latter, he surmised that the body also excretes wastes through what he called "insensible perspiration" that evaporates off the surface of the skin and by exhalation throughout the day. Because some foods cause a greater weight of perspiration, he surmised that less of that food's nutrients were actually absorbed into the body. Therefore foods that caused less perspiration were considered more nutritious. And foods that are lighter in texture are generally processed more efficiently than denser foods. Light fermented bread is thus more nutritious than crackers.[1] The significance of this research was his meticulous attention to running controlled experiments noting how sleep, exercise and other factors affect the body's perspiration. He recorded the results of his more than 30 years of data collection and expressed them in the new universal language of science: mathematics.

Santorio really never discovered much new apart from some scientific instruments, nor did he abandon Galenism. But the iatromechanical school of the latter seventeenth century conducted very important experiments into the nature of vacuums, how gases behave under pressure and with heat, and made a number of other landmark discoveries. In general, they began to explain human physiology in terms of mechanical processes, pressure gradients causing blood flow, mechanical breaking down of food explaining digestion and muscular contraction being controlled by tiny cells becoming rigid when irritated by a message sent down the nerve ending. Most importantly, they sought to achieve in the field of medicine the same mathematical precision that Isaac Newton had applied to physics. Unlocking the secrets of what they called the "animal economy" or basic functioning of the human body was merely a matter of figuring out how the machine worked. Much of this research was thus purely scientific or geared solely toward therapeutic remedies. What is significant is that with this exciting new work being done, the ordinary old business of prescribing diets and theorizing about the nature of foods became worn and unfashionable, and probably more importantly, unprofitable.

Writers on nutrition increasingly turned their attention to curing diseases by means of restricting diets. Topics like scurvy, gout and obesity and other therapeutic topics were now much hotter than how to maintain health through diet. This is due in part to the increasing professionalization of medicine. Physicians have to make a living in their practice, and preventative regimens do not pay the bills. Thus nutrition became a relatively minor clinical subfield as the profession increasingly focused on therapeutics, and medical texts included shorter and shorter sections on diet. The very definition of the term diet also began to narrow, excluding the "non-natural" factors and increasingly designating food intake, and in many cases a specific corrective diet. This is, of course the modern sense of the term—to go on a diet, which implies strict control and change to achieve specific goals, often weight loss.

Another related trend in the late seventeenth and eighteenth century might be termed the "self-help" movement. Considering physicians were still not proficient in curing most common ailments, it is not surprising that many people preferred to self diagnose and treat with simple home remedies, especially when one could avoid being bled, taking violent purgatives or going under the knife. This movement also contended that people have no use for physicians when in health, and there is certainly no need to strictly regulate diet when the mechanism is in good working order. This too was a backlash against the medical profession, but it ultimately weakened further any claim the medical profession might have had for dispensing dietary advice.

There were still some professional dietary treatises, and what is particularly interesting is the way they were forced to incorporate the latest scientific theories into what is still essentially an ancient humoral system. This sometimes merely meant appropriating the latest jargon to appear up to date and scientific. But there were also serious attempts to harmonize older and newer theories.

Louis Lemery's *Traité des aliments* of 1702 was one such work. Although his basic understanding of nutrition is still fundamentally Galenic, he mentions the role of respiration and circulation of the blood in distributing nutrients through the body, something absent in earlier dietary writings. He makes extensive use of new chemical theories by incorporating fermentation into his discussion of digestion and also mentions the effects of alkaline and acidic foods. There are also now four chemical constituents of food: "the terrestrial parts, the aqueous parts, the oily parts and the saline parts."[2] These are a step beyond simple humoralism, though clearly no laboratory-based chemical analysis was yet involved. The book is arranged like an encyclopedia, much as older dietaries were. The only difference is that now the odd chemical or sometimes even mechanical explanation is added to the definition. For example, his entry for peaches, as before mentions their excessive humidity and how easily they corrupt, but it includes the idea that they contain essential salts and very little oil.[3] In most cases these new ideas seem superficially tacked on to the older system.

But there is a major conceptual difference in the dietary theory of the eighteenth century, which is the increased emphasis placed on the flux of fluids and substances through the body. Humoral physiology certainly emphasized the importance of the texture and consistency of food and how fast it passes through the body, but it never focused so intently on the mechanical speed that fluids traverse the body's passageways. In Lemery, asparagus is easily passed not only because of its power to open the body's passages, but because of an abundance of essential salts that cuts through the body. It appears that this new focus has a good deal to do with the new attention to diseases like scurvy and gout, which were believed to be deposits of tartar left throughout the body resulting from an excessive diet and which could be corrected by eating a diet that promotes the passage of fluids.

Given the continued demand for dietary gurus, it is not surprising that eighteenth century diets tend to simplify and distort the importance of fluid transport for their sick and corpulent patients. Perhaps the most colorful of these popular practitioners was Scotsman George Cheyne, who himself conducted a life-long battle with his own obesity. Rather than discredit him among potential clients, as his obesity might today, people felt that this gave him a special empathy toward his patients, because he really could feel their suffering. Cheyne also mixed his dietary advice with a strange blend of mysticism, and in his mind to inhabit a thinner healthy body was also to be more righteous. Having been among the first generation of physicians in Edinburgh trying to reconcile Newtonian science with medicine, he could also claim a certain professional legitimacy, even though he now chose to take up common practice over scientific speculation.

Another patent abuse of the new focus on fluid transport was a book that promoted vegetarianism in mid-eighteenth-century Italy. Rather than present a moral stance, or economic justification for eating vegetables, Antonio Cocchi's *Del vitto pitagorico* (The pythagorean diet) of 1743 tried to justify a plant-based diet by referring to the new physiological theories. Because he did so in a superficial and haphazard way, he unleashed fierce criticism from his fellow physicians. Cocchi's argument rested on his contention that most people eat foods that are far too dry and difficult to digest. This slows down the "insensible perspiration" (a concept taken from Santorio), and prevents nutrients from passing through the body, reducing the quantity of nutrients absorbed and impeding the expelling of wastes. But a diet of fruits and vegetables and pure water would prevent clogs in the body, and the vegetables' scouring properties would even clean the passages effectively.[4] This is, in fact, a drastic departure from older theory that often pointed out the dangerous phlegmatic qualities of fruits and vegetables.

Cocchi was almost immediately attacked by other Italian physicians: Giuseppe Antonio Pujati and Giovanni Bianchi.[5] Their primary criticism was Cocchi's faulty and superficial use of science, insisting that he had taken a therapeutic regimen and falsely construed it as a proper regimen for maintaining health. Most humans require meat to be properly nourished, and they offered their own scientific evidence to prove this. What is interesting though, is that their theories are still fundamentally Galenic, no longer referring to the humors per se, but still relying on nutritional concepts over 2,000 years old.

Through the eighteenth century, not only did this lively forum for all varieties of new medical theory flourish, both scientific and quack, but new schools of physiology emerged as well, making it increasingly difficult for the dietary writer to keep abreast of the latest developments. This only exacerbated the tendency to simplify theory in an effort to boost the practitioner's reputation.

The first new school coalesced around Hermann Boerhaave at the University of Leiden in the Netherlands. In an attempt to thoroughly synthesize the chemical and mechanical schools, he suggested that bodily functions are controlled by a system of hydraulics, vascular channels suck up fluids or gases which themselves are subject to chemical change. This system could not account for everything though, and some of Boerhaave's students suggested another regulatory life force that flows up and down the nervous system, a kind of spirit or "animus" from which these people were called "animists." Some, like Georg Ernst Stahl tried to fully integrate the idea of a soul into the physiologic system. Further refining these ideas, another school, the "vitalists" appeared, followers of Albrecht von Haller. Then came the "Brunonians," followers of John Brown, who explained all health and sickness in terms of tension and relaxation or sthenic and asthenic disorders. Each of these presented a slightly different physiological system that incorporated different ideas about the role of diets and the nature of foodstuffs. For the most part, however, most of these theories still favored meat as the ideal aliment because it is most easily assimilated into our body and provides the greatest amount of energy. For correcting disorders though, some favored meat, others promoted vegetables. Some restricted alcohol, others prescribed it in moderation. What is remarkable though, is how the basic foundations of humoral physiology and the valuations it assigned to specific foods still remained relatively intact though Galenism had been long discredited. Despite the flurry of new theories, no one had yet devised a completely new way of thinking about food and its role in health.

By the end of the eighteenth century the authors who had written about food or "hygiene," a synonym for diet in its broader sense, became increasingly preoccupied with public hygiene. It is here that the term hygiene began to take on its modern connotation of cleanliness and freedom from infection, rather than the older maintenance of the "non-naturals." It is also at this time that a truly scientific understanding of nutrition began to emerge with the chemical discoveries of men like Antoine Lavoisier. Totally abandoning ancient elemental theory and replacing it with the system we now use with newly discovered elements like oxygen and hydrogen, Lavoisier was also able to describe the chemical processes of the body accurately and quantify them.

Needless to say, it was not long before all older physiological systems became outdated. In the course of the nineteenth century, Galenism and the system that had prevailed for over 2,000 years was finally completely dismantled as researchers like Justus von Liebig began to identify compounds that would later be called proteins, carbohydrates and fats, thus laying the foundations for the modern science of nutrition. Only in the early twentieth century was the role of vitamins identified.

NOTES

1. Santorio Santorio, *De medicina statica* (Paris: Natale Pissot, 1725), 356.

2. Louis Lemery, *Traité des Aliments* (Paris: Pierre Witte, 1705), ix. Available on line at http://www.bib.ub.es/grewe/showbook.pl?gw033.

3. Lemery, 22.

4. Antonio Cocchi, *Del vito pitagorico* (Florence: Francesco Moücke, 1743).

5. Giuseppe Antonio Pujati, *Riflessione sul vitto pitagorico* (Feltre, Italy: Odoardo Foglietta, 1751); Giovanni Bianchi, *Se il vitto Pittagorico di soli vegetabili sia giovevole per conservare la sanità* (Venice: Giambatista Pasquale, 1752). See also Ken Albala, "Insensible Perspiration and Oily Vegetable Humor" in *Gastronomica,* Summer 2002, 29–36.

CHAPTER 7

FOOD IN LITERATURE AND RELATED FOOD GENRES

There is a wealth of literary evidence that fills some of the gaps in our knowledge of early modern eating habits and attitudes toward food. Some of these sources yield only fictional depictions of meals or indirect clues in contexts that are not directly related to food, but others are actually about specific ingredients or relate an author's personal experience of eating. There were also several related genres that discussed food, most notably books about ancient eating habits. Thus in a sense the history of food as an academic discipline originated in this period.[1] The works discussed here, however, are drawn mostly from popular literature that features food prominently.

MEALTIMES

One detail that comes primarily from literary evidence is the time of day when meals were customarily taken. This was actually a matter of debate among dietary writers in the sixteenth century, but most of them deferred to the authority of ancient authors like Galen and recommended two meals per day. The first smaller meal, dinner, should be taken at around 11:00 a.m., and a larger meal, supper, follows six hours later at around 5:00 or 6:00 p.m. These authors reasoned that since the digestive powers are stronger during sleep when the digestive heat is withdrawn inward, and because there are more hours between the evening and morning meal, that supper should be larger. These recommendations follow ancient practice, and coincide with early modern custom in Spain and some parts of Italy like Venice and Genoa. But the rest of Europe followed a different pattern—eating the larger meal in the late morning and smaller meal in the evening. The evidence for this comes foremost from literary descriptions of meals that usually take place mid-day. Even in the vast majority of cookbooks that offer menus, the grander meal was held mid-day. Cookbook author Domenico Romoli, for example, has three or four courses for morning meals, but only one for the evening's "collation."

What is clear is that meal times gradually shifted, dinner being held later and later in the day. In the sixteenth century dinner was held around 11:00 a.m. By the seventeenth century it had crept up to 12:00 or 1:00 p.m. Samuel Pepys, the seventeenth-century English diarist, recorded several dinners he ate at 12:00 a.m. replete with heavy drinking. In the eighteenth century fashionable diners, and the gentry and business classes in the cities who sought to imitate them, ate dinner later and later in the afternoon. The English satirist Richard Steele wrote that dinner was becoming so late that it might be confused with breakfast.[2] Actually the usual dinner time was 2:00 or 3:00 p.m. by mid-century and by the late eighteenth century it was perhaps as late as 4:00 or 5:00 p.m. Only in more recent times has it come to rest in the evening, when supper consequently became less important. This development necessitated the invention of a new mid-day meal, lunch, which only became standard at the very end of the eighteenth century.

Even more elusive is evidence for breakfast. Judging from cookbooks and dietary literature there was no such meal, or at least it was only recommended for children, invalids and the elderly who have weak digestive systems and must eat smaller meals more frequently. Nevertheless, there was such a meal, and some people took it regularly. The word itself comes from the late Latin *disjejunare,* meaning "to un-fast" or break the fast of the evening. Remarkably, the word was contracted in the Romance languages to *disnare* or *disner* in Old French, or dinner in English. Thus the word dinner actually means breakfast. But the word is not recorded in English until 1463 in a royal account book that records expenses in breakfast, but it is not entirely clear whether this was an early dinner or another meal, the one we now know as breakfast, eaten first thing in the morning.

What appears to have happened is that as dinner moved later in the day, people were hungrier first thing in the morning, especially when the evening meal was relatively small. In countries where the evening meal was larger, breakfast did not become important. In southern

Von speiß vnd tranck.

ES rahten vnns nicht allein die ge-
treuwen erfahrnen ärtzet / sonder
Gott selbs durch die heylig Göttli-
che Schrifft/ zu messigkeit des lebens/daß
dardurch alle gute sitten erwachsen / vnnd
alle laster gedämmet werden. Dann wie
wir ohn vnderlaß vor Augen sehen / werden die schändtlichsten vnd schnödesten la-

D v ster

Figure 7.1 Dining scene. *From Ryff, Walter Hermann d. 1548. Spiegel unnd Regiment der Gesunndtheit. Frankfort : Heirs of C. Egenolff [for A. Lonicerus, J. Cnipius & P. Steinmeyer], 1574 P. 29. EPB 5679. Courtesy of Wellcome Library, London.*

Europe it is still not a proper meal, but merely coffee and perhaps a piece of bread or pastry. In England and the north the pattern was quite different. In 1661, Samuel Pepys recorded in his diary that he threw a New Year's breakfast that included oysters, meat, tongues and anchovies, but this was clearly a special occasion. Usually he merely took a "morning draught." By the eighteenth century breakfast still usually consisted of tea, coffee or chocolate accompanied by sweet breads or cakes, and was eaten around 9:00 or 10:00 in the morning. Only in the nineteenth century did it emerge as a full and sumptuous meal with bacon, eggs and even steaks.

Thus the three-meal-a-day pattern we are familiar with is a relatively recent phenomenon. The English afternoon meal called "tea" as a snack between lunch and dinner also did not emerge until the nineteenth century, but in the previous century there were similar snacks held after dinner, which meant that it was also held in the late afternoon.

This kind of evidence of course only relates to the meal patterns of the upper classes. From the comments of dietary writers who usually disapproved of common custom, it is certain that laboring people ate many more meals, usually a breakfast, dinner in the mid-morning, some form of snack at sundown and then a small supper late in the evening. This pattern also persisted despite the shift in meal times among elites.

The structure of the average meal can also be discerned through literary evidence. Ben Jonson's poem "Inviting a Friend to Supper" reveals that a proper supper began with olives, capers or salad, followed by mutton and chicken with a lemon sauce. Then a rabbit, and perhaps some wildfowl like larks, pheasant or woodcock. At the end appears pastry, digestive cheese and fruit washed down with wine from the Canary Islands and some "Tabacco." There is also an intriguing line which seems to suggest that some verses may appear on the pastry: "That will the pastrie, not my paper, show of." Apparently pastries were often sold wrapped in discarded sheets from printers' shops, which meant that Jonson's verses could indeed show up on the bottom of the pastry and he might in the end be forced to eat his words about all these promises of a fine meal.

FOOD FANTASY

Jonson was even more explicit in describing fantastic meals and people's secret food obsessions. In his play *The Alchemist* he has Sir

Epicure Mammon dream up a banquet inspired by the ancient Roman cookbook attributed to Apicius that includes tongues of carp, dormice and camels' heels, and other perversities like "The beards of barbel [a fish] served instead of salads, Oiled Mushrooms; and the swelling unctuous paps Of a fat pregnant sow, newly cut off, Drest with an exquisite and poignant sauce."[3] This obviously strays far from the realities of dining in early modern Europe, but it does at least give a glimpse of what Europeans might have dreamed about in their wildest fantasies. More down to earth are the insatiable cravings people have for roast pig in the play *Bartholomew Fair* by Jonson. One character even believes that there is "a natural disease of women called 'A longing to eat pig'" which he fears following his Puritanical logic might be a species of idolatry since the fair is sacred to Saint Bartholomew.[4] In the end, they submit and gorge themselves, and some characters appear to be transformed into pigs, sweating an unctuous fat as they roast in the sun.

More down to earth is the shopping list for a sheep shearing festival recited by a "clown" in Shakespeare's *The Winter's Tale*. The list includes three pounds of sugar, five pounds of currants, rice, saffron to color the warden (a kind of pear) pies, as well as mace, dates, nutmeg, ginger, prunes and raisins.[5] This is indirect evidence that an audience in late-sixteenth-century England did not find it ridiculous that such luxuries could be afforded by lowly shepherds, but it was nonetheless only on rare occasions. The clown says "what will this sister of mine do with rice? But my father hath made her mistress of the feast, and she lays it on." In other words, she is going all out for this bash and normally only the wealthy ate rice.

The literature of early modern Europe is filled with more explicit food fantasies, and none was so widespread as tales of the Land of Cockaigne, or in German Schlaraffenland. This was a magical dreamland where pigs ran around ready-cooked with knifes stuck in their backs. Pies fell off the roofs of houses and jugs produced an endless supply of wine. Even the buildings are made of food, with walls of sausages, windows of salmon, sturgeon and cod and tabletops of pancakes. Most importantly, all work was forbidden. One need only lay back and let the food fly into your mouth whenever you want it. In a certain sense this is a kind of mock inversion of paradise, or the Garden of Eden, except here people get to eat meat. In many versions there is also free love and no one ever grows old. There is no change of season; it is always spring. A fountain of youth keeps everyone young and healthy. What is interesting is that this is not a place filled with delicacies or fine spices. Most of the fantasy revolves around simple peasant food, but in never-ending quantities.

Presumably, when these stories were first concocted they provided ordinary people who faced the daily threat of real starvation a way to console their fears. Dreaming was a form of escape from the drudgery of everyday existence. Why they should have remained popular through the late Middle Ages when peasants were relatively well off and famines quite rare, is a mystery. And why relatively affluent regions such as Flanders, northern France and Italy would want to dream of insurmountable mounds of ordinary food is no less perplexing. Perhaps they merely became regular fixtures of the oral culture and remained popular for their entertainment value even after being written down. It may be rather like the story of Jack and the Beanstalk being told to countless children centuries after the story and economic setting have ceased to be relevant.

What is clear is that by the early modern period the printed versions of the Cockaigne story have twisted its original meaning entirely. It became a didactic tool ridiculing what were seen as grotesque peasant-like habits. In other words, it provided a model for how not to behave for comparatively wealthy townsfolk. Much the same could be said of Pieter Breughel's famous painting of Cockaigne, in which the figures are anything but attractive and worthy of emulation. Viewers would presumably walk away from the image with their own dreams of indulgence quelled.

One could also read the derisive feasts described in François Rabelais' *Gargantua and Pantagruel* in this light. That would at least explain why a serious-minded humanist and physician would waste his time writing about grotesque mounds of tripe, hams, smoked tongues, sausages and other ordinary peasant fare downed with gallons of wine. These are certainly not the foods his readers would have actively dreamed about. Either this was meant to be a negative object lesson, or as with the Cockaigne tales, the audience found this kind of low humor irresistibly funny. Probably both are at work. At one point, the giant Gargantua was advised by his mentors to wake up early and eat, but mostly to start drinking. "Early to rise brings little health / But early drinking's good for the health."[6] This is clearly a parody of the typical advice, but one meant to reveal hypocrisy among those dispensing such rules. That is, the text seeks to reform through low humor and sometimes even the crudest scatological jokes. The reader is drawn in by the humor, but is unwittingly fed a lesson.

Another type of food fantasy is the description of eating habits in imaginary lands. Thomas More's *Utopia* gives us the first of many of this kind and shows what a European humanist imagined the food of pure unspoiled people living in the state of nature might be. More discusses Utopian agriculture and the fact that all citizens rotate duty working on farms for two-year terms. Strangely they also have huge incubators for hatching chicks. Utopians eat together in big common halls, the women of each household taking turns cooking, and all the dirtiest jobs are left to the slaves (who are criminals). Most importantly, butchering animals is their job. "They do not allow their own citizens to grow accustomed to the slaughter of animals, as they think that constant practice in this gradually destroys the kindness and gentle feeling of our souls."[7] They are not vegetarians, but like us they don't like the idea of killing animals. Utopians also use grain, but only for bread, and they drink wine, or water flavored with honey and licorice. They also burn spices and incense. More even specifies their mealtimes: Utopians work three hours before the mid-day meal, rest for two hours then work three more before supper. Their food is described as pleasant but not excessive, full and hearty but not luxurious or refined. Like Rabelais, More's ultimate goal was to get Europeans to reexamine their own habits.

MANNERS AND MORALS

Sebastian Brandt's *Ship of Fools,* first published in Strassburg in 1494, is another satire, depicting the full panoply of human vices as a means of reform. The ship is bound for a fool's paradise, called Narragonia (*narren* means fool in German) and along the way each vice or folly is paraded forward, including the drunken glutton. One verse warns "The rich man reveled once so well/That on the morn he ate in hell." A few lines down Brandt specifies that the generous host provided nearly a whole cow, almonds, figs and rice—all expensive imports.[8] Although heavy-handed, it was one of the most popular books in sixteenth-century Germany, and influenced a whole generation of moralistic texts.

The funniest of these moralistic texts is another verse satire about Grobianus, patron saint of slobs, by Friederich Dedekind. Breaking every conceivable rule of polite behavior, Grobianus belches, wipes his nose and grabs food with his hands. Apart from being funny, this of course reinforces polite behavior. It is a lesson through inversion, tailor-made for bourgeois readers who might not know all the rules yet.

In England the work was translated as *The School of Slovenrie*. Among other things, it explains how the famous Greek orator Demosthenes learned to annunciate with marbles in his mouth, so the proper slob should do the same with his food. "In steede of hard stones thou thy mouth with breade and meat shalt fill. And rowling that within thy mouth, shalt full mouth'd speake thy will."[9] The reader has now learned what separates him from uncouth peasants—manners.

In early modern Europe there also flourished a serious genre of manuals designed to teach manners either to young boys as with Erasmus' *De civilitate morum puerilium* (On civil behavior of boys) of 1530, or adults as in Giovanni della Casa's *Galateo* of 1558. These works were designed not for the upper classes and those "to the manner born" who were raised knowing table manners, but are more likely directed at social aspirants who are seeking access to the court culture, and have to be taught proper table manners. They serve the same function as the satires mentioned above, but from an earnest vantage point.

Why such manners might have proliferated in the first place has generated a great deal of speculation among food writers. Most agree that ritualized modes of behavior reduce the threat of offending one's fellow diners, or even reduce the possibility of threatening them outright. For example, sharp-edged knives used to cut meat and often brought dangerously close to the mouth were replaced with knives with more rounded edges, and cuts of meat that would not require savage cutting. This is the same time that forks begin to be used. By distancing yourself from the very animal act of eating, by privatizing the dining space with individual plates and cups, not only does the meal become more civilized, but the risk of misunderstanding is mitigated. Along with this, bodily functions are increasingly hidden from sight or relegated to separate private rooms because they remind us that we are animals. Erasmus actually had to tell his readers not to blow their noses at the table, not to fart and not to pull half-chewed meat out of their mouths. (Discretely tossing it aside was preferable.) Obviously we have come a long way in defining polite behavior since then, but contrary to what we might think its primary function is not hygiene.

Just imagine yourself sitting at a table and briefly turning to talk to the person next to you. Suddenly, before you realize what has happened, a servant has snatched up your plate before you were done. Disappointment, anger, maybe abusive words would be hurled, and not only is the host embarrassed, but so is the poor servant who was just doing his job, and all the fellow diners as well. But a small ritual signal, perhaps a fork turned outward or placed on the napkin as a silent message to the servant that he may remove the plate is a sure way to avoid such misunderstanding. The small ritual makes dining safer and more civil. Ritualized acts of deference to superiors, and knowing exactly who is superior or inferior serves the same function. It prevents misunderstanding.

The growth of ritualized forms of table manners serves another function as well. It clearly delineates those who understand how to behave (the ins) from those who do not (the outs), whether that might be people of a lower social class, people from the country, foreigners or whatever. Rituals are a way to define group inclusion, and just as certain types of food go in and out of fashion, so elite groups tend to elaborate and complicate eating rituals once those below them have learned the rules. Or, in complete defiance, they begin to eat more informally in small intimate groups, as happened in mid-eighteenth century France and Britain, which was itself something new that others had to learn. As long as the latest fashion stays one step beyond the wealthy and socially mobile imitators it can survive.

But even when guests behaved at the table, hosts were not always equally as civil. There is another interesting and less known work by Erasmus dealing with food. It is the colloquy or dialogue designed to teach students Latin called *Opulentia Sordida* (On sordid opulence). In it he defends himself from accusations that he spent time at the house of the famous Venetian publisher Aldus Manutius as a paid proofreader, and while there ate sumptuously and was frequently found drunk. He claims that his host actually bought corrupted wine dregs and even watered that down. He also bought bad wheat mixed with clay for bread, and his guests were forced to wait until 1:00 or later for dinner, and 10:00 at night for supper. This was too long to wait for a meal, as wretched as it was, for when it did come it was a dish made of bean flour and seven lettuce leaves with vinegar, but no oil, for nine guests. Only on special occasions would he buy a kind of snail caught in the sewers, or stinking rotten tripe.[10] Apart from defending himself, Erasmus is also mocking what passes for Italian frugality, suggesting that it is actually stinginess. It is also an exhortation to hosts to treat their guests well, take their customs and eating habits into consideration, and at the very least see that they are fed. We can surmise from this dialogue that Erasmus, as a wandering scholar, was usually offered better fare, or at least expected it.

FOOD FARCE

There was another satirical food-related genre that flourished at this time, especially in Italy. Its goals were not so moralistic, in fact perhaps the opposite. These poems were mock odes to various foods, almost always items that were forbidden by physicians. They are thus defiant, and instead of reviling these dangerous foods, lift them to heroic status. Some of these were composed in Italian, like Firenzuola's "In praise of sausages." One part extols the noble virtues of bologna sausages asking, "Art thou not the true food for poets? All rich prelates and good nobles, Learned men, and those who have a good brain, Every beautiful and discrete gentlewoman spends her money most willingly for you .... "[11] It goes on to exclaim how they can be made from anything and cooked any way, but the best are those made with the author's own hands, fat and naturally red, the perfect food. By taking what was usually considered a lowly topic, eating sausages, and inverting its status to a topic worthy of verse, the author frustrates the reader's expectations, and the result is extremely funny.

Similar are the verses of Francesco Berni about all sorts of low topics elevated to noble status. They were extremely popular and widely imitated. His "In praise of peaches" one stanza of which reads "Oh fruit above all others blessed, good at the beginning, middle and after a meal, as a starter they're good but as dessert perfect."[12] The context of these comments is a heated argument that raged among dietary authors, some of whom believed that peaches at the end of the meal would corrupt before being digested and ruin one's health. Others claimed that they should precede a meal, but only when accompanied with wine to speed their passage. Berni is basically thumbing his nose at all the experts and saying taste is what matters and since peaches are divine they belong in every part of the meal. "If some say they are bad, come see me with one in my hand, and whether I'm alive or dead." In other words, experience shows that doctors have no clue what they are arguing about.

Some of these food poems were even composed in a made up language called "macaronic" Latin, a mixture (much like macaroni) of fake Latin, Italian and nonsense. They sound like what might happen if you gave an enthusiastic but untrained commoner the task of composing serious verse on his favorite topic—which of course would be food.

Heroic food poems were composed in other countries as well. Henry Fielding's "The Roast Beef of Old England" written in the eighteenth century is one example that warns "Then, Britons, from all nice Dainties refrain, Which effeminate Italy, France and Spain; And mighty Roast Beef shall command on the Main." More hilarious is Robert Burns famous "Ode to a Haggis." He calls the stuffed sheep's stomach "Great Chieftain o' the Puddin-race" and apparently the proper food for robust Scotsmen rather than the French ragout, or Spanish Olio, which were of course all the rage in dainty circles.

FOOD CONFESSIONS

Personal experiences related in diaries and essays are another literary form that reveals much about attitudes toward food. The French essayist Michel de Montaigne in his essay *On Experience* goes so far as to describe the way he eats, and how fixed he has become in his own habits. He admits that he cannot eat between meals, or take breakfast or even eat two full meals a day without feeling stuffed. Unlike his contemporaries, he disliked too many dishes and long drawn out meals. Just a few dishes, eaten quickly, but with a nice long rest afterwards is fine. He also confesses: "I could dine without a tablecloth, but to dine in the German fashion, without a clean napkin, I would find very uncomfortable. I soil them more than the Germans or Italians, and I make little use of either spoon or fork."[13] It is no wonder that he often found himself biting his fingers accidentally in his haste. He also mentions that he prefers meat undercooked but tender, that he dislikes most salads, and likes his wine diluted with one-half or one-third of water. There is scarcely any author who reveals more about his own quirky food preferences.

We also get a glimpse of real food neuroses from the diary of Renaissance artist Pontormo. In it he meticulously records every ounce he consumed, an egg here, some salad, a bit of bread there, a half glass of wine. In March 1554 he wrote "Monday evening after supper I felt very strong and well-disposed, I ate a lettuce salad, a good capon broth, and four quatrini of bread. Tuesday I had a lettuce salad and an omelet."[14] Pontormo appears to have been not only lonely and melancholic, but would not allow anyone to cook for him, lived as a recluse, and for some reason had an obsession with his health.[15]

Another autobiographical account of eating habits is found in the memoir of Ignatius Loyola, Spanish founder of the order of Jesuits. Determined to achieve sainthood, Ignatius wore torn shoes, let his hair and fingernails grow long, and fasted so intensely for an entire week that he was actually ordered by his superiors to eat something. Obedience being his primary duty, he had to eat, but did so unwillingly.[16]

One might be tempted to think that the ecstatic visions he had may have been induced by hunger.

Lady Mary Wortley Montague is another writer who occasionally relates in letters details about her preferences and things she experienced in her travels as an ambassador's wife in the early eighteenth century. For example, while in Vienna, she remarks about the magnificence of the dinners to which she has been invited. "I have been more than once entertained with fifty dishes of meat, all served in silver, and well dressed: the desert proportionable, served in the finest china. But the variety and richness of their wines is what appears most surprising."[17] This may have been all the more impressive considering that her friend, the poet Alexander Pope, had the following scathing remarks to say about her and her husband. The intent of the satire is to promote moderation rather than stinginess.

> Avidien and his wife (no matter which
> For him you'll call a dog, and her a bitch)
> Sell their Partridges, and Fruits,
> And humbly live on rabbits and on roots
> One half-pint bottle serves them both to dine,
> And is at once their vinegar and wine . . . .
> Oyl, tho' it stink, they drop by drop impart,
> But souse the cabbage with a bounteous heart.[18]

FOOD IN FICTION

The number of food references in early modern fiction would be impossible to recount here, but it would be remiss to neglect the way writers use eating habits and preferences as a way to delineate character. The reader needs only the briefest description of a meal to form a complete mental image of the person eating it. It is probably the quickest way to introduce a character. Picture the slob, someone daintily picking at a lettuce leaf, another chowing down on a huge bowl of spaghetti. We can already begin to fill in the other details about ethnicity, social class and occupation.

The most successful writers use food with brilliant effect. Miguel de Cervantes, for example opens his epic *Don Quixote* with a description of his hero's eating habits. We are told that his stew had more beef than lamb in it, he ate a *salpicón*—a simple stew, lentil soup on Fridays, bacon and eggs on Saturdays. All are indications of poverty. But he did indulge in a pigeon some Sundays that consumed three-fourths of his income. Spanish readers would immediately have identified the character as a poor man who sometimes lives beyond his means. These details are, of course, crucial to understanding why Quixote, a noble fallen on hard times, thinks he has to go on a chivalric quest. It is only after he becomes a knight-errant that he can stop worrying about food, because he has never read in his books about knights eating, unless invited to some special banquet in their honor. When in the field, knights eat whatever is at hand, which happens to be his companion's rustic fare: an onion, some cheese and a few crusts of bread.[19] His companion Sancho Panza is continually thinking about food, and his wildest dreams are about to be realized when invited to the wedding of Camacho the rich. There are huge cauldrons with whole sheep inside, suckling pigs stuffed into a steer, more than 60 wine skins, white breads, fritters dipped in honey, spices everywhere—all being prepared by an army of 50 buxom cooks. In the end all he gets are a few chickens, but the scene aptly describes the peasant mentality of Sancho—ever ready to gorge himself.[20]

Cervantes' exact contemporary, Shakespeare, also knew well the value of describing eating habits to disclose personality. From Cassius and his "lean and hungry look" in *Julius Caesar*, which immediately tells us he is scheming and untrustworthy, to Falstaff with his drunken carousing. Shakespeare also makes extensive use of food stereotypes, especially for ridiculing foreigners. In the *Merry Wives of Windsor*, one character Ford, sure that his wife can not be trusted decides "I will rather trust a Fleming with my butter, Parson Hugh the Welshman with my cheese, an Irishman with my acqua-vitae bottle ... "[21] All these peoples were supposedly inordinately fond of these foods.

Henry Fielding's *Tom Jones* is another resource for food history, though here the images are usually set in raucous taverns with plenty of grog and wenches. The book is introduced with a "bill of fare to the feast," in which the author provides a menu of the book's contents for the reader's perusal. We are told that the subject to be served is Human Nature, and if any one complains that this is too common, he insists that it will be finely prepared and dressed. For "the same animal which hath the honour to have some part of his flesh eaten at the table of a duke may perhaps be degraded in another part, and some of his limbs gibbeted, as it were, in the vilest stall in town. Where then lies the difference between the food of the nobleman and the porter, if both are at dinner on the same ox or calf, but in the seasoning, the garnishing, and the setting forth." In other words, the author will write like a talented chef cooks.[22] In the novel, Jones' appetites for food and sex are equally insatiable, and often go hand-in-hand. There is one notorious scene in which he makes a smooth transition from devouring a three-pound hunk of beef to devouring his companion, but not without some sighs and batting of eyelashes to distract him.[23]

NOTES

1. Janus Cornarius, *De conviviorum veterum* (Basil, 1548); Johann Wilhelm Stucki, *Antiquitatum convivialium* (Tiguri, 1582); Pedro Chacon, *De Triclinio* (Heidelberg, 1590). See also introduction to *Gastronomia del rinascimento,* ed. Luigi Firpo (Turin: UTET, 1974).

2. Ken Albala, "Hunting for Breakfast in Early Modern Europe," and Gilly Lehman, "Meals and Mealtimes, 1600–1800" in *The Meal, Oxford Symposium on Food and Cookery 2001* (Totnes, Devon: Prospect Books, 2002), 20–30 and 139–154.

3. Ben Jonson, *The Alchemist,* Act II, Scene i.

4. Jonson, I.vi.

5. Shakespeare, *The Winter's Tale,* Act IV, Scene iii.

6. François Rabelais, *Gargantua and Pantagruel,* tr. J.M. Cohen (Harmondsworth: Penguin, 1986), 82.

7. Thomas More, *Utopia,* tr. Peter K. Marshall (New York: Washington Square Press, 1965), 59.

8. Sebastian Brant, *The Ship of Fools,* tr. Edwin H. Zeydel (New York: Dover, 1944), 98.

9. Frederich Dedekind, *Grobianus in England,* Palaestra XXXVIII (Berlin: Mayer and Muller, 1904), 83.

10. Erasmus, *Opulentia Sordida.*

11. Agnolo Firenzuola, *Opere* (Firenze: Sansoni, 1963), 995.

12. Massimo Montanari, *Nuovo Convivio* (Bari and Rome: Editori Laterza, 1991), 34.

13. Montaigne, *Essays,* tr. J.M. Cohen (Harmondsworth: Penguin, 1958), 367.

14. Montanari, *Nuovo Convivio,* 82.

15. Rudolf and Margot Wittkover, *Born Under Saturn* (New York and London: W.W. Norton, 1963), 69–70.

16. Ignatius Loyola, *Autobiography,* tr. Joseph F. O'Callaghan (New York: Harper Torchbooks, 1974), 36.

17. Wortley-Montague, *Letters* (London: J.M. Dent, 1906), 65.

18. Alexander Pope, see Brigid Allen, *Food an Oxford Anthology* (Oxford: Oxford University Press, 1994), 333–334.

19. Miguel de Cervantes, *Don Quijote,* ed. Martín de Riquer (Barcelona: Planeta, 1980), 110 (Book I, ch. x).

20. Cervantes, Book II, ch. xx.

21. Shakespeare, *The Merry Wives of Windsor,* II, ii, 295.

22. Henry Fielding, *Tom Jones* (New York: Signet Classic, 1979), 28–29.

23. Fielding, 429–431.

CONCLUSION

If two women met in the street, one from the early sixteenth century, the other from the late eighteenth, they would certainly recognize each other, especially if they were peasant women. But put them in a city, give them some wealth, and the differences would become glaring. Their clothes would be different, one with her white wimple on her head, the other with a towering starched wig. They would speak a little differently, probably have different daily concerns, but in the end they would get along fine.

Now put these two women at a dinner table and we would have mayhem. One would reach with her hand for a gobbet of meat, the other gesturing toward the knife and fork. One would look around for the bowl of sauce, something spicy, sour and thickened with bread crumbs, the other would expect it on her plate, rich with butter, stock and garnished with something elegant like truffle slices. They would never agree when to eat or what order the foods should appear. Does one start with fruit and end with salad or the other way around? One would expect a gala banquet with sugar sculptures, the other a late intimate supper. One would wonder why there is meat on the table during Lent. The other would wonder what all the fuss is about. One would question the humoral balance of the foods served and whether they would agree with her particular complexion, the other would be worrying about treating her "vapors" by restricting her meal to vegetables.

Next send them to the market and it only gets worse. Potatoes and tomatoes, what are they? And why is the meat cut up into neat little unrecognizable pieces? I wanted a whole calf's head today. And why are these exotic goods so cheap? Just look at the price of sugar! In the kitchen they fare no better together. One pulls up her dress hem and squats before the fire. The other searches around for the stovetop.

All these differences between the two women point to the fact that eating changed dramatically over the course of 300 years. Manners have changed, the available foods and their prices, the way they are brought to market and sold, and of course what these women thought tastes good changed too. One can only imagine what either would think plopped down in modern America!

SUGGESTED FURTHER READINGS

GENERAL REFERENCE WORKS

Davidson, Alan. *The Oxford Companion to Food*. Oxford and New York: Oxford University Press, 1999.

Fernández-Armesto, Felipe. *Food: A History*. London: Macmillan, 2001.

Flandrin, Jean-Louis, and Massimo Montanari. *Food: A Culinary History*. Translated by Albert Sonnenfeld. New York: Columbia University Press, 1999.

Katz, Solomon H., ed. *The Encyclopedia of Food and Culture*. New York: Charles Scribner's Son's, 2003.

Kiple, Kenneth F., and Kriemhold Coneè Ornelas. *The Cambridge World History of Food*. Cambridge and New York: Cambridge University Press, 2000.

Larousse Gastronomique. New York: Clarkson Potter, 2001.

Tannahill, Reay. *Food in History*. New York: Crown, 1988.

Toussaint-Samat, Maguelonne. *History of Food*. Translated by Anthea Bell. Cambridge, MA: Blackwell, 1992.

Trager, James. *The Food Chronology*. New York: Henry Holt, 1995.

CHAPTER 1

Ambrosoli, Mauro. *The Wild and the Sown*. Translated by Mary McCann Salvatorelli. Cambridge and New York: Cambridge University Press, 1997.

Braudel, Fernand. *The Mediterranean*. Translated by Siân Reynolds. New York: Harper and Row, 1972.

———. *The Structures of Everyday Life: Civilization and Capitalism 15–18th Century, vol. I*. Translated by Siân Reynolds. New York: Harper and Row, 1981.

Cipolla, Carlo. *Before the Industrial Revolution.* Translated by Christopher Woodall. New York: W.W. Norton, 1993.

de Vries, Jan. *The Economy of Europe in an Age of Crisis, 1600–1750.* Cambridge and New York: Cambridge University Press, 1976.

Kerridge, Eric. *Agrarian Problems in the Sixteenth Century and After.* London: George Allen and Unwin, 1969.

Musgrave, Peter. *The Early Modern European Economy.* New York: St. Martin's Press, 1999.

Slicher van Bath, B.H. *The Agrarian History of Western Europe, A.D. 500–1800.* London: Edward Arnold, 1963.

Thirsk, Joan, ed. *Agrarian History of England and Wales.* Cambridge and New York: Cambridge University Press, 1967.

CHAPTER 2

Burnett, John. *Liquid Pleasures: A Social History of Drinks on Modern Britain.* London and New York: Routledge, 1999.

Camporesi, Piero. *Bread of Dreams.* Translated by David Gentilcore. Chicago: University of Chicago Press, 1989.

Coe, Sophie. *America's First Cuisines.* Austin: University of Texas Press, 1994.

Corn, Charles. *The Scents of Eden.* New York: Kodansha America, 1999.

Crosby, Alfred. *The Columbian Exchange: Biological and Cultural Consequences of 1492.* Westport, CT: Greenwood Press, 1972.

Dalby, Andrew. *Dangerous Tastes.* Berkeley: University of California Press, 2000.

David, Elizabeth. *Harvest of the Cold Months: The Social History of Ice and Ices.* New York: Viking, 1994.

Fiddes, Nick. *Meat: A Natural Symbol.* London and New York: Routledge, 1991.

Forster, Nelson, and Linda S. Cordell, eds. *Chilies to Chocolate.* Tucson: University of Arizona Press, 1992.

Fussell, Betty. *The Story of Corn.* New York: North Point Press, 1992.

Kurlansky, Mark. *Cod.* New York: Penguin, 1997.

———. *Salt: A World History.* New York: Walker and Company, 2002.

Mintz, Sidney. *Sweetness and Power.* New York: Penguin, 1985.

Pollan, Michael. *The Botany of Desire: A Plant's-Eye View of the World.* New York: Random House, 2001.

Root, Waverly. *Food.* New York: Simon and Schuster, 1980.

Rosenblum, Mort. *Olives.* New York: North Point Press, 1996.

Salaman, Redcliffe N. *The History and Social Influence of the Potato.* 3rd ed. Cambridge and New York: Cambridge University Press, 1985.

Schivelbusch, Wolfgang. *Tastes of Paradise.* Translated by David Jacobson. New York: Vintage, 1993.

Sokolov, Raymond. *Why We Eat What We Eat.* New York: Summit, 1991.

Unwin, Tim. *Wine and the Vine.* London and New York: Routledge, 1991.

Visser, Margaret. *Much Depends on Dinner.* New York: Grove Press, 1986.

Wright, Clifford. *A Mediterranean Feast.* New York: William Morrow, 1999.

Zuckerman, Larry. *The Potato.* New York: North Point Press, 1998.

CHAPTER 3

Shepherd, Sue. *Potted Pickled and Canned.* New York: Simon and Schuster, 2000.

Spang, Rebecca L. *The Invention of the Restaurant: Paris and Modern Gastronomic Culture.* Cambridge, MA: Harvard University Press, 2000.

Symonds, Michael. *A History of Cooks and Cooking.* Urbana and Chicago: University of Illinois Press, 2000.

Trubeck, Amy. *Haute Cuisine: How the French Invented the Culinary Profession.* Philadelphia: University of Pennsylvania Press, 2000.

CHAPTER 4

Hartley, Dorothy. *Food in England.* London: Little, Brown, 1954.

Mennell, Stephen. *All Manners of Food.* Oxford: Blackwell, 1985.

Paston-Williams, Sara. *The Art of Dining.* London: National Trust, 1993.

Peterson, T. Sarah. *Acquired Taste. The French Origins of Modern Cooking.* Ithaca and London: Cornell University Press, 1994.

Revel, Jean-François. *Culture and Cuisine.* Translated by Helen R. Lane. New York: Da Capo, 1982.

Sim, Alison. *Food and Feast in Tudor England.* New York: St. Martin's Press, 1997.

Wheaton, Barbara Ketcham. *Savoring the Past: The French Kitchen and Table from 1300 to 1789.* New York: Touchstone, 1983.

CHAPTER 5

Bell, Rudolph. *Holy Anorexia.* Chicago: University of Chicago Press, 1985.

Burke, Peter. *Popular Culture in Early Modern Europe.* New York: Harper Torchbook, 1978.

Bynum, Caroline Walker. *Holy Feast and Holy Fast: The Religious Significance of Food to Medieval Women.* Berkeley: University of California Press, 1987.

Darnton, Robert. *The Great Cat Massacre.* New York: Random House, 1984.

Henisch, Bridget Ann. *Fast and Feast*. University Park: Pennsylvania State University Press, 1976.

Spenser, Colin. *The Heretic's Feast: A History of Vegetarianism*. Hanover, NH, and London: University Press of New England, 1995.

Thomas, Keith. *Religion and the Decline of Magic*. New York: Charles Scribner's Sons, 1971.

CHAPTER 6

Albala, Ken. *Eating Right in the Renaissance*. Berkeley: University of California Press, 2002.

Fieldhouse, Paul. *Food and Nutrition: Customs and Culture*. 2nd Edition. Cheltenham: Stanley Thornes, 1996.

Mikkeli, Hiekki. *Hygiene in the Early Modern Medical Tradition*. Helsinki: Finnish Academy of Sciences, 1999.

Tremolieres, J. "A History of Dietetics," in *Progress in Food and Nutrition Science* 1, no. 2 (1975): 65–114.

CHAPTER 7

Allen, Brigid. *Food and Oxford Anthology*. Oxford and New York: Oxford University Press, 1995.

Digby, Joan, and John Digby, eds. *Food for Thought*. New York: William Morrow, 1987.

Elias, Norbert. *The History of Manners*. Translated by Edmund Jephcott. New York: Pantheon Books, 1982.

Jeanneret, Michel. *A Feast of Words: Banquets and Table Talk in the Renaissance*. Translated by Jeremy Whiteley and Emma Hughes. Cambridge: Polity Press, 1991.

Pleij, Herman. *Dreaming of Cockaine*. Translated by Diane Webb. New York: Columbia University Press, 2001.

Spenser, Colin, and Claire Clifton. *The Faber Book of Food*. London: Faber, 1993.

Visser, Margaret. *The Rituals of Dinner*. New York: Grove Weidenfeld, 1991.

SUBJECT INDEX

RECIPE INDEX

RECIPE INDEX

About the Author

KEN ALBALA is an associate professor in the History Department at the University of the Pacific, Stockton, California. He specializes in food history and is the author of *Eating Right in the Renaissance* (2001).